STECK-VAUGHN
CONNECTIONS

Basic Skills in Science

REVIEWERS

Jim Barlow
Retired Vice-Principal
of Adult Education
Waterloo Region District
School Board
Educational Consultant
and Author
Kitchener, Ontario

William Burns
Instructor
San Mateo County
Office of Education
Palo Alto, California

Sherri Claiborne
Literacy Coordinator
Claiborne County
Adult Reading Experience
(CCARE)
Tazewell, Tennessee

Bill Freeland
Almonte Adult School
Almonte, California

Joanie Griffin-Rethlake
Adult Education Division
Harris County Department
of Education
Houston, Texas

Jim Scheil
Jersey City Adult Education Center
Jersey City, New Jersey

STECK-VAUGHN
COMPANY
A Division of Harcourt Brace & Company

www.steck-vaughn.com

Acknowledgments

Executive Editor: Ellen Northcutt

Project Editor: Julie Higgins

Design Manager: Jim Cauthron

Media Researchers: Claudette Landry, Christina Berry

Cover Design: Donna Neal

Cover Production: Donna Neal and Alan Klemp

Electronic Production: PC&F, Inc.

Photograph Credits: Cover, p. i and title page, p. ii: radiotelescope, volcano, mictoscope, butterfly, chambered nautilus, magnifying glass, lightbulb © PhotoDisc; p. 13 © PhotoDisc; p. 15, 17 Courtesy NASA; p. 21 Courtesy American Cancer Society; p. 28a, 28b © Science Photo Library/Photo Researchers; p. 33 © Bonnie Kamin/PhotoEdit; p. 39, 45 © PhotoDisc; p. 47 © Biophoto Associates/Science Source/Photo Researchers; p. 51 © Discover Magazine; p. 57 © Michael J. Balick/Peter Arnold, Inc.; p. 63 © PhotoDisc; p. 69 © E.R. Degginger/Animals Animals; p. 75, 81 © PhotoDisc; p. 87 © O. Louis Mazzatenta/National Geographic; p. 92, 100 © PhotoDisc; p. 103 © Mark Humphrey/AP/Wide World; p. 105 © Superstock; p. 111 © Stephen Saks/Photo Researchers Inc.; p. 113 © PhotoDisc; p. 117 © Alexander Lowry/Photo Researchers; p. 123, 125 Courtesy NASA; p. 129 *Sojourner* ®, *Mars Rover* ® and spacecraft design and images © copyright 1996–97, California Institute of Technology. All rights reserved. Further reproduction prohibited.; p. 134 © Superstock; p. 143 Courtesy District of Columbia Fire Department; p. 145a © Robert Brenner/PhotoEdit; p. 151a © PhotoDisc; p. 151b © David Young-Wolff/PhotoEdit; p. 153 © Robert Brenner/PhotoEdit; p. 157a CORBIS/Canadian Museum of Civilization; p. 157b, 163 © Tony Freeman/PhotoEdit; p. 169 © PhotoDisc; p. 174 © David Young-Wolff/PhotoEdit; p. 183 © Chip Hires/Liaison; p. 185 © Tom Prettyman/PhotoEdit; p. 187 © PhotoDisc; p. 191 © Jonathan Daniel/AllSport; p. 193 © John Swart/AllSport; p. 197 © George Widman/AP/Wide World; p. 198a © PhotoDisc; p. 203 © Euroelios/Phototake; p. 208 © SuperStock.

Illustration Credits: Maryland Cartographics, Inc. pages 1, 2, 4, 6, 8, 106, 107, 114, 136, 159, 164, 170, 171, 179, 186, 191, 217, 218

University Graphics: pages 22, 113

PC&F, Inc.: pages 29, 131, 141, 147, 180, 198, 205, 221

Contents

To the Student

How to Use This Book

This book allows you to build upon what you already know to improve your science skills. You will increase your knowledge and understanding of the four areas of science by reading interesting articles on many different topics. These topics are divided into the four units described below.

UNITS

Unit 1: Life Science Life science is the study of living things, where they live, and how they affect each other. In this unit, you will develop such thinking skills as making inferences and predictions, classifying, and comparing and contrasting. The graphic illustrations in this unit also provide practice in skills such as understanding diagrams and reading maps, timelines, and graphs. This unit contains articles about the human body ranging from skin cancer to genetic screening. It also has articles about plants, animals, evolution, the environment, and ecosystems.

Unit 2: Earth and Space Science Earth and space science is the study of Earth and the universe. This unit covers skills such as distinguishing fact from opinion and reading tables and weather maps. You will read about weather, the greenhouse effect, water resources, the solar system, and the planet Mars.

Unit 3: Chemistry Chemistry is the study of matter and how it changes. This unit includes skills such as understanding chemical formulas, comparing and contrasting, making predictions, and reading line graphs. You will gain an understanding of chemistry by reading articles about the chemistry of household cleaners, chemical reactions in cooking, mixtures and solutions, combustion, and nuclear reactions.

Unit 4: Physics Physics is the study of energy and forces and how they affect matter. In this unit, you will practice reading diagrams, making inferences, summarizing information, and drawing conclusions. You will read articles about how machines work, force and motion, computers and electronics, and laser surgery.

INVENTORY AND POSTTEST

The Inventory is a self-check of what you already know and what you need to study. After you complete all of the items on the Inventory, the Correlation Chart tells you where each skill is taught in this book. When you have completed the book, you will take a Posttest. Compare your Posttest score to your Inventory score to see your progress.

SECTIONS

All the units are divided into sections. Each section is based on the Active Reading Process. Active reading means doing something *before reading, during reading,* and *after reading.* By reading actively, you will improve your reading comprehension skills.

SETTING THE STAGE

Each section begins with an activity that helps you prepare to read the article. This is the activity you do *before reading.* Each activity will have you preview the article to find out what you are about to learn. Then you will relate the subject of the article to your own opinions, knowledge, or experience. Finally, this activity will list vocabulary words. These words and others appear in the article in **bold type.** All words in bold type are defined in the glossary at the end of the book.

THE ARTICLE

The articles you will read are about interesting topics in science. As you read each article, you will see a Skills Lesson. Here you learn a reading or science skill, and you do a short activity. After completing the activity, continue reading the article. Two Skills Lessons appear in every article. These are the activities you do during reading.

THINKING ABOUT THE ARTICLE

These are the activities you do *after reading.* Here you answer fill-in-the-blank, short-answer, or multiple-choice questions. Answering these questions will help you decide how well you understood what you just read. The final question in this section relates information from the article to your own real-life experiences.

ANSWERS AND EXPLANATIONS

Answers and explanations to every exercise item are at the back of this book, beginning on page 227. The explanation for multiple-choice exercises tells why one answer choice is correct and why the other answer choices are incorrect.

STUDY SKILLS

Good study skills are important. Here are some things you can do to improve your study skills.

- Find a quiet place to study.
- Organize your time by making a schedule.
- Take notes by restating important information in your own words.
- Look up any words you don't know in a dictionary or in the glossary at the back of this book.
- Make a list of concepts and skills on which you need to work. Take time to go back and review this material.

Inventory

Use this Inventory before you begin Section 1. Don't worry if you can't answer all the questions. The Inventory will help you find out which skills you are strong in and which skills you need to practice. Read each article, study any graphics, and answer the questions that follow. Check your answers on page 227. Then enter your scores on the chart on page 11.

The Plant Cell

All living things are made of cells, the working units of the body. Plant cells differ from animal cells. Plant cells have a cell wall for strength. They also have a chemical called chlorophyll for making food. The food gives the plant cell energy and substances needed for growth. The diagram shows the structures of a plant cell and describes the function of each structure.

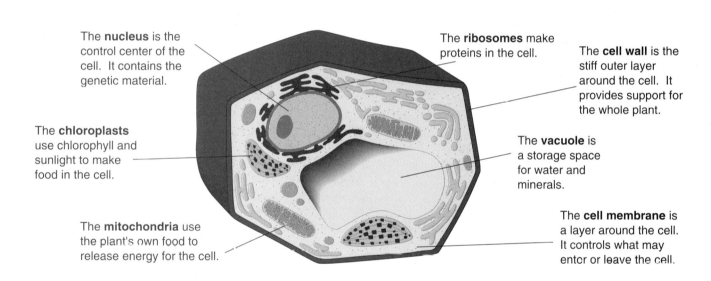

The **nucleus** is the control center of the cell. It contains the genetic material.

The **ribosomes** make proteins in the cell.

The **cell wall** is the stiff outer layer around the cell. It provides support for the whole plant.

The **chloroplasts** use chlorophyll and sunlight to make food in the cell.

The **vacuole** is a storage space for water and minerals.

The **mitochondria** use the plant's own food to release energy for the cell.

The **cell membrane** is a layer around the cell. It controls what may enter or leave the cell.

Fill in the blank with the word or words that best complete each statement.

1. The control center of a cell is its _____.

2. The _____ makes the plant cell stiff.

Circle the number of the best answer.

3. A plant cell needs water when its
   (1) nucleus is empty.
   (2) chloroplast is empty.
   (3) vacuole is empty.
   (4) ribosome is empty.
   (5) cell membrane is empty.

The Muscles of the Arm

Pick up a cup of coffee. You bend your elbow and raise your lower arm. This action is caused by a muscle in the upper arm. Now put down the cup of coffee. You straighten your elbow and move your lower arm down. This action is caused by another muscle in the upper arm.

Muscles work in pairs. The biceps muscle bends the elbow joint. The triceps muscle straightens the elbow joint. Why does it take two muscles to operate one joint? Muscles pull, but they cannot push. A muscle works by contracting, or shortening. When the biceps contracts, it pulls on the bones of the lower arm. The elbow joint bends. When the triceps contracts, it pulls on the same bones but in the opposite direction. When one muscle is contracting, its partner is relaxing.

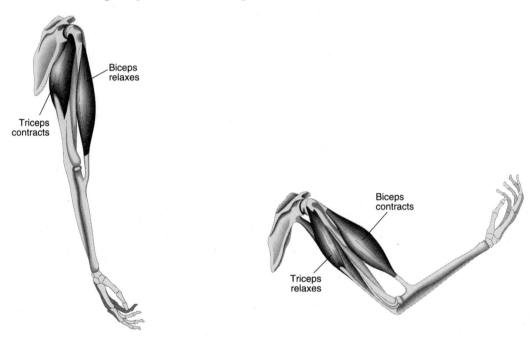

Fill in the blank with the word or words that best complete each statement.

4. When a muscle _____ , it gets shorter.

5. When one muscle in a pair is contracting, the other muscle is

    _____ .

Circle the number of the best answer.

6. The large muscles at the back of the thigh bend the knee joint. Where are the muscles that straighten the knee joint?
    (1) at the back of the thigh
    (2) at the front of the thigh
    (3) at the front of the lower leg
    (4) at the back of the lower leg
    (5) at the hip

Bacteria

Bacteria are simple one-celled organisms. They can be found just about anywhere. The action of bacteria can be good for people, or it can be harmful. The bacteria that turn milk into cheese or yogurt are useful. These same bacteria also turn the milk in your refrigerator sour. Then they are not so useful.

If sour milk and yogurt are made by the same bacteria, why does one taste so bad? The difference is in how the bacteria are controlled. When yogurt is made, the bacteria are killed before they make the product too sour. In your refrigerator, the bacteria keep on going. The result is that the milk gets much too sour. The bacteria that make milk sour use the sugar in the milk for energy. Their waste product, lactic acid, is the sour substance you taste in the spoiled milk.

The activity of bacteria depends on the temperature. People are often surprised when they find that food has gone bad in the refrigerator. Keeping food cool does slow down the bacteria. However, it does not stop their action. Freezing food does stop the action of bacteria. But it does not necessarily kill the bacteria. So food that has been in the freezer can spoil after it has been defrosted.

Bacteria can be killed by high temperatures. Milk and other dairy products are pasteurized. In this process, the milk is heated to a high temperature, then quickly cooled. The heat kills the bacteria. But once you take the milk home and open it, new bacteria may get in. Then the spoiling process begins.

Fill in the blank with the word or words that best complete each statement.

7. _____, which is a waste product of bacteria, makes spoiled milk taste sour.

8. Milk is turned into yogurt by the action of _____.

Circle the number of the best answer.

9. How does the pasteurizing process affect bacteria?
   (1) Pasteurizing kills bacteria with high temperatures.
   (2) Pasteurizing kills bacteria with low temperatures.
   (3) Pasteurizing slows bacteria with low temperatures.
   (4) Pasteurizing slows bacteria with high temperatures.
   (5) Pasteurizing poisons bacteria with chemical preservatives.

The Flower

The reproductive organ of a plant is the **flower**. Flowers come in many shapes and sizes. Some are large and bright. Others are so small, you might not notice them.

Flowers make pollen. The pollen contains sperm, which is made in the anthers of the flower. The pollen is carried from one flower to another by insects, birds, or the wind. When pollen from one flower reaches another flower of the same kind, the sperm in the pollen joins with the egg, which is made in the ovary of the flower. The fertilized egg becomes a seed. The seed begins the next generation.

Flowers that are pollinated by insects such as bees often are bright in color. They have large petals, which give the bees a place to land. Many of these flowers also make nectar. This sweet juice attracts bees to the flower. When the bees drink the nectar, some of the sticky pollen gets on their bodies. This pollen rubs off when the bees get to the next flower.

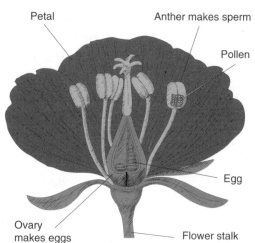

The flowers of many trees and grasses are pollinated by the wind. These flowers usually have tiny petals. Some have no petals at all. The pollen is dry and dusty. These features make it easy for the pollen to blow from one plant to another.

Identify each of the following as a characteristic of a plant that is pollinated by insects or by the wind. Write *insects* or *wind* in the space provided.

10. Sticky pollen _____

11. Sweet nectar _____

12. Very small petals _____

13. The flower shown on this page _____

Circle the number of the best answer.

14. Which part or parts of the flower are necessary for reproduction?
    (1) petals
    (2) anthers
    (3) ovary
    (4) petals and anthers
    (5) anthers and ovary

Go on to the next page.

Biomes

You probably know that Earth's climate is coldest near the poles and warmest near the equator (an imaginary circle drawn around the Earth halfway between the poles). The climate determines the living things that are found in any area. Large regions with the same climate throughout have the same kinds of living things. A large region with a certain climate and certain living things is called a **biome**.

There are many kinds of biomes on Earth. Most of the eastern and northeastern United States is a forest biome. This biome is home to many kinds of trees and birds. There are also many **mammals**, such as deer, foxes, squirrels, and chipmunks.

Most of the central United States is a grassland biome. Because this biome is drier than the forest biome, there are few trees. The animals of the grassland feed on the many kinds of grasses there. Once there were huge herds of bison grazing the grasslands. Now there are herds of sheep and cattle. The most common wild animals are small. These are rabbits, prairie dogs, and badgers.

Much of the southwestern United States is a desert biome. It is so dry that few plants can grow there. Rain is sometimes heavy in the desert, but it does not rain often or for long. Then it dries up quickly. The cactus plant survives here because it is able to store water. Most of the animals of the desert live underground to escape the heat. They come out at night or early morning when it is cool. Small animals feed on the plants and their seeds. In turn, these animals are food for coyotes, hawks, and rattlesnakes.

Fill in the blank with the word or words that best complete each statement.

15. The _____ biome is home to many trees and deer.

16. The _____ biome is home to rabbits and prairie dogs.

17. A desert plant that can store water is the _____.

Circle the number of the best answer.

18. In general, the biomes of the United States change as you move from east to west because the climate becomes
    (1) cooler.
    (2) drier.
    (3) windier.
    (4) less sunny.
    (5) wetter.

The Water Cycle

When you are caught in a sudden rainstorm, you probably don't think about where all that water came from. But you are experiencing one step in the water cycle. The **water cycle** is the circulation of water on Earth and in its atmosphere.

Water covers more than half of the planet. This surface water is found in oceans, lakes, and rivers. Surface water constantly evaporates. Water in the atmosphere condenses and forms clouds. When the clouds become too heavy, the water falls as rain. Rain, snow, and sleet are forms of **precipitation**. When it rains, some water soaks into the ground and some moves along the land to rivers and lakes.

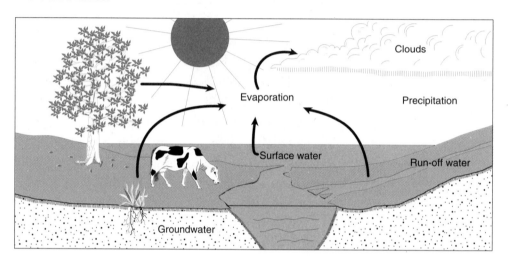

Match the part of the water cycle with its description. Write the letter of the part of the cycle in the blank at the left.

Description

_____ **19.** rain and snow

_____ **20.** lakes and oceans

_____ **21.** water that soaks into the soil

_____ **22.** water that condenses in the atmosphere

_____ **23.** water flowing over the top of the soil

Part of the Water Cycle

a. clouds

b. groundwater

c. precipitation

d. run-off water

e. surface water

Rocks

Have you ever washed your hands with gritty soap? The soap probably had ground pumice in it. Pumice is a kind of rock. This rock forms when lava from a volcano cools and hardens. **Igneous rocks**, such as pumice and granite, form when melted rock hardens. Some buildings are made of granite.

Over a long period of time, wind and water can wear down rocks. Small pieces of the rocks are blown or washed away. These pieces may settle slowly and form layers. The particles are called sediment. Slowly the layers harden, forming **sedimentary rocks**. Sandstone, limestone, and shale are sedimentary rocks. Sedimentary rocks are not as hard as igneous rocks. Sandstone and limestone wear away much faster than granite.

Igneous and sedimentary rocks can be changed into new forms. This is caused by high temperatures or great pressure. Rocks formed in this way are called **metamorphic rocks**. Marble is a metamorphic rock. You may have seen statues made of marble.

Fill in the blank with the word or words that best complete each statement.

24. Rocks that form as layers of hardened particles are called

    _____.

25. Rocks that form under high temperatures or great pressure are called

    _____.

Circle the number of the best answer.

26. Which of these is an example of an igneous rock?
    (1) granite
    (2) limestone
    (3) marble
    (4) sandstone
    (5) shale

27. An area where many igneous rocks are found may once have had
    (1) many rivers.
    (2) large amounts of sediment.
    (3) high pressure.
    (4) volcanoes.
    (5) earthquakes.

The Atom

All matter is made up of atoms. An **atom** is made up of three types of particles. **Protons** are particles with a positive electrical charge. **Neutrons** have no charge. Protons and neutrons are found in the **nucleus**, or core, of an atom. All atoms of a particular element have the same number of protons. The number of neutrons can vary.

Orbiting around the nucleus are **electrons**, particles with a negative electrical charge. Electrons are much lighter than protons or neutrons. The number of electrons in an atom is equal to the number of protons. That means the amount of positive and negative electric charge is the same, so overall an atom has no charge. If an atom gains or loses an electron, it is called an **ion**. An ion has a charge.

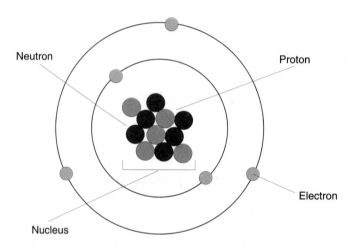

Match the name of the particle with its description. Write the letter of the particle in the blank at the left. Letters may be used more than once.

		Description		Particle
_____	28.	has no electric charge	a.	proton
_____	29.	not found in the nucleus	b.	neutron
_____	30.	has a positive electric charge	c.	electron
_____	31.	a negatively charged ion has an extra one		
_____	32.	all atoms of an element have the same number of these		

States of Matter

On Earth, all matter is found in three states: **solid, liquid**, and **gas**. The table below shows the properties of these states. The state of matter of a substance depends on its temperature. Each substance changes state at different temperatures. At low temperatures, substances are solids. Sugar, salt, and plastic are solids at room temperature. If a solid is heated, it changes to a liquid. Water and alcohol are liquids at room temperature. If a liquid is heated, it changes to a gas. Air is a mixture of substances that are gases at room temperature.

State	Temperature Range	Shape	Volume
solid	lowest	definite (does not change)	definite (does not change)
liquid	middle	not definite; takes the shape of its container	definite (does not change)
gas	highest	not definite; takes the shape of its container	not definite; expands to fill the volume of its container

Circle the number of the best answer.

33. In which state or states of matter does the volume stay the same?
    (1) solid only
    (2) liquid only
    (3) gas only
    (4) solid and liquid only
    (5) solid, liquid, and gas

34. What happens if you cool a liquid enough to make it into a solid?
    (1) Its shape changes from not definite to definite.
    (2) Its shape changes from definite to not definite.
    (3) Its volume changes from not definite to definite.
    (4) It will be in its highest temperature range.
    (5) None of its properties changes.

Forces

A **force** is a push or pull. In a tug of war, two teams pull on a rope. Each team exerts a force on the rope. The forces act in opposite directions. If the two forces are equal, there is no movement. The forces are said to be balanced.

Suppose an extra player joins one team. The extra player increases that team's force. Now the forces are not balanced, and there is movement. A change in movement is called acceleration. The rope accelerates, moving in the direction of the greater force. The team with the extra player wins.

If you hold a ball in your hand, the forces on the ball are balanced. **Gravity** pulls down on the ball. Your hand exerts an upward force that balances the force of gravity. If you let go of the ball, your force changes, but gravity does not. Gravity "wins," and the ball accelerates in the direction of the pull of gravity.

If you throw a ball, the forces involved get more complicated. When you throw the ball, you exert a force on it. The forward force of your hand is opposed by the force of **friction** between the ball and the air. These forces are not balanced. Because your force is greater, the ball moves in the direction you throw it. Once the ball leaves your hand, you exert no force on it. Friction continues to act on the ball. This force is not balanced, so it changes the motion of the ball. The ball slows down. At the same time, gravity pulls on the ball. This downward force is not balanced by another force. So the ball falls down as it moves forward.

Fill in the blank with the word or words that best complete each statement.

35. A _____ is a push or a pull.

36. A change in movement is called _____.

Circle the number of the best answer.

37. Which of the following is an effect of an unbalanced force?
    (1) acceleration
    (2) gravity
    (3) friction
    (4) a push
    (5) a pull

Check your answers on pages 227–228.

Inventory Correlation Chart

Science

The chart below will help you determine your strengths and weaknesses in the four content areas of science.

Directions

Circle the number of each item that you answered correctly on the Inventory. Count the number of items in each row that you answered correctly. Write the number in the Total Correct space in each row. (For example, in the Life Science row, write the number correct in the blank before *out of 18*). Complete this process for the remaining rows. Then add the four totals to get your total correct for the whole 37-item Inventory.

Content Areas	Items	Total Correct	Pages
Life Science (Pages 12–101)	1, 2, 3 4, 5, 6 7, 8, 9 10, 11, 12, 13, 14 15, 16, 17, 18	_____ out of 18	Pages 20–25 Pages 32–37 Pages 50–55 Pages 56–61 Pages 80–85
Earth and Space Science (Pages 102–141)	19, 20, 21, 22, 23 24, 25, 26, 27	_____ out of 9	Pages 116–121 Pages 128–133
Chemistry (Pages 142–181)	28, 29, 30, 31, 32 33, 34	_____ out of 7	Pages 144–149 Pages 150–155
Physics (Pages 182–215)	35, 36, 37	_____ out of 3	Pages 184–189

TOTAL CORRECT FOR INVENTORY _____ out of 37

If you answered fewer than 34 items correctly, look more closely at the four content areas of science listed above. In which areas do you need more practice? Page numbers to refer to for practice are given in the right-hand column above.

Life Science

If you look closely at your skin, you'll see lines and pores. If you look at skin under a microscope, you will see many tiny cells. All living things are made up of cells, the smallest units of life.

Life science is the study of living things. One part of life science is the study of the cell. Discoveries about cells often make the news. Someday they may change the way we live.

Another part of life science is the study of organisms: the plants, animals, and other forms of life—including us—that are made of cells. The study of the human body, for example, helps us look and feel our best.

Finally, part of life science is the study of how organisms relate to one another and to their environments. People are facing many decisions about their world. Why is it important to protect our forests and beaches? Learning about life science can help you understand yourself and your world.

○ What are your concerns about diet, exercise, and health?

○ What can you, as just one person, do to contribute to a healthy environment?

SECTIONS

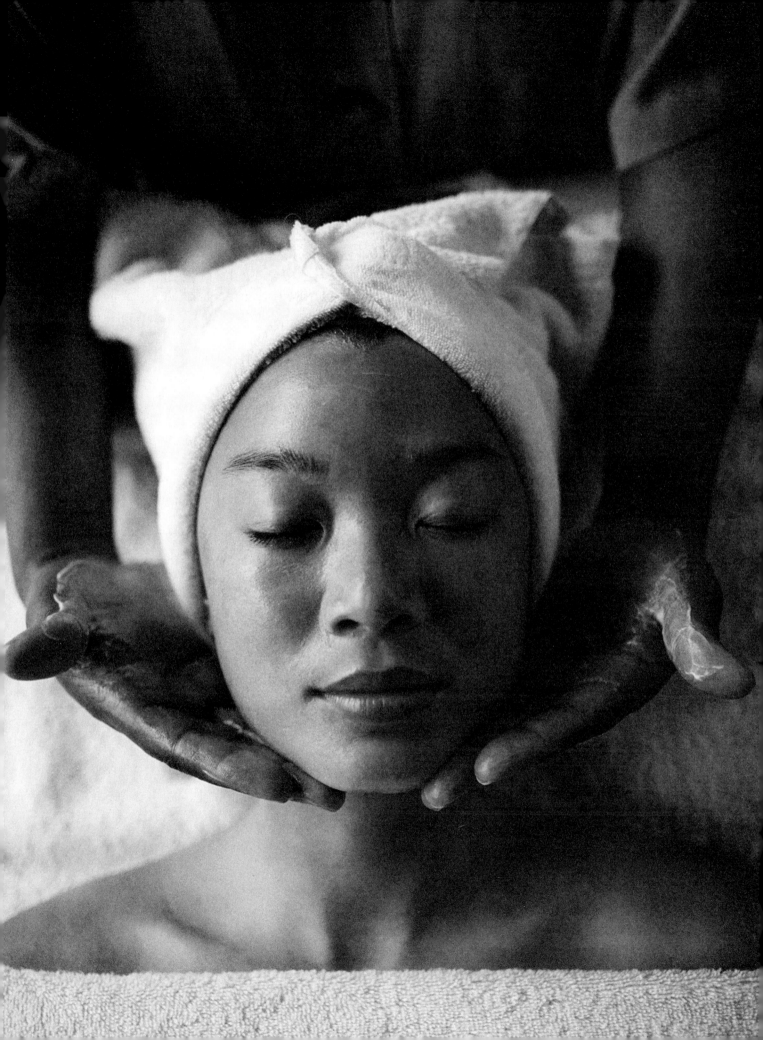

Scientific Methods

Setting the Stage

When former astronaut John Glenn returned to space at age 77, he enjoyed being weightless. While he moved about the space shuttle, scientists observed the way his body functioned. Someday people of all ages may be in space. Can babies be born there? To begin to answer such a question, scientists gather information and test ideas.

PREVIEW THE ARTICLE

You will get a better understanding of what you read if you look over an article before reading it. Look at the title of this article and the headings, or subtitles.

Read the title and the headings on pages 15–17. What are some things you can expect to learn about scientific methods from this article?

_____

_____

RELATE TO THE TOPIC

This article is about the methods used in science. It explains some processes that scientists go through to figure out how nature works. It describes an actual experiment aboard the space shuttle to show science in action.

You often hear of new scientific findings in the news. How do you think knowledge of scientific methods can help you decide whether a science news story is true or not?

_____

_____

VOCABULARY

scientific methods	**observation**	**hypothesis**
experiment	**conclusion**	

An Experiment in Space

When people fly in space, they are not affected by the pull of Earth's gravity. Being weightless may be fun, but it can also cause problems. Some astronauts get space-motion sickness. Others come back from long flights with weak bones and muscles. Some scientists worry that such conditions may limit the future of space travel.

It is important to understand how weightlessness affects the body. Flights to distant planets may take years. People may live and work for long periods in space stations. How will their bodies react? Will they be able to raise families?

Weightless astronauts aboard the space shuttle

Scientific Methods

Questions like these are not easy to answer. To find answers, scientists have ways to get information and test ideas. These processes are **scientific methods.** The basic scientific method includes four main steps. These steps are observation, hypothesis, experiment, and conclusion.

Observation

A high school student named John Vellinger became curious about weightlessness. Through **observation,** he learned about what was already known. He watched astronauts on TV. He read as much as he could. He wondered how weightlessness would affect people in space for long periods. Would they be able to raise animals for food? Would they be able to have children? The answers to these questions may be important if people are to go on long voyages in space.

Hypothesis

Once scientists observe things, they try to explain them. A **hypothesis** is a possible explanation of how something works. It is based on many observations. Would weightlessness affect the development of an **embryo,** an unborn living thing in an early stage of life? One hypothesis is that an embryo would not be affected by weightlessness.

Making Predictions   A hypothesis is useful because it is the basis for predicting—or foretelling—what will happen. For example, Vellinger might predict that a chicken embryo would hatch normally in space. A **prediction** is a good guess about the future.

Reread the first paragraph on this page.

Which of the following statements is a better prediction of what will happen next? Circle the letter of the correct answer.
   a.   Vellinger will try to develop chicken embryos in the weightlessness of space to see whether they hatch normally.
   b.   Vellinger will try to develop young chicks in the weightlessness of space to see if they grow to adulthood.

Experiment

Scientists must test whether a hypothesis is supported by facts. They do this with an **experiment.** With help from scientists, Vellinger designed an experiment to test whether weightlessness would affect chicken embryos. NASA chose his experiment for a space shuttle mission.

Vellinger decided to use 64 fertilized chicken eggs. He divided the eggs into two groups. One group of eggs would spend five days in space on the shuttle *Discovery.* This group was the **experimental group.** The other group of eggs would stay on Earth. The second group was the **control group.** The two groups differed in only one way. The group of experimental eggs would be weightless for five days. The eggs in the control group would remain in Earth's gravity.

Vellinger then divided both the experimental and control groups. Sixteen eggs from each group were fertilized nine days before the shuttle launch. The other 20 eggs in each group were fertilized just two days before the launch. This meant that some embryos in the experimental group would be "young" and some would be older when they were launched into space.

What happened in the experiment? Did the evidence support the hypothesis? If so, all 64 eggs should have hatched after the normal 21-day development period. Instead, something surprising happened. None of the younger embryos that had been aboard the shuttle survived. Yet the older group that had also spent time in space hatched normally.

 Check your answer on page 228.

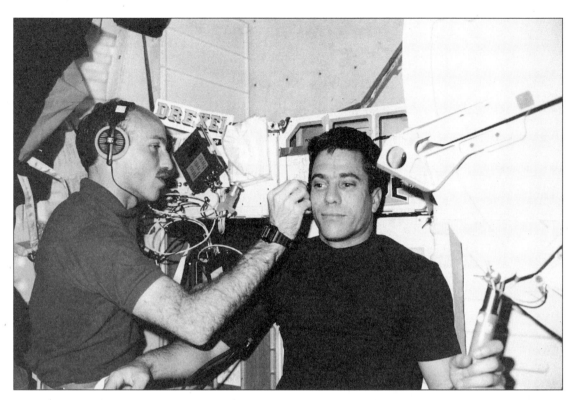

Astronaut John E. Blaha participates in an experiment on the space shuttle *Discovery*.

Using the Glossary or Dictionary   When you read, you may see words you do not understand. Circle any words you do not know. You can look up the meaning of words in **bold print** in the glossary at the back of this book. Other unfamiliar words can be found in a dictionary.

Match each term with its correct definition. Use the glossary or dictionary.

_____ **1** experiment   a.   an unborn living thing in an early stage of life

_____ **2** embryo   b.   the act of noting a fact or event in nature

_____ **3** observation   c.   a procedure that tests a hypothesis

Conclusion

The results of an experiment are stated in a **conclusion.** This experiment shows that our hypothesis was not supported by what happened. Our conclusion is that weightlessness does seem to affect embryos. But it does not seem to affect embryos at different stages of growth in the same way. The embryos that died were all weightless during the first third of the 21-day development period. The embryos that hatched were in the second third of the development period when they were weightless.

Astronaut John E. Blaha, the pilot of *Discovery,* said, "What looked like a simple experiment may have . . . generated thousands of questions." With the results of this experiment, scientists will make new hypotheses and do more experiments. Someday they may be able to answer the question: can people have children in outer space?

Thinking About the Article

Practice Vocabulary

The terms below are in the passage in bold type. Study the way each term is used. Then complete each sentence by writing the correct term in the blank.

| scientific methods | hypothesis | observation |
| experiment | conclusion | |

① In science, ways of getting information and testing ideas are called

_____ .

② Through _____ , scientists note things that happen in nature. They try to figure out why or how these things happen.

③ The scientists then come up with an explanation, called a(n)

_____ , that will explain the observations.

④ Scientists test this explanation by doing a(n) _____ that is designed to see if the explanation is correct.

⑤ The results of this work are stated in a(n) _____ .

Understand the Article

Circle the letter of the correct answer.

⑥ How did the control and experimental groups of chicken embryos differ?
   a. The control group developed under normal gravity, and the experimental group developed in weightlessness.
   b. The control group consisted only of older embryos, and the experimental group consisted only of younger embryos.

⑦ What were the results of the chicken embryo experiment?
   a. All the embryos in the experiment hatched.
   b. All the embryos that stayed on Earth hatched, but only the older embryos that were weightless in space hatched.

⑧ What conclusion can you draw from this experiment?
   a. Weightlessness does not seem to affect embryo development.
   b. Weightlessness does seem to affect embryo development.

⑨ What hypothesis do these results suggest about space travel?
   a. Women may be unable to bear children on long space voyages.
   b. Young children may not grow and mature in space.

Apply Your Skills

Circle the number of the best answer for each question.

10 Use your glossary to help you determine the best definition for the word *hypothesis*.
(1) a question
(2) the answer to a question
(3) an observation
(4) a procedure for testing an observation
(5) a possible explanation for something observed

11 All of the following are examples of observation except
(1) watching embryos develop on Earth.
(2) watching embryos develop on the space shuttle.
(3) measuring the length of time it takes the embryos to hatch.
(4) drawing a conclusion about the results of the experiment.
(5) noting how many embryos fail to hatch.

12 Which of the following is the best prediction of what would happen if duck eggs fertilized at different times were taken aboard a shuttle flight?
(1) None of the eggs would hatch.
(2) Eggs that were fertilized nine days before the launch would hatch.
(3) Eggs that were fertilized two days before the launch would hatch.
(4) All of the eggs would hatch.
(5) The baby ducks would be abnormal.

Connect with the Article

Write your answer to each question.

13 Why do you think it is important to test a hypothesis by experimenting?

_____

_____

_____

14 Suppose you were in charge of shuttle experiments. A pregnant woman has volunteered to go into space to test the effects of weightlessness on a human embryo. Would you let her go? Why or why not?

_____

_____

_____

The Cell

Setting the Stage

Sitting in the warm sun feels good. It feels so good that many people find it hard to believe the sun can be harmful. Still, the sun can cause skin to burn painfully. Even worse, it can eventually cause skin cancer. Harmful rays in sunlight can cause skin cells to grow in abnormal ways.

PREVIEW THE ARTICLE

One way to preview an article is to look at the photographs and diagrams. They will give you a general idea of what the article is about.

Look at the photograph on page 21 and the diagram on page 22. What are some things you can expect to learn about cells from this article?

_____

_____

RELATE TO THE TOPIC

This article is about skin cancer, the abnormal growth of skin cells. It explains the types of skin cancer, how sunlight can cause it, and how you can prevent it. It also shows a normal cell.

Have you or someone you know ever had any problems from staying out in the sun? Describe what happened.

_____

_____

VOCABULARY

cell	cytoplasm	ribosomes
mitochondria	nucleus	cell membrane

Check your answers on page 229.

Sunlight and Skin Cancer

Each year, millions of Americans relax at beaches or swimming pools and in the mountains. Many people work outdoors in the sun. Some people go to tanning parlors to get a bronzed look. However, exposure to **ultraviolet light,** a type of light given off by the sun and by tanning lamps, can cause skin cancer. In fact, there are almost 1,000,000 new cases of skin cancer in the United States each year. That makes skin cancer the most common cancer in this country. Skin cancer is also the easiest form of cancer to treat and cure.

Types of Skin Cancer

There are three types of skin cancer. They are called basal cell, squamous cell, and melanoma.

The most common and least dangerous skin cancer is **basal cell skin cancer.** About 750,000 people develop this type of skin cancer each year. Basal cell skin cancer often appears on the hands or face. It may look like an open sore, reddish patch, mole, shiny bump, or scar. Basal cell skin cancer grows slowly and rarely spreads to other parts of the body. When found early and removed, basal cell skin cancer can almost always be cured.

Squamous cell skin cancer is more dangerous than basal cell skin cancer. It affects about 200,000 people each year. Squamous cell skin cancer looks like raised pink spots or growths that may be open in the center. This cancer grows faster than basal cell skin cancer. Squamous cell skin cancer can spread to other parts of the body. If it is not treated, this type of skin cancer may lead to death.

The most dangerous of the three types of skin cancer is **melanoma.** There are about 41,600 new cases each year. This type of skin cancer may grow in a mole or on clear skin. Melanomas are oddly shaped blotches that turn red, white, or blue in spots. They become crusty and bleed, and they grow fast. When melanomas reach the size of a dime, it's likely that they have spread and become deadly. About 7,300 people die of melanoma each year in the United States.

Finding the Main Idea   One way to make sure you understand what you read is to find the main idea of each paragraph. A paragraph is a group of sentences about one **main idea** or topic. The main idea is usually stated in one sentence which is called a **topic sentence.**

Reread the first paragraph on this page. The first sentence is the topic sentence. It makes a general statement about the topic of the paragraph. All the other sentences give details about the topic.

Which of the following is the main idea of this paragraph?
    a.   Melanoma is the most dangerous type of skin cancer.
    b.   Thousands of people die of melanoma each year.

How Sunlight Causes Skin Cancer

The human body is made of many cells. A **cell** is the smallest unit of a living thing that can carry on life processes such as growing, responding, and reproducing itself. A typical animal cell is shown here. This is a normal cell, not a cancer cell.

An Animal Cell

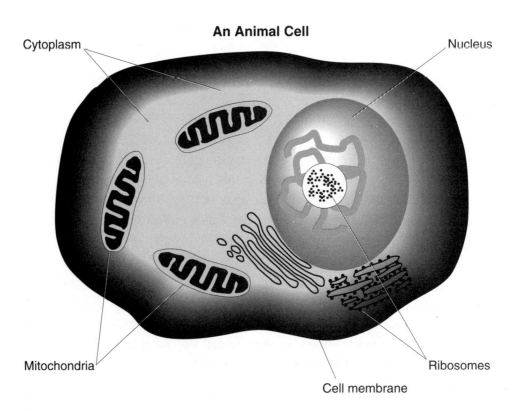

Cytoplasm

Nucleus

Mitochondria

Ribosomes

Cell membrane

Check your answer on page 229.

A cell has many parts. A jellylike material, called **cytoplasm,** makes up most of the cell. **Ribosomes** are cell parts that make the proteins the cell needs to grow. **Mitochondria** give the cell the energy it needs to grow and reproduce.

The part of the cell that controls all cell activities is the **nucleus.** When a normal cell reproduces, it divides into two cells. Each new cell gets its own complete copy of the nucleus. The ultraviolet rays in sunlight can cause changes in the nucleus of a skin cell. When this happens, the cells divide abnormally. Cancer is cell division that is out of control.

The **cell membrane** covers the cell. Most cells stop dividing when they touch another cell. However, cancer cells keep dividing, even if they crowd the cells near them.

Using Headings   One way to find information is to read the headings in an article. Headings give you an overview of what the material is about. Headings are phrases printed in large, bold, or colored type, so you can see them easily. For example, the heading for the next section is "Preventing Skin Cancer." From this heading, you know that the section discusses how to protect yourself from skin cancer.

Suppose you were looking for information about different kinds of skin cancer. Under which of the following headings would you look? Circle the letter of the correct answer.

a.   Types of Skin Cancer
b.   How Sunlight Causes Skin Cancer

Preventing Skin Cancer

The color of your skin has a lot to do with how likely you are to get skin cancer. In general, people with light skin are the most likely to get skin cancer. People with darker skin, including most Asians and Hispanics, are less likely to get skin cancer. African Americans are least likely to get skin cancer.

Here are some things you can do to protect yourself from skin cancer.

- Spend less time in the sun, especially between 10 A.M. and 3 P.M.

- Wear long sleeves and a hat to protect your skin.

- Always wear a sunscreen with an SPF (Sun Protection Factor) of at least 15. Apply it to all of the exposed areas of your body, including the tops of your ears and your lips. Use a sunscreen even on cloudy days. Sunscreens may not protect against melanomas, but they do give important protection against sunburn and less harmful skin cancers.

- Do not use tanning parlors.

- Check your skin for new growths or sores that do not heal. If you find any of these, see a doctor right away. Early treatment for skin cancer is very important.

Thinking About the Article

Practice Vocabulary

The terms below are in the passage in bold type. Study the way each term is used. Then match each term to its meaning by writing the correct letter in the blank.

_____ ❶ cell membrane

_____ ❷ cytoplasm

_____ ❸ cell

_____ ❹ nucleus

_____ ❺ mitochondria

_____ ❻ ribosome

a. the outer covering of a cell

b. the control center of a cell

c. smallest unit of a living thing that carries on life processes

d. the jellylike material that makes up most of the cell

e. the cell part that makes proteins

f. the parts of the cell that provide energy

Understand the Article

Write or circle the answer to each question.

❼ Describe the three types of skin cancer.

_____

_____

_____

❽ How can sunlight cause skin cancer?
   a. The ultraviolet rays in sunlight cause bacteria and viruses to grow on skin.
   b. The ultraviolet rays can cause skin cells to grow and reproduce abnormally.

❾ What is the relationship between skin color and the likelihood of getting skin cancer?
   a. The lighter the skin, the more likely a person is to get skin cancer.
   b. The darker the skin, the more likely a person is to get skin cancer.

❿ List three ways to protect yourself from skin cancer.

_____

_____

_____

Check your answers on page 229.

Apply Your Skills

Circle the number of the best answer for each question.

⑪ What is the main idea of the first paragraph under the heading "Preventing Skin Cancer" on page 23?
  (1) Clothing protects the skin from the harmful effects of the sun.
  (2) Skin color is closely related to the risk of developing skin cancer.
  (3) African Americans are least likely to develop skin cancer.
  (4) People with darker skin, including most Asians and Hispanics, are less likely to get skin cancer.
  (5) People with light skin are most likely to develop skin cancer.

⑫ What is the main idea of the first paragraph on page 21?
  (1) Millions of Americans enjoy the sun.
  (2) Many people work outdoors in the sun.
  (3) Sunlight can cause skin cancer.
  (4) A million Americans get skin cancer each year.
  (5) Skin cancer can usually be treated and cured.

⑬ Under which heading in the article would you find information about protecting yourself from skin cancer?
  (1) The Cell
  (2) Sunlight and Skin Cancer
  (3) Types of Skin Cancer
  (4) How Sunlight Causes Skin Cancer
  (5) Preventing Skin Cancer

Connect with the Article

Write your answers in the space provided.

⑭ Why would it be a good idea to have any moles checked periodically by a doctor?

_____

_____

_____

⑮ How will you protect your skin the next time you go to the beach or some other sunny place?

_____

_____

_____

Blood Vessels

Setting the Stage

We've been hearing the message for years: Americans eat too many fatty foods, and fat is bad for your heart. Some people have heard this message and changed their diets, eating more fruits, grains, and vegetables. They are eating less meat and dairy foods, which have lots of fat. But it's also true that fat gives food a satisfying flavor, so many people find it hard to cut down. For those who can't resist that bag of chips, there are new, low-fat versions of snack products to try.

PREVIEW THE ARTICLE

Sometimes the illustrations in an article give you an overview of what the article is about.

Look at the illustrations on pages 27 through 29. What are some things you can expect to learn about food and health from this article?

_____

_____

RELATE TO THE TOPIC

This article is about fats and cholesterol and how they affect the heart. It explains that cutting down on fats in the diet can help prevent heart disease.

Describe an experience that you or someone you know has had with heart disease or with dieting to help prevent heart disease.

_____

_____

VOCABULARY

cholesterol   saturated fat   monounsaturated fat

polyunsaturated fat   arteries

Eating Right for a Healthier Heart

Food labels can be confusing. They are full of words like *cholesterol, saturated fat, polyunsaturated fat,* and *monounsaturated fat.* Since eating too much fat and cholesterol can cause heart disease, it's important to know what's in your food.

Help with Reading the Labels

Many people confuse cholesterol and fat, although these substances are not the same. **Fats** are substances that provide energy and building materials for the body. Fats are found in oils, butter, milk, cheese, eggs, meat, and nuts. When the body takes in more food of any kind than it needs, it stores the extra food as fat. **Cholesterol** is a fatlike substance found in all animals, including humans. Some foods, such as egg yolks and shellfish, contain cholesterol. But most of the cholesterol in our bodies is made from the saturated fats in the foods we eat.

Saturated fat is a type of fat that is solid at room temperature. Most saturated fats come from animal products such as butter, cheese, meat, and egg yolks. Some vegetable oils, such as palm oil, also have saturated fat. Saturated fat increases cholesterol in the blood.

Monounsaturated fat is a type of fat found in some vegetable products, including olive oil, peanut oil, and peanut butter. Some scientists think monounsaturated fat lowers the body's cholesterol. Others believe it has no effect on cholesterol.

Polyunsaturated fat is a type of fat found in some vegetable foods and fish. Corn oil, almonds, mayonnaise, soybean oil, and fish are common sources of this fat. Polyunsaturated fat lowers the amount of cholesterol in the blood.

Fried foods, potato chips, and lunchmeats are usually high in fat and cholesterol.

The Effect of Fat and Cholesterol

Your body needs fat. Fat insulates the body from hot and cold. Fat stores energy. The body uses fats to build cells. Fats are needed to absorb certain vitamins. Women need fat to help regulate menstruation.

Your body also needs cholesterol. Cholesterol is an important part of all animal cells. It also helps protect nerve fibers. The body needs cholesterol to make vitamin D and other substances.

Using the Index   Is the word *cells* familiar? Cells were mentioned in the article on skin cancer. You can find other discussions of cells in this book by using the index on pages 261–266. An index lists words alphabetically, with the page numbers on which the words appear.

Turn to the index and find the word *cells.* It is on page 261, in alphabetical order under the letter C. Cells are discussed on pages 12, 20, and 22–23, as well as other pages. Now look up *fat* in the index. The index tells you that fat is mentioned on pages 26–29 and _____ .

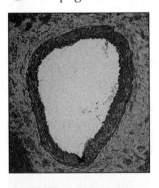

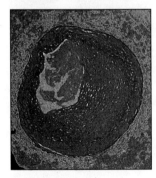

Cross sections of a healthy artery (top) and an artery clogged with plaque (bottom)

If fat and cholesterol have so many benefits, what is the problem? The problem is that too much fat and too much cholesterol can be harmful. The average person should eat no more than about 65 grams of fat per day. Many people have trouble keeping their fat intake within these guidelines. Also, the body can make cholesterol.

What happens when there is too much fat and cholesterol in the diet? Extra cholesterol circulates in the blood. There it forms deposits called **plaque** on the inside walls of arteries. Too much fat can add to this problem. **Arteries** are large blood vessels that carry blood to all parts of the body. When they are clogged with plaque, arteries cannot carry as much blood. The heart must work harder to pump the same amount of blood through them. When the flow of blood to the heart muscle is blocked, a heart attack occurs. The person may die.

Studies have shown that people with a lot of cholesterol in their blood are most likely to have heart attacks. Reducing blood cholesterol can lower the risk of having a heart attack. The best way to do this is to eat less food that is high in cholesterol and saturated fats.

Food Companies Respond

Since so many people are looking for foods low in cholesterol and saturated fat, food companies have responded. One chain of fast-food restaurants stopped frying potatoes in beef fat, which is saturated. Now they use a mixture made mostly of vegetable oil. They also added a salad bar and put more chicken and fish, which have less fat than beef, on the menu.

Check your answer on page 230.

Some snack food companies have switched from saturated to polyunsaturated fats. Many have cut the fat content of their products. Some are using a controversial fat substitute called Olestra. Still, you have to read the labels carefully. "No cholesterol" does not mean "no saturated fat." Also, even low-fat versions of some products may still have a lot of fat.

Percent of Total Calories from Various Nutrients

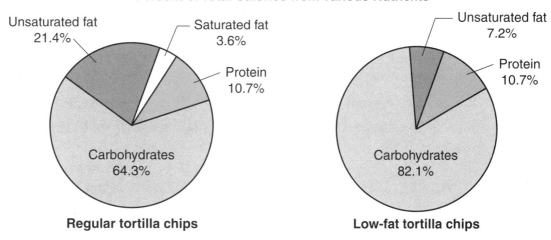

Regular tortilla chips   **Low-fat tortilla chips**

Reading a Circle Graph   Think of a **circle graph** as a pie. The circle is the whole pie. Each wedge is a piece of the pie. In the circle graphs above, the whole pie is the total percent of calories in one serving of tortilla chips (100%). Each wedge shows the percent of calories for one nutrient. Big wedges show big percents, and small wedges show small percents. For example, most of the calories in tortilla chips come from carbohydrates: 64.3 percent for the regular chips and 82.1 percent for the low-fat chips.

Look at the circle graphs to answer these questions.

1 What percent of the calories in the regular chips comes from unsaturated fat?
a. 21.4%   b. 3.6%

2 The regular tortilla chips have about _____ times the amount of unsaturated fat as the low-fat chips.

What You Can Do

There are some simple things you can do to reduce your chances of heart disease. Start with your diet. Eat less meat, eggs, butter, ice cream, cheese, whole milk, and snack foods. If you must eat some snack foods, try low-fat versions. Eat more grains, fruits, and vegetables. You also should get more exercise. Walking, running, swimming, and other aerobic exercises all help lower the body's cholesterol level. Stop smoking—that's also bad for your heart. Last, have your cholesterol level checked by your doctor. If it is too high, your doctor will probably suggest a diet and exercise.

Thinking About the Article

Practice Vocabulary

The terms below are in the passage in bold type. Study the way each term is used. Then match each term to its meaning by writing the correct letter in the blank.

_____ ❶ cholesterol

_____ ❷ saturated fat

_____ ❸ monounsaturated fat

_____ ❹ polyunsaturated fat

_____ ❺ artery

a. a fat found in some vegetable products like olive oil

b. a fat that is solid at room temperature and usually comes from animals

c. a large blood vessel that carries blood to all parts of the body

d. a fatlike substance found in all animals

e. a fat found in some vegetables and fish

Understand the Article

Write or circle the answer to each question.

❻ What are fats?
   a. substances that provide energy and building materials for the body
   b. substances found only in animals, including humans

❼ What happens to the extra cholesterol that the body cannot use?

   _____

   _____

❽ Why does the heart have to work harder in a person with clogged arteries?
   a. The arteries become narrower, so the heart has to work harder to pump the same amount of blood through them.
   b. The heart becomes weaker because the person is not getting exercise.

❾ What can you do to reduce your chance of getting heart disease? Circle the letter next to each action that will help.
   a. Eat more meat, butter, and eggs.
   b. Eat more grains, fruits, and vegetables.
   c. Get more exercise.
   d. Stop smoking.
   e. Have your cholesterol level checked.

Check your answers on page 230.

Apply Your Skills

Circle the number of the best answer for each question.

10 This article discusses the effect of fat on the heart. Use the index to find the page(s) that have information about exercise and the heart.
(1) 26–28
(2) 33
(3) 95
(4) 148–151
(5) 201–203

11 According to the circle graph on page 29, low-fat tortilla chips do not have any calories from
(1) unsaturated fat.
(2) saturated fat.
(3) any kind of fat.
(4) carbohydrates.
(5) protein.

12 If you were on a low-salt diet, which tortilla chips would be better for you?
(1) The regular chips would be better because they have less salt.
(2) The low-fat chips would be better because they have less salt.
(3) The low-fat chips would be better because they have less fat.
(4) Both types of chips would be okay.
(5) You cannot tell because the graphs do not show the salt content.

Connect with the Article

Write your answer to each question.

13 Avocados, which are fruit, contain a large amount of saturated fat. Does this surprise you? Why or why not?

_____

_____

_____

14 Suppose you want to reduce the amount of fat in your diet. Which foods would be easiest for you to give up? Which would be hardest for you to give up? What would you eat instead?

_____

_____

_____

Check your answers on page 230.

Bones and Muscles

Setting the Stage

One of the simplest activities—walking—is good for your health. Walking strengthens the heart, muscles, and bones. Because walking is a low-impact exercise, there is little chance of damaging your bones, muscles, or joints. Best of all, walking doesn't require expensive gear, special clothing, or lessons. In this section you will learn about the benefits of walking and other exercise to your muscles, ligaments, and bones.

PREVIEW THE ARTICLE

You can begin to think about what you will be reading by looking at the title of the article, the headings (subtitles) within the article, and the titles of the pictures and diagrams.

Read the headings on pages 33–35. What are some things you can expect to learn about bones and muscles from this article?

_____

_____

RELATE TO THE TOPIC

This article is about walking as a kind of exercise. It explains the benefits of walking and shows its effects on muscles and joints.

Suppose you wanted to convince a friend to start an exercise program. Why might you recommend walking as a way to get started? What are some of the points you would make to sell your friend on the importance of exercising regularly?

_____

_____

VOCABULARY

aerobic   osteoporosis   joint

sprain   ligaments

Walking for Fitness

Strolling through the mall or around town is a pleasant way to spend time. But did you know that by walking faster, you can improve your fitness and health? Walking at a fast pace gives the heart, lungs, muscles, and bones a good workout.

The Benefits of Walking

Walking is easy and it's convenient. You don't need expensive equipment, special clothing, or lessons to walk. All you need is a good pair of shoes and a little time. You can walk anywhere—around the block, on a track, or even indoors. Some malls open early so walkers can exercise before the shoppers arrive.

Walking is easy on the body. It doesn't jar the joints as jogging or tennis does. That makes walking safe for many people. In fact, doctors often recommend walking to patients recovering from heart attacks, operations, or some injuries.

Walking is a safe and inexpensive way to exercise.

Walking can be an aerobic exercise like jogging, swimming, or cycling. An **aerobic** exercise requires the body to take in extra oxygen. It strengthens the heart, because the heart is required to beat faster. It also increases the amount of oxygen taken in by the lungs. As you exercise, your heart delivers the oxygen-rich blood to your muscles, which helps them grow stronger.

Studies have shown that brisk walking may reduce the risk of heart disease, stroke, and high blood pressure. Other studies have shown that a brisk walk three times a week may lower cholesterol, lower stress, and even provide protection against certain types of cancer.

Walking uses up stored fat. Walking burns about the same number of calories per mile as jogging. It just takes longer to walk a mile than to jog. People who walk regularly and do not increase the amount they eat can lose weight slowly.

Improving Bones and Muscles

Walking uses major muscle groups in the legs, abdomen, and lower back. Walkers who exercise their arms as they walk can make the muscles of the upper body stronger, too.

Muscles work in pairs to move bones. The diagram below shows that when you push off the ground with your foot, you straighten your ankle. To do this, the calf muscles of the leg contract, or shorten. At the same time, the shin muscles relax, or lengthen. Then as you swing your leg forward, your foot lifts up. To bend the ankle this way, the shin muscles contract. At the same time, the calf muscles relax. This repeated movement improves the tone of the leg muscles.

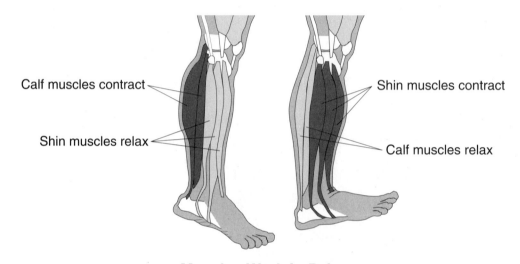

Calf muscles contract

Shin muscles relax

Shin muscles contract

Calf muscles relax

Muscles Work in Pairs

Exercise that increases muscle strength also benefits the bones. Exercise causes muscles to pull on the bones. As a result, the bones become stronger and more solid. This can help prevent **osteoporosis,** a condition of brittle bones. This problem affects many older people, especially women.

Finding the Implied Main Idea   Sometimes the main idea of a paragraph is not stated. Instead, it is hinted at, or **implied**. To find the implied main idea, you have to think about how the details in the paragraph are related to each other and to the topic of the article.

Reread the paragraph on this page that begins, "Exercise that increases. . . ." It discusses the effect of exercise on bones. The implied main idea is that *walking can benefit bones,* even though the word *walking* is never used.

Read the first paragraph on this page. What idea is implied?
a.   Walking reduces pain in your lower back.
b.   Walking strengthens muscles throughout your body.

Check your answer on page 230.

Easy on the Joints

Walking is considered one of the safest forms of exercise because it doesn't jar the joints of the body. A **joint** is the place where two or more bones come together. There are several types of joints. Most allow some kind of movement. For example, a hinge joint works like the hinge on a door. The hinge allows the door to open and close. A hinge joint allows your knee to bend and straighten.

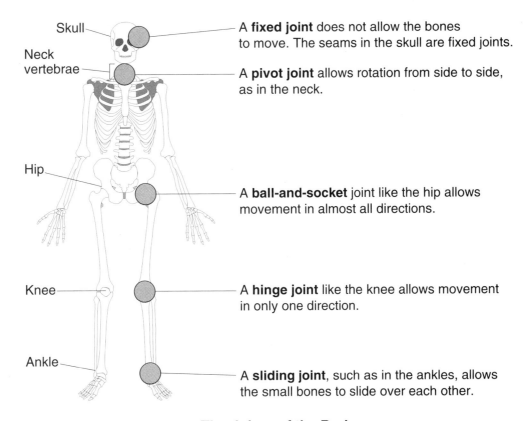

Skull

Neck vertebrae

Hip

Knee

Ankle

A **fixed joint** does not allow the bones to move. The seams in the skull are fixed joints.

A **pivot joint** allows rotation from side to side, as in the neck.

A **ball-and-socket** joint like the hip allows movement in almost all directions.

A **hinge joint** like the knee allows movement in only one direction.

A **sliding joint**, such as in the ankles, allows the small bones to slide over each other.

The Joints of the Body

Some physical activities, such as jogging, can put a lot of stress on joints. In some cases, runners sprain a leg or ankle. A **sprain** is a joint injury in which the ligaments are stretched too far or torn. **Ligaments** are strong bands that connect bones at joints. A ligament stretches much like a rubber band. Unlike joggers, walkers rarely hurt their ligaments.

Comparing and Contrasting   Sometimes writers explain an idea by telling how it is similar to another idea. This is called **comparing**. In the first paragraph, the movement of a hinge joint is compared to opening and closing a door. At other times, writers explain how things are different. This is called **contrasting**.

The last paragraph on the page explains that runners get sprains. What contrasting idea is given in the paragraph?

a.   A sprain is an injury to a ligament.

b.   Walkers seldom injure their ligaments.

Check your answer on page 230.

Thinking About the Article

Practice Vocabulary

The terms below are in the passage in bold type. Study the way each term is used. Then complete each sentence by writing the correct term in the blank.

aerobic   **osteoporosis**   **joint**

sprain   **ligaments**

1 The _____ in the neck allows rotation from side to side.

2 A torn _____ is a common injury for runners.

3 A(n) _____ exercise improves the condition of your heart and lungs.

4 People with _____ have brittle bones.

5 You might _____ an ankle if you run on a hard, uneven surface.

Understand the Article

Write the answer to each question.

6 Name three health benefits that result from walking.

_____

_____

_____

7 Why is it necessary for muscles to work in pairs?

_____

_____

_____

_____

8 You decide to go for a fast walk to get some exercise. How can you tell whether you are walking fast enough for your exercise to be aerobic?

_____

_____

_____

Check your answers on page 230.

Apply Your Skills

Circle the number of the best answer for each question.

9 One way that jogging and walking are similar is that
  (1) both strengthen the muscles of the upper body.
  (2) both require special equipment.
  (3) both are easy on the body.
  (4) neither cause sprains.
  (5) both can be aerobic exercises.

10 Why do walking and jogging burn about the same number of calories per mile?
  (1) Both walking and jogging reduce the risk of heart disease.
  (2) It takes longer to walk a mile than to jog one.
  (3) Any kind of exercise can help you lose weight.
  (4) Both kinds of exercise help to increase muscle strength.
  (5) Runners are more likely to sprain their ankles.

11 Reread the paragraph below the diagram on page 35. What main idea is implied?
  (1) Sprains heal slowly.
  (2) Ligaments stretch or tear easily.
  (3) Walking does not put a lot of stress on joints.
  (4) Joint injuries are painful.
  (5) Jogging is an unsafe form of exercise.

Connect with the Article

Write your answer to each question.

12 Choose one of the types of joints from the diagram on page 35. Explain how the joint works by comparing it to a common object.

_____

_____

_____

13 Suppose you want to start an exercise program to lose weight and improve your overall health. Would you choose walking or jogging? Why?

_____

_____

_____

5

The Reproductive System

Setting the Stage

The maternity ward of a hospital is a joyful place. Healthy babies, wrapped and secure, are held by beaming relatives. In contrast, the neonatal intensive care unit is upsetting. Tiny babies are hooked up to tubes and monitors. They lie in incubators to keep warm. Nurses and worried parents hover over them. Some of these babies develop into normal children, but others have difficulties all their lives. Although all birth defects and problems cannot be prevented, pregnant women can help their babies by being careful about what they eat and drink.

PREVIEW THE ARTICLE

The title and headings of an article provide an outline of the article. So it can be helpful to look at the title and headings before you begin to read. That will give you an overview of the article.

Read the title and headings on pages 39–41. What are some things you can expect to learn from this article about having a healthy baby?

_____

_____

RELATE TO THE TOPIC

This article describes how an unborn baby develops. It explains how drugs like alcohol can pass from mother to baby. It tells what birth defects and problems certain drugs are linked with.

Suppose you wanted to persuade a friend that she should not have alcoholic drinks while she is pregnant. What reasons would you use?

_____

_____

VOCABULARY

zygote   uterus   embryo

placenta   fetus

Check your answers on page 231.

Having a Healthy Baby

Scientists once thought that almost all birth defects were **hereditary.** This means that the problem was passed from parent to child through the father's sperm or the mother's egg. People did not think that what a mother did could affect the health of her unborn child.

Then in the 1950s and 1960s, many pregnant women in Europe took a drug called *Thalidomide.* Thousands of these women had babies born with misshapen arms and legs. Over a thirty-year period in this country, millions of women took a drug called *DES.* This drug prevented miscarriages. But by 1970, daughters of many of these women had cancer. Studying the effects of these two drugs helped scientists focus their research. Since then, scientists have learned that unborn babies are affected by what their mothers eat, drink, and smoke.

A mother and her healthy baby

The Development of an Unborn Baby

In nine months, a new human being develops from one cell into an organism with billions of cells. A developing baby goes through three stages before it is born. First it is a zygote, then an embryo, and finally a fetus.

Zygote. A sperm from the father joins with the egg produced by the mother. This fertilized egg is called a **zygote.** The zygote divides and forms a hollow ball of cells. By the tenth day, the zygote attaches to the **uterus,** or womb. During this early stage, there is no exchange of substances between the mother and the zygote.

Embryo. From the third to the eighth week, the developing baby is called an **embryo.** The embryo is attached to the uterus by the placenta. The **placenta** is a structure that allows substances to pass between the embryo and the mother.

The placenta is like a filter. The mother's blood passes along one side of the placenta. The embryo's blood passes along the other side. The two bloodstreams are separated by thin blood vessels. Food substances and oxygen pass from the mother's blood to the embryo's. Waste and carbon dioxide pass from the embryo's blood to the mother's. Other substances in the mother's blood, such as drugs or chemicals, can pass through, too.

During this stage, the baby's main body organs and systems form. Birth defects are most likely to occur at this time. A harmful substance in the mother's blood can cause serious damage to the embryo.

Fetus. From the third to the ninth month, the developing baby is called a **fetus.** During these months, the fetus grows. Harmful substances are less likely to cause birth defects during this stage because the main systems and body have been formed. If damage occurred in the embryo stage, the damaged organ or system in the fetus may not work properly.

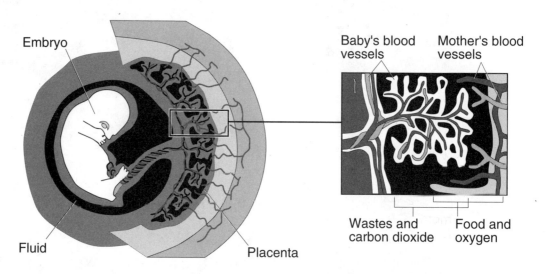

The Exchange of Substances Between Mother and Embryo

Finding the Main Idea of a Diagram A diagram is a picture that helps you see how something looks or works. Like a paragraph or an article, a diagram has a main idea. You can figure out the main idea by looking at the diagram or by studying its title. Look back at the diagram on page 22. The title tells you the main idea: this is what an animal cell looks like.

Which of the following tells the main idea of the diagram above?
 a.   Substances pass between mother and embryo.
 b.   The embryo is attached to the mother by the placenta.

Check your answer page 231.

The Effects of Drugs

What happens when a pregnant woman smokes a cigarette, drinks a beer, or takes an aspirin? It's hard to prove what is harmful and what is not. But over the years, scientists have started to link some substances with certain problems.

Cocaine. The mother's use of cocaine can cause a miscarriage, early labor, or stillbirth (death of the fetus). Cocaine babies are often underweight. They may have damage to the brain, lungs, urinary system, or sex organs.

Cigarettes. The nicotine in cigarettes makes the blood vessels in the placenta shrink. Less oxygen and fewer nutrients reach the developing baby. Smoking has been linked to miscarriages and stillbirths. Babies born to smokers are often underweight at birth.

Finding Details Details are specific facts that describe or explain the main idea of a paragraph, article, or diagram. For example, the main idea of the previous paragraph is that smoking cigarettes during pregnancy can affect the baby. A detail that supports this main idea is that the babies of smokers often are underweight at birth.

Place a check mark beside any details that you can find in the paragraph about smoking cigarettes during pregnancy.

_____ a. Nicotine shrinks placenta blood vessels.

_____ c. Smoking is linked to stillbirths.

_____ b. Nicotine can damage the baby's brain.

_____ d. Fewer nutrients reach the baby's blood.

Alcohol. A condition called **fetal alcohol syndrome (FAS)** can occur when the mother drinks alcohol while pregnant. Children with FAS may have abnormal heads, faces, arms, or legs. They often have low birth weights. Some are mentally retarded.

Common Medications. Most common medications seem to pose no risk to the developing baby. This does not mean there are no risks. It just means no risks have been proven. However, some risks are suspected. Taking a lot of aspirin may cause bleeding or longer labor. Some aspirin substitutes taken late in pregnancy may cause problems with the baby's breathing.

Preventing Birth Defects

There is no way to guarantee a healthy baby. But women can help lower the risks to their babies. A pregnant woman should eat a well-balanced diet. She should get regular medical care. A woman who is pregnant should not smoke or drink alcohol. She should not take cocaine or other illegal drugs. Also, she should check with her doctor before taking any medicines.

Thinking About the Article

Practice Vocabulary

The terms below are in the passage in bold type. Study the way each term is used. Then complete each sentence by writing the correct term in the blank.

zygote　　　　　**uterus**　　　　　**embryo**

placenta　　　　　**fetus**

1 The fertilized egg, called a(n) _____, attaches to the wall of the _____, or womb, by the tenth day.

2 From the third to the eighth week, the developing baby is called a(n) _____.

3 The _____ is a structure through which substances pass between mother and baby.

4 From the third to the ninth month, the developing baby is called a(n) _____.

Understand the Article

Write or circle the answers to each question.

5 What two drugs helped focus research on what happens when a woman takes drugs during pregnancy?

_____

6 List the three stages of a baby's prebirth development in the proper order.

_____

7 During which stage of development is the most serious damage to the unborn baby likely to occur?

_____

8 List three drugs that have been linked with problems for babies.

_____

9 What can a pregnant woman do to help ensure she has a healthy baby? Circle the letter next to each correct answer.

a. Eat a well-balanced diet.

b. Not smoke at all.

c. Drink alcohol in moderation.

d. Check with her doctor before taking medicine.

Check your answers on page 231.

Apply Your Skills

Circle the number of the best answer for each question.

10 The diagram on page 40 has two parts. The main idea of the part on the left is that
   (1) the embryo stage is from three to eight weeks.
   (2) the placenta is part of the mother, not the baby.
   (3) the embryo is connected to the placenta, which is connected to the mother.
   (4) the baby and mother exchange substances via the placenta.
   (5) food and oxygen pass from the mother to the baby.

11 Harmful substances are least likely to cause birth defects in the last few months of pregnancy. The reason for this is that, by the last few months of pregnancy,
   (1) all of the body organs have formed.
   (2) the placenta blocks harmful substances.
   (3) the fetus has stopped growing.
   (4) the fetus can control what it takes in.
   (5) the fetus is not connected to the placenta.

12 A pregnant woman who wants to have a healthy baby should
   (1) eat a well-balanced diet.
   (2) stop smoking if she smokes.
   (3) stop drinking alcohol if she drinks.
   (4) use drugs only with the advice of a doctor.
   (5) do all of the above.

Connect with the Article

Write your answer to each question.

13 Many states have laws that require alcoholic beverages to have a warning label stating the dangers of drinking while pregnant. Do you think this is a good law? Give a reason for your answer.

_____

_____

_____

14 If you had a friend who was pregnant and you saw her lighting a cigarette, what would you do? Why?

_____

_____

_____

Genetics

Setting the Stage

Do you have the same color eyes or hair as your mother? Do you have a nose shaped like your father's? Parents pass on features like these to their children. Unfortunately, parents can also pass on certain diseases. Tests can find out if people are likely to get a disease passed on by their parents.

PREVIEW THE ARTICLE

A good way to get an overview of what you will be reading is to scan the headings in the article. These tell you what each section of the article will be about.

Read the headings on pages 45–47. What are some things you can expect to learn about genetics from the article?

_____

_____

_____

RELATE TO THE TOPIC

This article is about genetics. It explains how some features, including diseases, are passed from parents to children. It also discusses testing people to see whether they have inherited traits or have genetic material that will cause disease.

Think about your appearance. Which of your features look like those of your parents or children?

_____

_____

_____

VOCABULARY

traits   heredity   genetics

dominant trait   recessive trait

Genetic Screening

When Kristi Betts was fifteen, her mother came down with Huntington's disease. This disorder, which starts in middle age, slowly attacks the brain. People with Huntington's lose control over their physical and mental functions. This takes place over a period of about twenty years. There is no treatment or cure.

At first, Kristi was concerned only for her mother. Then she realized that she and her sisters and brothers were at risk for Huntington's disease, too. You cannot catch Huntington's disease like a cold or the flu. You **inherit** the disease. This means that you receive genetic material from one or both of your parents that causes you to develop the disease. Huntington's disease is passed on in the same way as brown eyes or curly hair. Each child of a parent with Huntington's disease has a chance of inheriting it.

How Traits Are Passed from Parent to Child

All organisms inherit features, or **traits,** from their parents. Some traits, such as hair color, are easily seen. Others, such as blood type, cannot be seen. **Heredity** is the passing of traits from parents to their young, or offspring. Traits are passed on when organisms reproduce. The study of how traits are inherited is called **genetics.**

Each parent gives its offspring genetic material for a form of the trait. In some cases, one form of the trait shows and the other does not. The form of the trait that shows whenever it is present is called the **dominant trait.** The form of the trait that doesn't always show is called the **recessive trait.** In humans, for example, dark hair and dark eyes are dominant traits. Light hair and light eyes are recessive traits. A person must inherit a recessive trait from each parent in order for it to show.

A four-generation birthday party

Scientists show how traits combine by using a diagram called a **Punnett square,** which shows all the possible combinations of traits among the offspring of two parents. Look at the Punnett square on the left. It shows the combinations that may result when one parent has the trait for Huntington's disease and the other parent does not. The trait for Huntington's disease is a dominant trait. It is labeled with a capital H. The healthy form of the trait is recessive. It is labeled with a lowercase h.

Mother

	H	h
h	Hh	hh
h	Hh	hh

Father

In this Punnett square, the mother with the trait for Huntington's disease is shown on top. She has a dominant and a recessive form of the trait. The healthy father is shown on the left. He has two recessive forms of the trait. When these two people have a child, each gives one form of the trait to the child. Their traits can combine as shown in the four boxes. A child who inherits a dominant and a recessive form (Hh) or two dominant forms (HH) will develop Huntington's disease as an adult. A child who inherits two recessive forms (hh) will not develop the disease.

Finding Details   Details are very important in science. When you come to a passage with a lot of details, slow down. The previous paragraph explains how to read the Punnett square. Reread the paragraph one sentence at a time. If you read slowly and carefully, you will understand the details. For example, you will find out that the father is healthy because he has two recessive forms of the trait for Huntington's. The mother has Huntington's because she has one dominant and one recessive form of the trait.

Look back at the paragraph to find the details to help you answer these questions.

1 Will a child who inherits hh develop Huntington's disease? _____

2 Will a child who inherits Hh develop Huntington's disease? _____

Testing for Inherited Disorders

You can see from the Punnett square above that Kristi Betts had a two out of four chance of inheriting Huntington's disease. At one time, people had to live with this uncertainty. Since Huntington's disease doesn't appear until middle age, young people with an ill parent didn't know their own fate. But now people at risk can be tested. **Genetic screening** is the name for tests that can tell people if they have inherited certain disorders.

It is hard to decide whether to be tested for Huntington's disease. Is it better to know or not know if you are going to get the disease? Kristi decided it was better to know. She was lucky. She found out that she had not inherited Huntington's disease.

Unlike Huntington's, many genetic diseases are recessive. When two recessive forms combine, the child inherits the disorder even though both parents may be healthy. There are tests to see if adults carry the recessive traits for certain disorders, such as sickle-cell anemia.

Check your answers on page 231.

Genetic Screening of the Unborn

Genetic screening of fetuses is becoming more common, even among people with no history of genetic disease in their families. For example, **amniocentesis** is a test that can be performed after the sixteenth week of pregnancy. This test can detect several disorders caused by genetic abnormalities, including Down syndrome. **Down syndrome** is a disorder caused by the presence of an extra **chromosome.** Children who have Down syndrome are mildly to severely mentally retarded. They may also have other health problems.

The developing baby receives genetic material from each parent in the form of chromosomes. Each baby should have 23 pairs of chromosomes, with one in each pair coming from the mother, and the other coming from the father. In amniocentesis, the baby's chromosomes are photographed and examined. The extra chromosome 21 in this photograph indicates that this baby has Down syndrome.

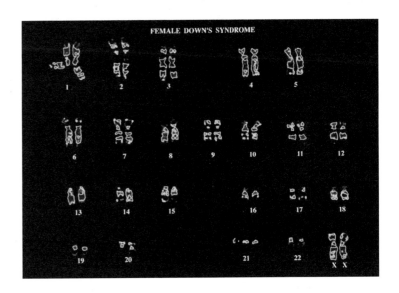

When genetic screening shows a disorder, prospective parents must decide what to do. Genetic counselors help them explore their choices. People may decide not to have children. They may also accept the outcome and risk the possibility of having a disabled child. Some people believe that genetic screening is wrong. Others feel that the knowledge, even if it is bad news, is worth having.

Distinguishing Fact from Opinion   **Facts** are things that can be proved true. **Opinions,** on the other hand, are beliefs. They may or may not be true. When reading science, it's important to distinguish fact from opinion. One way to do this is to look for words that signal an opinion: *believe, feel, think,* and *opinion.* For example, in the previous paragraph the phrase "Some people believe" signals that an opinion is coming.

Write the words *fact* or *opinion* next to each statement. If the statement includes an opinion, circle the word that signals an opinion.

❶ Genetic counselors help parents explore their choices. _____

❷ Some people feel that even bad news is knowledge worth having. _____

Thinking About the Article

Practice Vocabulary

The terms below are in the passage in bold type. Study the way each term is used. Then complete each sentence by writing the correct term in the blank.

traits   **heredity**   **genetics**

dominant trait   **recessive trait**

1 In humans, dark hair is a _____ that always shows when it is present.

2 _____, or characteristics, are features inherited from parents.

3 _____ is the study of how traits are inherited.

4 The passing on of traits from parents to their children is called

_____.

5 Light hair is a _____.

Understand the Article

Write or circle the answer to each question.

6 Unlike a cold or pneumonia, Huntington's disease is not spread by contact with other people's germs. How is Huntington's disease transmitted?
a.   You inherit it from a parent.
b.   You get it from contact with poisonous chemicals.

7 Name a human trait that is dominant.

_____

8 Name a disease that results when a child inherits two recessive forms of the trait.

_____

9 Name a disorder that can be identified by performing amniocentesis.

_____

10 What is the job of a genetic counselor?

_____

_____

Apply Your Skills

Circle the number of the best answer for each question.

11 Which of the following is a genetic screening test for a fetus?
- (1) Huntington's disease
- (2) amniocentesis
- (3) Punnett square
- (4) heredity
- (5) Down syndrome

12 According to the Punnett square on page 46, what is the chance that a child of a parent with Huntington's disease will inherit the disease?
- (1) zero out of four
- (2) one out of four
- (3) two out of four
- (4) three out of four
- (5) four out of four

13 Which of the following statements includes an opinion rather than a fact?
- (1) To test whether a person has inherited a disease, he or she undergoes genetic screening.
- (2) A person with one parent who has Huntington's has a chance of inheriting the disease.
- (3) Some young people think it is better to be tested and know whether they will develop Huntington's in middle age.
- (4) Some parents undergo amniocentesis to find out whether their unborn babies have Down syndrome or other disorders.
- (5) Children born with Down syndrome are mildly to severely retarded and may have other health problems.

Connect with the Article

Write your answer to each question.

14 If both of your parents had Hh traits for Huntington's, what would be your chances of inheriting this disease?

_____

15 If you were about to become a mother or father, would you want genetic screening done during pregnancy? Why or why not?

_____

_____

_____

Bacteria and Viruses

Setting the Stage

Have you ever been trapped in a small space with people who are coughing, sneezing, and blowing their noses? If so, you probably resigned yourself to catching a cold. After all, there's a reason this illness is called the common cold: Most people have at least two colds each year. But even worse than a cold is the flu. Although most people recover from the flu after a few weeks, other people go on to develop pneumonia, which can be deadly.

PREVIEW THE ARTICLE

You can improve your comprehension by scanning the diagrams, photos, and captions of an article before you begin to read. These give you clues about what the article is about. They help you understand the details of what you will be reading.

Look at the photo and diagrams on pages 51–53. Read the captions and titles. What are some things you can expect to learn from this article?

_____

_____

RELATE TO THE TOPIC

This article is about viruses and bacteria that cause some common diseases. It explains what causes a cold, the flu, and pneumonia, and how you can catch these diseases. It also tells what these illnesses are like.

Think back to a time when you had a bad cold, the flu, or even pneumonia. How do you think you caught it? What were your symptoms? What did you do to make yourself feel better?

_____

_____

VOCABULARY

virus	influenza (flu)	pneumonia
bacteria	antibiotics	

Colds, Flu, and Pneumonia

First you feel a small ache or a tickle in your throat. Soon your nose is running, your head is congested, and your eyes are watering. Your throat is now sore, too. Yes, it's another cold.

Catching a Cold

In spite of what your mother may have told you, getting wet and chilled won't give you a cold. Instead, you catch a cold from a sick person near you.

Scientists disagree about how colds are passed from one person to another. Jack Gwaltney, a scientist at the University of Virginia, thinks that colds are passed by touch. Gwaltney says that people with colds have many cold-causing viruses on their hands. When these people touch something, such as a telephone, they leave viruses on the surface. You come along and touch the telephone. Then you touch your nose or eyes, and the virus settles in.

Another scientist, Elliot Dick from the University of Wisconsin, disagrees with Gwaltney. As an experiment, Dick gathered sixty card players for a twelve-hour poker game. Twenty players had colds. Of the forty healthy players, half wore braces or collars that kept them from touching their faces. The other half were free to touch their faces. Players in both healthy groups caught colds. Since players who could not touch their faces also got sick, Dick believes that cold viruses are spread through the air. Someone who is sick sneezes or coughs, and you breathe in the virus. Soon you are sick, too.

Elliot Dick's cold virus experiment

Treating a Cold

Protein covering

Genetic material

A Rhinovirus

Stroll through any drugstore and you'll see hundreds of sprays, pills, capsules, and syrups to make the cold sufferer feel better. Many of these products do help. But none can cure a cold. For years, scientists have been trying to find a cure for the common cold. The problem is that colds are caused by about 200 different viruses. About half of all colds are caused by a group of viruses called **rhinoviruses.**

Just what is a virus? A **virus** is a tiny particle made up of genetic material with a protein covering. The genetic material holds directions for making more viruses. The protein covering protects the virus.

Finding Details in a Diagram   Besides providing a general picture of something, a diagram has many specific things, or details, in it. You have to look carefully to find the details. Often there's help: The most important details are labeled. The words with lines pointing to parts of the diagram are called *labels.* Labels direct your attention to important details. In the diagram of a rhinovirus above, labels point out two details: the protein covering and the genetic material.

Now look at the diagram of a bacterial cell on the next page. List the details you can find in this diagram.

_____   _____

_____   _____

Viruses are not cells, and they are not made of cells. They don't grow. To make more viruses, they must be inside a living cell. For example, a rhinovirus latches onto a cell in the nose. The virus injects its genetic material into the cell and uses the cell's materials to make more viruses. Then the cell bursts open and dies. The new viruses are released to infect other cells.

Infections caused by viruses are hard to cure. The best way to fight viruses is to stop them before they invade. Researchers are looking for ways to block the rhinoviruses from attaching to cells in the nose.

The Flu

Another illness caused by a virus is **influenza,** usually called the **flu.** The difference between a cold and the flu is sometimes hard to feel. A cold usually starts slowly, with a scratchy throat. Other symptoms follow in a day or two. Usually there is little or no fever. In contrast, the flu starts quickly. Within twelve hours you may have a fever over 101 degrees. Besides having a sore throat, stuffy nose, and a cough, you ache and feel very tired. Recovering from the flu can take up to three weeks. Although there are some drugs to help people feel better, there is no cure.

Check your answers on page 232.

One defense against the flu is to get a flu vaccination each year. A **vaccination** is an injected dose of a dead or weakened disease-causing agent. This causes the body to form antibodies. An **antibody** is a substance the body makes to fight a disease. Once antibodies form, you are protected against that specific agent. This protection lowers your chance of getting the disease.

Pneumonia

People weakened by a bad cold or the flu are more likely to develop pneumonia. Symptoms include a high fever, chest pain, breathing problems, and a bad cough. **Pneumonia** is an infection of the lungs caused by a virus or bacterium. **Bacteria** are one-celled organisms and are many times larger than viruses. A bacterial cell is shown in the following diagram.

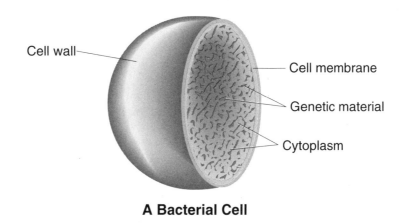

Cell wall
Cell membrane
Genetic material
Cytoplasm

A Bacterial Cell

About 90 percent of flu-related pneumonia is caused by bacteria. As the infection takes hold, the lungs produce fluid and mucus to fight the bacteria. The fluid blocks the air passages in the lungs. The person has trouble breathing and may have to go to a hospital. He or she is given **antibiotics,** drugs that fight bacteria. The antibiotics kill the disease-causing bacteria, and the person gets better.

Making Inferences   When you read, you can sometimes figure out things that the author hints at but doesn't actually tell you. A fact or idea that is not stated in the text but that you figure out is an **inference.** Reread the first paragraph about pneumonia. The author says that people who have the flu sometimes develop an infection called pneumonia. One thing you can infer is that a good way to avoid getting pneumonia is to avoid getting the flu.

Which of the following ideas can be inferred from the information in the paragraph that begins "About 90 percent"? Circle the letter of the correct inference.
   a.   About 10 percent of flu-related pneumonia is caused by a virus.
   b.   Antibiotics can help cure pneumonia caused by a virus.

Thinking About the Article

Practice Vocabulary

The terms below are in the passage in bold type. Study the way each term is used. Then match each term to its meaning by writing the correct letter in the blank.

_____ ❶ virus

_____ ❷ influenza

_____ ❸ pneumonia

_____ ❹ bacteria

_____ ❺ antibiotic

a. one-celled organisms

b. an infection of the lungs caused by bacteria or a virus

c. an illness caused by a virus; also called the flu

d. a drug that fights bacteria

e. a tiny particle made of genetic material and a covering

Understand the Article

Write or circle the answer to each question.

❻ Scientists Jack Gwaltney and Elliot Dick disagree about the common cold. What do they disagree about?
   a. Gwaltney thinks colds are caused by one type of virus, and Dick thinks they are caused by many types.
   b. Gwaltney thinks colds are spread through touch, and Dick thinks they are spread through the air.

❼ What can cause each of the following diseases? Write _bacteria_ and/or _virus_ in the space provided.

   a. a cold _____

   b. the flu _____

   c. pneumonia _____

❽ How does a virus make more copies of itself?
   a. It splits in half, as in cell division.
   b. It takes over a cell and uses cell materials to copy itself.

❾ What is a vaccination?

   _____

   _____

❿ What is an antibody?

   _____

   _____

Check your answers on page 232.

Apply Your Skills

Circle the number of the best answer for each question.

11 Which of the following is *not* a structure in a bacterial cell?
(1) cell wall
(2) cell membrane
(3) antibody
(4) genetic material
(5) cytoplasm

12 From the information in this article, you can infer that the best way not to get a cold is to
(1) avoid touching anything that people with colds touch.
(2) avoid breathing air in spaces where people with colds are.
(3) avoid people with colds.
(4) stay dry and warm in the winter.
(5) get a vaccination against colds.

13 You can infer that antibiotics are not used to treat colds and the flu because
(1) they do not fight viruses.
(2) they do not fight bacteria.
(3) people with colds or the flu do not go to the hospital.
(4) they cost too much to use them on colds and the flu.
(5) they are used to prevent colds and the flu.

Connect with the Article

Write your answer to each question.

14 Winter is the season when most cases of colds, flu, and pneumonia occur. Why do you think that is so?

_____

_____

_____

15 What can you do to keep yourself and your family healthy next winter?

_____

_____

_____

_____

8 Plants

Setting the Stage

When you reach into the medicine cabinet for an aspirin, do you realize you are using a drug that comes from a plant? Aspirin is a compound that comes from the bark of the willow tree. It has been used for thousands of years to relieve fever and pain by many peoples, including Native Americans and ancient Greeks. Many medicines we use today come from plants, especially rain forest plants. Scientists are working to find these useful plants before the rain forests disappear.

PREVIEW THE ARTICLE

You can get the most from your reading by scanning the diagrams, photos, and tables of an article before you begin to read. These give you clues to what the article is about. They help you understand the details of what you will be reading.

Look at the photo, diagram, and table on pages 57–59. Read the captions and title of the diagram and the table. What are some things you expect to learn about plants from this article?

_____

_____

RELATE TO THE TOPIC

This article is about plants that are used as medicines. It describes the parts of a plant and explains how scientists test plants for possible use as drugs.

People use plants for many purposes, not just as medicines. Think about how you use plants. Describe one or two ways that you use plants.

_____

_____

VOCABULARY

roots   stem   bark

leaves   buds   flowers

   Check your answers on page 233.

Medicines from Plants

In South America, the juice from a fungus (a mushroom or a mold) is used to treat earaches. In Indonesia, pressed plants are used to cure tetanus (lockjaw). In India and Nepal, coleus is used to get rid of body worms. These are just a few of the plants that are used as medicines. People have been using plants to treat and cure diseases for thousands of years. Plant medicines work in two ways. Some affect the body's chemistry. Others affect the bacteria and viruses that cause diseases.

Searching for Medicinal Plants

There is an urgent need to search for plants that can be used as medicines. The tropical rain forests contain two-thirds of the world's plant **species,** or kinds of plants. Many of these species have not yet even been identified. But the rain forests are disappearing at a rapid rate. Useful plants may become extinct before they can be identified and studied.

This vine can be brewed into a tea that is used to treat stomachaches. It grows in rain forests.

One scientist is using a shortcut to find useful plants. Dr. Mark Plotkin has been working with native shamans, or traditional healers, in the Amazon rain forest. These healers have a knowledge of plants that dates back thousands of years. They use about three hundred different plants as medicines. Dr. Plotkin has to work quickly, though. Most young people in the Amazon rain forest are more interested in modern ways. As a result, the shamans' knowledge is dying out. The plants they use may soon be gone, too.

Scientists must test a plant if they think it may be a source for a medicine. An extract, or strong solution, is made from the plant. The extract is placed in test tubes that contain cancer cells, bacteria, or viruses. Extracts that seem to work as a medicine are tested on mice. Then the extract is broken down into its chemical parts. The parts are tested until the active chemical is found. Then scientists must figure out how much of the extract is safe to use. Many plant products are poisonous in large doses.

Parts of a Plant

Medicines have been made from all parts of plants. Often only one part of a plant can be used to make a medicine. The diagram shows the parts of a typical seed plant.

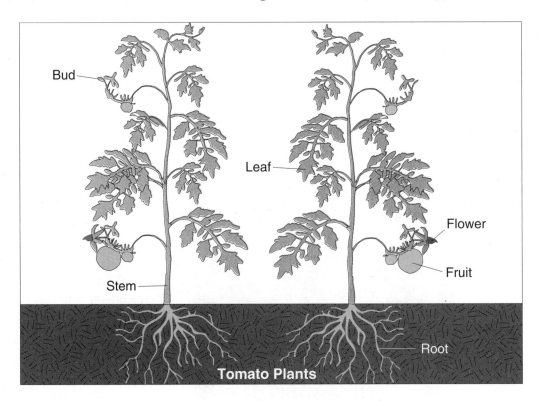

The **roots** of a plant hold the plant in the ground. They also absorb minerals and water from the soil. The **stem** supports the plant. It also transports water and minerals from the roots to the top of the plant. **Bark** is the outer part of the stem of a woody plant. **Leaves** use sunlight to change water and carbon dioxide into food for the plant. **Buds** are areas of growth. New leaves or flowers grow from buds. **Flowers** are the reproductive organs of plants. Flowers develop into fruits. The fruits contain the seeds, which will grow into new plants.

Getting Meaning from Context You may not understand every word you read in science. But sometimes you can figure out the meaning of words you don't know from clues nearby. Reread the description of the stem in the paragraph above. Can you guess what the word *transport* means? Look at the **context**—the rest of the words in the sentence. There are clues. Water and minerals are moving up from the roots to the rest of the plant. The stem is carrying water and minerals. The word *transport* means "to carry or move."

In the paragraph that describes the parts of a plant, what does *reproductive organs* mean? Circle the letter of the correct meaning.

a. the parts of the plant that produce offspring

b. the parts of the plant that produce many copies of the leaves

Check your answer on page 233.

Using Plant Medicines

Even in modern cultures, plants are the source of many drugs. There are more than 265,000 different plant species known in the world. Less than one percent of them have been tested as medicines. Yet about 25 percent of all medicines have come from that tiny number of plants. Many medicines are made directly from natural plant products. Others are synthetic, or artificial, copies of the plants' helpful substances. These synthetic substances make more medicine available than people could gather from the plants alone. The table shows some of these medicines and their plant sources.

Medicines and Their Plant Sources

Medicine	Plant Source	Use
quinine	cinchona bark	treating malaria
curare	several tropical plants	muscle relaxant during surgery
digitalis	purple foxglove	treating heart disorders
vinca alkaloids	rosy periwinkle	treating Hodgkin's disease and leukemia
expectorant	horehound	in cough syrup to discharge mucus
menthol	peppermint leaves	in pain relievers and decongestants
valepotriates	root of valerian	sedative
reserpine	roots of several shrubs	sedative; treating high blood pressure
salicylate	wintergreen	in liniments to soothe muscle aches
taxol	bark of Pacific yew	treating ovarian and other cancers

The table shows that many common medicines come from plants. For example, Valium, a well-known sedative, is a synthetic form of substances found in the roots of the valerian plant. (Sedatives are medicines that help people relax.) Horehound is used to make cough syrups and throat lozenges.

Some plants are used in the treatment of serious diseases, such as cancer. Many forms of chemotherapy use natural products from plants. One recent discovery is taxol. It is used to treat ovarian cancer. So far, taxol cannot be made in a laboratory. The Pacific yew must be harvested to produce natural taxol.

Summarizing Information   When you **summarize** something, you condense, or shorten, a larger amount of information into one or several sentences. You state the major points of a larger body of information in a few words. Reread the previous paragraph about treating cancer. This paragraph can be summarized as follows: Plant products, such as taxol, are used in chemotherapy to treat cancer.

Which of the following statements is a good summary of this article? Circle the letter of the best summary.

    a.   People have been making medicines from all parts of plants for thousands of years.

    b.   A typical seed plant has roots, stems, leaves, and flowers.

Check your answer on page 233.

Thinking About the Article

Practice Vocabulary

The terms below are in the passage in bold type. Study the context in which they appear. Then match each plant part to its function by writing the correct letter in the blank.

_____ **1** leaf

_____ **2** stem

_____ **3** bark

_____ **4** flower

_____ **5** bud

_____ **6** root

a. transports water to leaves

b. reproductive organ of the plant

c. absorbs water and minerals from soil

d. outer part of the stem of a woody plant

e. area of growth

f. makes food for the plant

Understand the Article

Write or circle the answer to each question.

7 List two ways that plants work as medicines.

_____

_____

8 Why do scientists test plants in laboratories before trying them on people? Circle the letter of each correct reason.
   a. They have to find out which chemical in the plant is active.
   b. They cannot find volunteers to take the plant extracts.
   c. They have to figure out how much of the plant extract to use.
   d. They have to see whether the plant destroys cancer, bacteria, or viruses.

9 Why has Dr. Mark Plotkin been working with shamans in the Amazon rain forest?

_____

_____

10 According to the table on page 59, how are reserpine and valepotriates alike? Circle the letter of each correct similarity.
   a. Both are made from roots.
   b. Both are sedatives.
   c. Both are used in cough syrups.

Check your answers on page 233.

Apply Your Skills

Circle the number of the best answer for each question.

⑪ Reread the last paragraph on page 57. What does the phrase *active chemical* mean? Use context clues to help you figure out the meaning.
  (1) the extract of the plant
  (2) the strong solution that contains cancer cells, bacteria, or viruses
  (3) the chemical that works as a medicine
  (4) the most poisonous chemical in the plant
  (5) the amount of chemical that is safe to use

⑫ Which of the following best summarizes the diagram on page 58?
  (1) Tomato plants have leaves, flowers, and fruit.
  (2) Good soil is necessary to anchor a flowering plant in the ground.
  (3) A typical seed plant has roots, stems, buds, leaves, flowers, and fruit.
  (4) The fruits of a tomato plant develop from its flowers.
  (5) Although tomatoes are called vegetables, they are really fruits.

⑬ Reread the first paragraph under the heading "Searching for Medicinal Plants" on page 57. What does the word *species* mean?
  (1) type of culture
  (2) type of organism
  (3) medicines that come from plants
  (4) treatment for a disease
  (5) type of sedative

Understand the Article

Write your answer to each question.

⑭ What are two ways modern culture has helped limit the use of rain forest plants as medicines?

_____

_____

_____

⑮ Have you or someone you know ever used any of the medicines listed on page 59? If so, write why the medicine was used. If not, describe some other medicine you have taken.

_____

_____

_____

Animal Behavior

Setting the Stage

People have been intrigued by dolphins for thousands of years. Stories of dolphins befriending children and swimmers come from all parts of the world. The dolphin shows at marine parks and aquariums are extremely popular. People even pay to swim with dolphins at resorts and parks. Today, scientists are studying dolphins to discover how these animals communicate in the wild and in captivity.

PREVIEW THE ARTICLE

The headings of an article tell you what each section of the article is about. By scanning these before you begin to read, you will have a better idea of what the article will cover.

Look at the headings on pages 63–65. What are some things you can expect to learn about dolphins from this article?

_____

_____

RELATE TO THE TOPIC

This article is about one very specific aspect of animal behavior, dolphin communication. It describes the sounds dolphins make and what they are used for. It also tells about a project to teach dolphins an artificial language.

Have you ever seen dolphins, either in the wild or at an aquarium? Or have you seen dolphins on TV or in the movies? Describe the dolphins you saw.

_____

_____

VOCABULARY

mammals	sound waves	echolocation
density	language	

Check your answers on page 233.

How Do Dolphins Communicate?

At a signal from their trainer, the dolphins leap out of the pool, curve high over the water, and then dive back in. They perform beautifully, and the audience at the marine park loves them. While they resemble fish, they are actually **mammals.** Dolphins are not just charming entertainers. They are the subject of many research studies, including several on how dolphins communicate. In the wild, dolphins communicate using a variety of sounds. They use whistles, grunts, and repetitive clicks, many of which humans cannot hear. In captivity, they have been taught to communicate using simple sign language.

Signature Whistles

One type of sound that dolphins use is the whistle. To most people, all dolphin whistles sound alike. But research indicates that each dolphin has its own unique signature whistle.

Studying signature whistles is difficult. Although people can hear the whistles underwater, we cannot locate a whistle's source. Even when underwater microphones are used to pick up the whistles, their source cannot be pinpointed. One solution to this problem is to isolate a single dolphin for a short time and record its whistle. Another solution, invented by Peter Tyack of Stanford University, is a device called a vocalight. The vocalight is attached to a dolphin's head by a suction cup. A microphone inside the vocalight picks up sounds, which are displayed as lights. The louder the sound, the more lights go on.

Tyack used vocalights to study two dolphins, Spray and Scotty, at the Sealand aquarium in Brewster, Massachusetts. One dolphin had green lights and the other red. Tyack and his colleagues observed the dolphins and recorded the number and color of the lights. Tyack found that each dolphin made two types of whistles. One type was Spray's signature, and the other type was Scotty's. Each dolphin used the other's signature whistle some of the time, perhaps as a label or a name. And each signature whistle had many variations in duration, pitch, and shape of the sounds. Tyack thinks that the dolphins could detect these variations.

Most dolphins at marine parks and aquariums are bottlenose dolphins.

Spray died after these experiments, leaving Scotty alone. Two years later, Tyack returned to test Scotty's whistles. He found that Scotty no longer used Spray's favorite whistle. His whistles had become shorter and quieter. Tyack thinks this is evidence that the whistles are a form of social communication among dolphins.

Echolocation

In addition to whistles, dolphins use high-pitched clicks to identify objects. The dolphin produces a burst of sound from its head. The **sound waves** strike objects and bounce back. The waves are then received in the dolphin's lower jaw and interpreted. This process, called **echolocation,** is similar to a submarine's use of sonar.

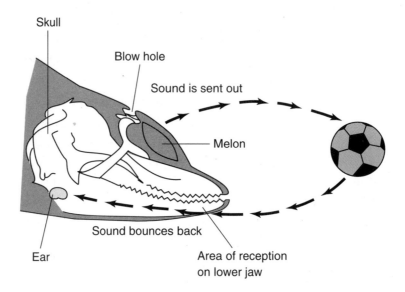

Skull

Blow hole

Sound is sent out

Melon

Sound bounces back

Ear

Area of reception on lower jaw

Through echolocation, a dolphin can "see" the shape of objects. In addition to providing information about an object's surface, echolocation provides information on **density.** A dolphin can sense the amount of matter in a particular amount of space. For example, a dolphin can detect a swimmer's lungs, which are less dense than the rest of his or her body because they are filled with air. In this way, echolocation is similar to ultrasound, which provides images of the inside of the human body.

Classifying Grouping things that are similar helps us understand how nature works. Putting things into groups is called **classifying.** In this article, we have seen that scientists classify the sounds that dolphins make. One classification, discussed on page 63, is the whistle.

Reread this page and look for the sound classifications described here.

The sounds used in echolocation are classified as —————————————.

Check your answer on page 233.

Teaching Dolphins Artificial Language

Dolphins do communicate in the wild, but so far there is no evidence that their communication is a form of language. A **language** is a system of sounds, symbols, signs, or gestures that refer to objects or ideas and that can be combined in many different ways to produce different meanings. Human language uses sounds to represent meaning and grammar to combine sounds into an infinite number of messages.

Can dolphins be taught a simple language? Louis M. Herman and his colleagues at the University of Hawaii thought so. They taught four captive dolphins two artificial languages. One language uses computer-generated high-pitched "words." The other language uses hand and arm movements (sign language) to signify words. Each language has about forty words, including nouns such as *channel, gate, person,* and *ball;* verbs such as *fetch;* and modifiers such as *right, left, surface,* and *bottom.* Herman wanted to know if the dolphins could learn these words and understand the difference between them.

The dolphins were able to learn both what each word referred to and how to interpret the order of words. For example, the dolphins could distinguish between two sign language sentences such as "right hoop left Frisbee fetch" and "left hoop right Frisbee fetch." The first sentence means "take the Frisbee on the left to the hoop on the right," and the second means "take the Frisbee on the right to the hoop on the left." Herman's experiments seem to provide further evidence of dolphins' ability to understand and communicate.

One dolphin, Ake, went beyond responding as trained. She was able to invent responses to unusual situations. For example, there were two large paddle-shaped switches labeled "yes" and "no." If Ake was asked to move an object and it was not in the pool, she pressed the "no" paddle. If she was given a command that was impossible to carry out, such as "fetch the water to the person," she ignored it. If she was given a command with too many nouns, such as "fetch the water and the hoop to the person" she ignored the word "water" and simply fetched the hoop. Herman sees these untaught responses as evidence that dolphins have learned the grammar rules of the artificial language and can use them to interpret new messages.

Drawing Conclusions   A **conclusion** is an idea that follows logically from facts or evidence. Scientists are careful not to draw a conclusion unless they have evidence to support it. For example, Ake's ability to make up her own responses to unusual messages and situations supports Herman's conclusion that dolphins can learn grammar rules and use them to interpret new messages.

Which of the following is a conclusion that can be drawn from the evidence provided by the artificial language experiments? Circle the letter of the correct answer.

    a.   Dolphins can learn "words" that refer to specific objects or ideas.

    b.   Dolphins use language to communicate in the wild.

Thinking About the Article

Practice Vocabulary

The terms below are in the passage in bold type. Study the way each term is used. Then complete each sentence by writing the correct term in the blank.

mammals	**sound waves**	**echolocation**
density	**language**	

1. Scientists taught dolphins, which are marine _____,

   an artificial _____ that involved gestures.

2. Dolphins send out _____ from their heads and receive them in their lower jaws.

3. Through _____, dolphins can identify objects in the environment.

4. In addition to sensing the shape of an object, a dolphin can sense its

   _____ .

Understand the Article

Write or circle the answer to each question.

5. How did Peter Tyack solve the problem of identifying the source of underwater sounds?

   _____

   _____

   _____

6. What is a dolphin's signature whistle?

   _____

   _____

7. How does echolocation work?
   a. by bouncing sound waves off objects in the environment
   b. by creating light signals that represent sounds in the environment

8. What led Louis Herman to conclude that dolphins could learn the grammar rules of the artificial language and use them to interpret new messages?
   a. Ake was able to create new responses to unusual situations.
   b. Ake was able to fetch the Frisbee and hoop when commanded.

Apply Your Skills

Circle the number of the best answer for each question.

9 According to the article, dolphins are classified as
   (1) fish.
   (2) rodents.
   (3) mammals.
   (4) primates.
   (5) amphibians.

10 Scotty's whistles changed after Spray died. Tyack cited this fact as evidence supporting his conclusion that dolphin signature whistles are
   (1) unique.
   (2) stable over many years.
   (3) inaudible to the human ear.
   (4) a form of social communication.
   (5) a language with "words" and "grammar."

11 Dolphins have been taught a simple language with gestures and sentences made of gestures. From this fact you can conclude that dolphins
   (1) have the ability to learn and think.
   (2) use language in the wild.
   (3) don't really need to use sounds.
   (4) live in groups of 10 to 25 dolphins.
   (5) have unique signature whistles.

Connect with the Article

Write your answer to each question.

12 Do you think that dolphins' ability to communicate is one of the reasons they are such a popular attraction at marine parks and aquariums? Explain your answer.

_____

_____

_____

13 Have you or someone you know ever tried to train an animal such as a dog or cat? Describe this experience. What did this experience teach you about animal communication?

_____

_____

_____

Setting the Stage

Roaches, silverfish, carpenter ants, termites, aphids—the list of insect pests is long. One destructive pest is the gypsy moth. Gypsy moths are leaf-eating insects that have damaged millions of acres of trees. People have tried many methods of wiping out these pests at each stage of their life cycle. Still, gypsy moths continue to spread in the United States.

PREVIEW THE ARTICLE

The headings of an article provide an outline of the article's contents. That's why it's important to read the headings before you start to read the article. You will have an overview of what the article is about.

Read the headings on pages 69–71. What are three things you can expect to learn about gypsy moths from this article?

_____

_____

_____

RELATE TO THE TOPIC

This article is about an insect pest, the gypsy moth. It describes the life cycle of the moth and ways that people use to control its spread.

If you had to describe the stages of the human life cycle that you have experienced so far, what stages would you include? How would you describe each stage?

_____

_____

VOCABULARY

life cycle	**egg**	**caterpillar**
pupa	**adult**	

Check your answers on page 234.

Fighting the Gypsy Moth

You probably take the trees in your neighborhood for granted. Yet in the Northeast, gypsy moth caterpillars have stripped the leaves off millions of oak, birch, aspen, gum, and other trees. People in the northeastern United States have been fighting the gypsy moth for a hundred years.

The Spread of the Gypsy Moth

A Frenchman brought gypsy moth eggs from Europe to Massachusetts in the 1860s. He hoped to breed the moths with American silk-producing moths. Unfortunately, several moths escaped from his house. Fifty years later, the gypsy moth had spread throughout the Northeast. Today many scientists, government agencies, and private citizens are fighting the gypsy moth as far south as Virginia and as far west as Michigan. The moths have been seen even in California and Oregon.

Gypsy moth caterpillars do a great deal of damage. They will eat every leaf on trees they like, such as oak trees. However, they skip other types of trees, such as spruce. Healthy trees can survive a gypsy moth attack. The leaves usually grow back the next year. But trees weakened by disease or inadequate rainfall may die after a year or two.

In addition to damaging trees, gypsy moth caterpillars make a mess. They leave half-eaten leaves everywhere. Their droppings ruin the finish on cars. The caterpillars make their way onto porches, screens, and windows. When they die, the smell of decay is terrible.

Oak tree leaves damaged by gypsy moth caterpillars

The Life Cycle of the Gypsy Moth

To find ways to get rid of gypsy moths, scientists study the insect's life cycle. A **life cycle** is the series of changes an animal goes through in its life. There are four stages in the life cycle of a gypsy moth.

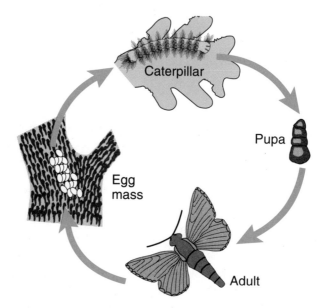

The Gypsy Moth's Life Cycle

❶ **Egg.** Gypsy moth eggs are laid during the summer. Each female lays from 75 to 1,000 eggs in a clump called an **egg mass.** Egg masses are tan and slightly fuzzy.

❷ **Caterpillar.** Gypsy moth eggs hatch into caterpillars. The caterpillars climb up trees to find leaves to eat. They grow to more than two inches long.

❸ **Pupa.** During the pupa stage, the caterpillar encloses itself in a case for about two weeks. Its body changes into a moth.

❹ **Adult.** When the pupa case breaks open, the adult moth comes out. Adult gypsy moths do not eat, so they do not live long. The female gives off a smell that attracts males. After mating, the male dies. The female lives long enough to lay eggs, and then she dies.

Identifying Sequence   The order in which things happen is called **sequence**. Often, things that happen in sequence are numbered, as in the description of the gypsy moth life cycle on this page.

❶   In the life cycle of a gypsy moth, what stage comes after the caterpillar?

_____

❷   What stages come before the adult stage?

_____

Check your answers on page 234.

A life cycle is often shown in the circular style used on page 70. However, it can also be shown in a timeline, such as the one below.

Life Cycle of a Gypsy Moth

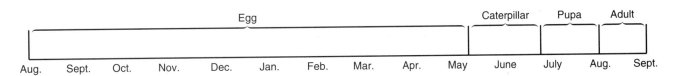

| Egg | Caterpillar | Pupa | Adult |

Aug.　Sept.　Oct.　Nov.　Dec.　Jan.　Feb.　Mar.　Apr.　May　June　July　Aug.　Sept.

Reading a Timeline　A **timeline** is another way to show a sequence. In addition to showing the sequence of events, a timeline shows when an event happens. When you see a timeline, look at its title first. That will tell you what the timeline is about. This one is about the life cycle of the gypsy moth. Next, look at the labels. The labels along the bottom of this timeline are months. The labels at the top show the stages of a gypsy moth's life. For example, you can see that most adult moths emerge in August and die in September. This stage only lasts a month.

1 How long does the caterpillar stage of the life cycle last? _____

2 When do adult moths begin to emerge from the pupa stage?

Controlling the Gypsy Moth

The gypsy moth damages trees during the caterpillar stage. The caterpillars can be killed by spraying the trees. Some sprays are chemicals that can harm other animals and the environment. Other sprays contain bacteria that kill only the moths. Caterpillars can be caught by wrapping sticky tape around trees. When the caterpillars climb, they get stuck on the tape and die. Gypsy moths can also be killed by destroying their eggs. Egg masses can be found on trees, buildings, fences, and outdoor furniture. They can be scraped into a bucket of kerosene, bleach, or ammonia. These chemicals kill the eggs.

Pupa cases can be removed from trees and crushed. Adult males can be caught in scented traps, which contain a bait that smells like a female moth. The male flies into the trap and dies there.

Some birds prey on gypsy moths. Birds that eat the moths can be attracted into an infested area. People can put out food, water, and nesting materials to encourage the birds to stay. Another natural control method uses parasites. A **parasite** is an organism that lives on or in another organism and harms it. Many parasites have been released in areas with gypsy moths.

Diseases can lower the number of moths. One year there was a very rainy spring, and many moths died of a fungus disease. Perhaps one day scientists will be able to use the fungus to kill gypsy moths.

Thinking About the Article

Practice Vocabulary

The terms below are in the passage in bold type. Study the way each term is used. Then complete each sentence by writing the correct term in the blank.

life cycle	egg	caterpillar
pupa	adult	

1. The _____ is the first stage of the gypsy moth's life.

2. The caterpillar is enclosed in a case during the _____ stage.

3. During the _____ stage, the gypsy moth crawls around and damages trees.

4. A mature gypsy moth, capable of laying eggs, is in the _____ stage.

5. An animal goes through stages during the course of its life, which are called its _____ .

Understand the Article

Write the answer to each question.

6. How were gypsy moths introduced into the United States?

_____

_____

_____

7. What damage does the gypsy moth caterpillar do?

_____

_____

Match the stage of the gypsy moth's life cycle with the control method used during that stage.

_____ 8 egg   a. spraying insecticide

_____ 9 caterpillar   b. soaking in ammonia, kerosene, or bleach

_____ 10 pupa   c. putting out scent traps

_____ 11 adult   d. crushing

Check your answers on page 234.

Apply Your Skills

Circle the number of the best answer for each question.

12 Which of the following is the correct sequence of stages in the gypsy moth life cycle?
  (1) egg, pupa, caterpillar, adult
  (2) egg, adult, pupa, caterpillar
  (3) egg, pupa, adult, caterpillar
  (4) egg, caterpillar, adult, pupa
  (5) egg, caterpillar, pupa, adult

13 According to the timeline, which is the longest stage of the gypsy moth life cycle?
  (1) egg
  (2) egg mass
  (3) caterpillar
  (4) pupa
  (5) adult

14 During the month of March, which control method can people use to destroy gypsy moths?
  (1) Crush the pupa cases.
  (2) Spray the caterpillars with insecticide.
  (3) Kill the caterpillars by catching them on sticky tape.
  (4) Put out scented bait traps for adult male moths.
  (5) Soak the egg masses in kerosene, bleach, or ammonia.

Connect with the Article

Write your answer to each question.

15 What other animals do you know about that look different at different stages of the life cycle? Pick one of these animals and describe how it looks and acts during different parts of its life cycle.

_____

_____

_____

16 Describe an experience you or someone you know has had with gypsy moths or other insect pests. What did you do to control them?

_____

_____

_____

11 The Environment

Setting the Stage

When you take the garbage out, notice how much your family tosses away each day. Paper and plastic packaging, food leftovers, cans, jars, old clothes, and junk—where does it all go? In recent years, more and more garbage is being recycled. Still, most of it winds up in landfills. With little air or water to help break it down, the garbage is preserved for years and the environment suffers.

PREVIEW THE ARTICLE

One way to preview an article before reading it is to read the first sentence of each paragraph. The first sentence of a paragraph often expresses the main idea, so reading these sentences will give you an overview of the whole article.

Read the first sentence of each paragraph on pages 75–77. What are some things you can expect to learn about garbage and the environment?

_____

_____

_____

RELATE TO THE TOPIC

This article is about garbage. It describes the types of garbage we produce and explains where the garbage goes. It tells what happens to garbage in landfills and compost piles.

How is garbage disposed of in your community? Must materials such as newspapers and glass be separated? Describe how your family handles garbage.

_____

_____

VOCABULARY

organic   inorganic   degrades

decomposers   aerobic

Where Does the Garbage Go?

Each day the average American tosses out more than four pounds of **municipal solid waste.** Most people call it garbage. Whatever you call it, on average, each person throws away three-quarters of a ton of garbage per year. For all Americans, that is 210 million tons per year total. That figure doesn't include the billions of tons produced each year by industry and farms.

What We Throw Away

Garbage contains two kinds of materials. **Organic** materials come from things that were once alive. Paper, food waste, yard waste, and wood are all organic. **Inorganic** materials come from things that were never alive. They include plastics and metals.

Most garbage is organic. Paper makes up about 40 percent of all garbage. Yard waste makes up about 14 percent. The rest is glass, metals, plastics, and other materials, including food, rubber, and disposable diapers.

Where does all this garbage go? About 27 percent is **recycled,** or processed to be used again. Newspapers, aluminum cans, glass jars, some plastic containers, and yard waste can be recycled. Seventeen percent of garbage is **incinerated,** or burned. Dumping garbage in the ocean is no longer allowed. More than half of our garbage winds up in **landfills,** which are modern versions of the town dump.

A truck unloading garbage into a landfill

You can learn a lot about people by looking at what they throw away. This bar graph shows what people threw out in 1970 and in 1995.

Municipal Solid Waste: What's in it, 1970 and 1995

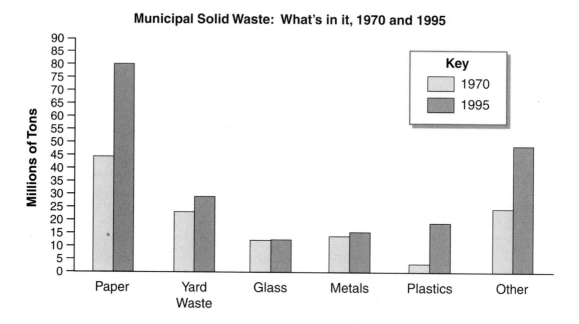

Reading a Bar Graph   **Bar graphs** are used to compare sets of information. The height of the bars shows you at a glance the amounts of each item. To read a bar graph, first look at the title to find the main idea. This graph compares the amount of each type of garbage in two different years. Then read the words along the vertical line to see what measurement is being used. In this case, the items are measured in millions of tons. The words along the horizontal line identify the items shown in the bars—types of garbage. Finally, look at the key, which tells what symbols are used. The color bars show 1995 figures. The black bars show 1970 figures. To find an amount of garbage, line up the top of the bar with the vertical scale. For example, in 1970 less than 5 million tons of plastics was tossed. Almost 20 million tons was thrown out in 1995.

1   About how many tons of paper were thrown away in 1970? In 1995?

_____

2   Which garbage items decreased from 1970 to 1995?

_____

What Happens in a Landfill?

Inorganic materials break down very slowly, if at all. They may remain for hundreds of years. That is why these materials should be recycled, not dumped. Organic garbage **degrades,** or breaks down, through the action of living things. Living things that break down organic materials are called **decomposers.** Many labels claim that products are "biodegradable," which means they will break down. But these labels can be misleading.

Check your answers on page 234.

Many people think that organic garbage will degrade in a landfill. But this is not always true. Most bacteria that are decomposers are **aerobic,** which means they need oxygen to live. In a landfill, there is no oxygen below eight to ten feet. Since the aerobic bacteria cannot survive, the garbage remains, even if it is "biodegradable." The University of Arizona's Garbage Project dug up an old landfill. They found hot dogs, carrots, and corn cobs—all intact. A newspaper from 1952 was still readable.

What Happens in a Compost Pile?

Many communities are composting some garbage, especially yard waste, instead of disposing of it in landfills. In **composting,** organic material is broken down by aerobic bacteria, fungi, insects, and worms. Unlike landfills, compost piles have oxygen to keep bacteria alive. The oxygen is provided by turning the garbage periodically. After a while, the garbage turns into a soil-like mixture called compost. This can be added to soil for gardening or farming.

People have been composting in their yards for years. Large-scale composting is fairly new. In 1985, there was no large-scale composting. Today, over 3,000 communities compost their yard waste. About 30 percent of all yard waste is composted.

Applying Knowledge to Other Contexts General ideas can be put to use in new, specific situations. Scientists are always trying to apply ideas to new situations to solve problems. In the previous two paragraphs, the author describes an old idea, composting. She tells how this old idea is being used in a new, specific way.

For years, households reused many items, such as rubber bands and aluminum foil. In what context is this idea of reusing things being applied today?
 a. large-scale community and commercial recycling programs
 b. developing aerobic landfill systems

What You Can Do

Some cities encourage recycling with "pay as you throw" programs. In Seattle, for example, the more garbage you make, the more you pay to have it taken away. There are many things you can do to reduce the amount of garbage you throw away. You may not save money unless you live in a city like Seattle, but you will help save the environment.

- Buy products in containers that can be used more than once. Buy items that have recyclable packaging.

- Reuse plastic bags and deli containers, glass jars, cardboard, paper, and foil.

- Take part in your community's recycling program.

- If you have a yard, start a compost pile. Even if you compost only yard waste and some food, you can make a big difference.

Labels such as this show that a product can be recycled.

Check your answer on page 235.

Thinking About the Article

Practice Vocabulary

The terms below are in the passage in bold type. Study the way each term is used. Then complete each sentence by writing the correct term in the blank.

organic   **inorganic**   **degrades**

decomposers   **aerobic**

① When waste breaks down through the action of living things, it

_____ .

② _____ materials are made from substances that were never alive.

③ Paper and food waste are examples of _____ materials.

④ _____ are organisms that break down organic garbage.

⑤ In a compost pile, organic waste is broken down by

_____ bacteria.

Understand the Article

Write or circle the answers to each question.

⑥ Is each of the following organic or inorganic garbage? Write *organic* or *inorganic* on each line.

   a.   newspaper _____   c.   raked leaves _____

   b.   old portable radio _____   d.   glass jar _____

⑦ Which categories of garbage increased from 1970 to 1995?

_____

⑧ Why does most organic garbage not degrade in a landfill?
   a.   The garbage is preserved by the weight and pressure of additional garbage on top of it.
   b.   There is no oxygen below 8 to 10 feet, so aerobic bacteria cannot degrade the organic garbage there.

⑨ How is oxygen supplied in composting?
   a.   The air circulates through passages in the compost pile.
   b.   The garbage is turned periodically to expose it to the air.

Apply Your Skills

Circle the number of the best answer for each question.

10 According to the bar graph on page 76, the largest category of garbage by weight in both 1970 and 1995 was
(1) paper.
(2) yard waste.
(3) glass.
(4) metals.
(5) plastics.

11 According to the bar graph on page 76, the weight of which of the following wastes increased by about six times between 1970 and 1995?
(1) paper
(2) yard waste
(3) glass
(4) metals
(5) plastics

12 Organic materials do not break down deep in landfills because there is no oxygen to support the decomposers, aerobic bacteria. Which of the following methods of preserving food uses the same principle?
(1) vacuum-packing
(2) refrigerating
(3) pickling
(4) salting
(5) drying

Connect with the Article

Write your answer to each question.

13 Choose one category of waste from the bar graph on page 76. List as many items as you can think of that would fall into this category of garbage. In what ways can people reduce their contribution of this waste to the waste stream?

_____

_____

_____

14 What items do you recycle regularly? If you do not recycle now, what items would be easiest for you to recycle?

_____

_____

Ecosystems

Setting the Stage

What do Brazil nuts, mahogany, and natural rubber have in common? They are all products of tropical rain forests. Tropical rain forests are warm, humid areas. They have a wide variety of plants and animals. Although rain forests cover only a small part of Earth, they benefit the whole world. The rain forests are disappearing because of farming, logging, and ranching.

PREVIEW THE ARTICLE

One way to preview an article before reading it is to look at the photos, diagrams, maps, and other illustrations. These will give you an overview of the whole article.

Look at the illustrations on pages 81–83. What are some things you can expect to learn about rain forests?

_____

_____

_____

RELATE TO THE TOPIC

This article is about tropical rain forests. It explains how tropical rain forests help regulate the temperature of Earth. It describes how destruction of rain forests may contribute to global warming.

What tropical foods and other products do you buy? List them on the lines below.

_____

_____

VOCABULARY

tropical rain forest   ecosystem   photosynthesis

respiration   carbon dioxide–oxygen cycle

Check your answers on page 235.

Tropical Rain Forests

Do you like rice cereal with bananas? Coffee with sugar? Did you know that the foods in this breakfast first came from a **tropical rain forest?** Tropical rain forests are the source of many foods that are now grown commercially.

Take a look around you. Offices, libraries, and department stores may have furniture made of mahogany or teak. These woods grow in tropical rain forests. Check out your medicine cabinet. One out of every four drugs has ingredients that first came from tropical rain forest plants.

What Is a Tropical Rain Forest?

A tropical rain forest is a large ecosystem. An **ecosystem** is an area in which living and nonliving things interact. Tropical rain forests are found near the **equator** (the imaginary line that goes around the middle of the Earth, halfway between the poles). In these areas, there is a great deal of rainfall, and it is warm throughout the year. The temperature may vary more from day to night than from season to season.

The conditions in tropical rain forests support a wealth of plant and animal life. More than half of all types of plants and animals live in tropical rain forests. The variety of life is tremendous. For example, just one square mile of rain forest in Peru has 1,450 types of butterflies. Together, the United States and Canada have only 730!

A tropical rain forest

The Global Effects of the Rain Forests

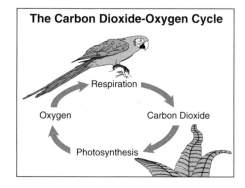

The Carbon Dioxide-Oxygen Cycle

Respiration

Oxygen   Carbon Dioxide

Photosynthesis

The plants of the rain forests absorb carbon dioxide from the atmosphere. Through the process of **photosynthesis,** plants use energy from sunlight to combine carbon dioxide and water to make food. This process gives off oxygen. Oxygen is used by animals for respiration. **Respiration** is the process by which living things use oxygen to get energy from food. This process gives off carbon dioxide. Carbon dioxide is also given off when fuels are burned and when organic material, such as plants and animals, decompose. The carbon dioxide is then used by plants, completing the **carbon dioxide–oxygen cycle.**

Recognizing Cause and Effect   There are many situations in which one thing (a cause) makes another thing (an effect) happen. For example, plants make their own food during photosynthesis (cause). The process of photosynthesis results in plants' giving off oxygen (effect). Science is full of cause-and-effect relationships. Watch for words such as *cause, effect, because, result, leads to, due to, therefore, thus,* and *so.* These words often signal cause-and-effect relationships.

In the previous diagram and paragraph, you learned about the carbon dioxide–oxygen cycle. If more forests were planted, what would be the effect on the amount of carbon dioxide in the air?

a.   There would be less because more plants would use carbon dioxide for photosynthesis.

b.   There would be more because plants give off carbon dioxide during photosynthesis.

The amount of carbon dioxide in the air affects Earth's temperature. Carbon dioxide absorbs heat and helps keep Earth warm. The role of carbon dioxide and other gases in warming the Earth is known as the **greenhouse effect.** By taking carbon dioxide from the air, the plants of the rain forests help control Earth's temperature.

Destruction of the Rain Forests

About 40,000 square miles of tropical rain forests are destroyed each year by farmers, ranchers, and loggers. Many tropical countries don't have enough farmland. So farmers clear forests and burn the trees. When the soil is no longer able to nourish crops, they move on and clear new places. Ranchers cut down trees to make room for their cattle. Loggers also destroy the forests by cutting down trees for the wood.

This destruction affects the carbon dioxide–oxygen cycle in two ways. First, many trees are burned to clear the land. This burning adds tons of carbon dioxide to the air. Second, destroying trees leaves fewer plants to take carbon dioxide from the air. Scientists think that more carbon dioxide in the air is causing **global warming,** a worldwide increase in temperature.

Tropical rain forests cover about one-twentieth of Earth's land area. They are found along the equator, as shown in the map below. Large areas of the rain forests have already been destroyed.

The World's Tropical Rain Forests

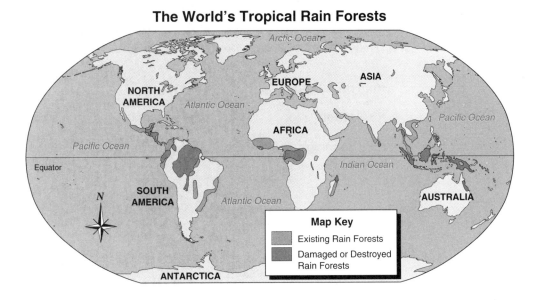

Reading a Map   To study a map, first look at the title. It tells you what the map shows. This map shows the world's tropical rain forests. Then look for the map key. The map key tells you how information is shown on the map. In this map, existing rain forests are in a dark color, and damaged or destroyed forests are in gray. Look at the compass rose in the lower left. It shows the directions north, south, east, and west.

Study the map above. Which of the following continents has the smallest area of tropical rain forest? Circle the letter of the correct answer.

    a.   North America   c.   Africa
    b.   South America   d.   Asia

Stopping the Destruction

People in tropical countries do not destroy the forests on purpose. In these countries, the forests are a source of land, fuel, food, and cash. It's not possible to keep farmers, ranchers, and loggers out of the rain forests. Many countries are now trying to save some areas in the forests by making them off-limits. Some areas are set aside for tourism. In addition, new methods of farming and logging can help people use the forests without destroying them.

Other countries can help, too. They can buy products, such as Brazil nuts, that are grown without damaging the forests. They can refuse to buy products that damage the forests. This includes tropical woods, such as teak. It also includes beef ranched on lands that were once tropical rain forests.

Check your answer on page 235.

Thinking About the Article

Practice Vocabulary

The terms below are in the passage in bold type. Study the way each term is used. Then complete each sentence by writing the correct term in the blank.

tropical rain forests	**ecosystem**	**photosynthesis**
respiration	**carbon dioxide–oxygen cycle**	

1. An area in which living and nonliving things interact is called a(n)

    _____ .

2. _____ is a process by which living things use oxygen to get energy from food.

3. The _____ describes how carbon dioxide and oxygen circulate through the world.

4. _____ is a process by which plants use carbon dioxide, water, and energy from sunlight to make food.

5. Some scientists think that the destruction of the

    _____ is contributing to global warming.

Understand the Article

Write or circle the answer to each question.

6. What are some foods we eat that originally came from tropical rain forests?

    _____

    _____

7. What role do animals play in the carbon dioxide–oxygen cycle?
    a. Animals take in oxygen and give off carbon dioxide during the process of respiration.
    b. Animals take in carbon dioxide and give off oxygen during the process of photosynthesis.

8. Which three industries are most destructive to the tropical rain forest? Explain why.

    _____

    _____

    _____

Check your answers on page 235.

Apply Your Skills

Circle the number of the best answer for each question.

9 All of the following are effects of rain forest destruction <u>except</u>
   (1) more land for farming and ranching.
   (2) increased carbon dioxide in the air.
   (3) global warming.
   (4) loss of plant and animal species.
   (5) more photosynthesis.

10 People burn more fuel now than ever before. The effect of this is that the amount of carbon dioxide in the air has
   (1) increased.
   (2) decreased.
   (3) first increased, then decreased.
   (4) first decreased, then increased.
   (5) remained the same.

11 Refer to the map on page 83. Which of the following statements is <u>not</u> true?
   (1) Most tropical rain forests are located near the equator.
   (2) Australia has tropical rain forests.
   (3) All tropical rain forests are located south of the equator.
   (4) There are no tropical rain forests in Antarctica.
   (5) South America has a large area of tropical rain forests.

Connect with the Article

Write your answer to each question.

12 List three ways that tropical rain forests are important to human health and to the health of Earth's ecosystems.

_____

_____

_____

13 What can you do to help prevent the destruction of tropical rain forests?

_____

_____

_____

_____

13 Evolution

Setting the Stage

In one scene in the movie *Jurassic Park,* two dinosaurs hunt children hiding in a kitchen. As we look on in horror, the dinosaurs turn the knob and open the kitchen door. They are able to do this because they are *Velociraptors,* dinosaurs with flexible wrists that allow them to swivel their hands. But did you know that flexible wrists are also characteristic of birds? A flexible wrist allows powered flight. This, and many other shared characteristics, have led some scientists to believe that birds and dinosaurs are related.

PREVIEW THE ARTICLE

Before you start to read, look over the headings on pages 87–89. These will give you a general idea of what the article is about. Write three things you can expect to learn by reading this article.

_____

_____

_____

RELATE TO THE TOPIC

This article is about the theory of evolution. It explains how birds may have evolved from small dinosaurs with feathers.

What birds live in your area? List them on the lines below.

_____

_____

_____

_____

VOCABULARY

adaptation   mutation   natural selection

evolution   convergence

Check your answers on page 236.

Dinosaurs with Feathers

Mammals have fur or hair, fish have scales, and dinosaurs have—feathers? New fossils indicate that some dinosaurs did indeed have feathers. A **fossil** is a trace of an organism that lived in the distant past. By comparing fossils over time, scientists can trace the development of species over time. Some scientists think that these feathered fossils settle the longstanding debate over the dinosaur-bird link. According to this view, feathered dinosaurs provide evidence that modern birds evolved from dinosaurs.

Dinosaur-Bird Links

The first scientist to suggest that birds and dinosaurs are related was Thomas Henry Huxley. His theory was based on the 1861 discovery of a primitive bird fossil, *Archaeopteryx* (ar-kee-AHP-tuhr-iks). This creature had many similarities to dinosaurs, including clawed fingers and a long bony tail. It also had feathers. While most scientists believed Huxley was right, there was little proof. Birds are so fragile that they are rarely preserved as fossils. **Paleontologists,** scientists who study prehistoric life, predicted that the fossils of birdlike dinosaurs would be found. Now they have been proved right. In the late 1990s, two fossil species of birdlike dinosaurs were found in northeastern China by a team of Chinese, Canadian, and American scientists.

One species is *Protoarchaeopteryx* (proh-toh-ar-kee-AHP-tuhr-iks). It is similar in many ways to the fast, meat-eating dinosaur *Velociraptor* (vuh-LAH-suh-rap-tuhr), made famous by the movie *Jurassic Park*. *Protoarcheopteryx* had a cluster of long feathers at the end of its tail.

The other species, *Caudipteryx* (caw-DIP-tuhr-iks), was even more feathery. Feathers covered the arms, much of the body, and the tail. Some feathers were tiny and soft like down, and others were large and stiff like quills.

A model of the feathered dinosaur *Caudipteryx*

The Usefulness of Feathers

Despite the feathers, neither *Protoarchaeopteryx* nor *Caudipteryx* could fly. Instead, scientists think that the short feathers may have provided insulation. The long feathers may have been used by males to attract females. Many modern birds have down to keep warm and colorful courtship displays of feathers.

Once feathers developed, they may have given these dinosaurs a competitive edge. They may have enabled these dinosaurs to run faster or balance better than their nonfeathered relatives. Eventually, feathers may have enabled gliding or flying. A trait, such as feathers, that makes an organism better able to live in its environment is called an **adaptation.** Another example of an adaptation is an arctic fox's white fur. The color helps the arctic fox blend into the background of snow. Its enemies have trouble seeing it, so the fox has a better chance of surviving.

Many adaptations occur through mutation. A **mutation** is a change in genetic material. Mutations happen by chance and most are harmful. But sometimes a mutation causes a trait, like feathers on a dinosaur or white fur on a fox, that helps an organism survive.

Making Inferences   An **inference** is a fact or idea that follows logically from what has been said. Readers make inferences all the time from the information in what they read. Review the previous paragraph about mutations. The author states in the paragraph that some mutations cause traits which can help an organism to survive. From what the author says, you can infer that harmful mutations can cause an individual to die.

Which of the following can you infer from the paragraph about adaptations? Circle the letter of the correct inference.
   a.   White fur is a useful adaptation any place that foxes live.
   b.   White fur is a useful adaptation only in places with lots of snow.

Evolution through Natural Selection

There are always variations in any population due to mutation. When feathers first appeared, a few dinosaurs may have had them. A dinosaur with this adaptation was more likely to survive, reproduce, and pass the trait to offspring. A dinosaur without this adaptation was more likely to die before it reproduced.

Charles Darwin, a nineteenth-century English scientist, called this process natural selection. **Natural selection** means that the organisms best suited to their environments are most likely to survive and reproduce. Natural selection is sometimes called *survival of the fittest*. What is *fit* depends on the situation. In this case, feathers may have helped some dinosaurs in the competition for resources. However, survival of an individual organism is not enough. It must reproduce to pass on the adaptations to its offspring.

Check your answer on page 236.

The above illustration depicts evolution from dinosaurs to birds.
Source: Portia Rollings/NGS Image Collection

The make-up of a population of organisms changes slowly. Those with useful adaptations reproduce more than others. The useful traits will appear in more of the offspring. Over time, the adaptation may be found in most of the population. This gradual change of a species over time is called the theory of **evolution.**

Convergence

Not all scientists are convinced that the Chinese feathered dinosaurs prove that birds evolved from dinosaurs. They argue that birds and dinosaurs could have developed traits such as feathers independently, a process called **convergence.** Convergence results in similarities among groups of animals that are not closely related through evolution. For example, crows, bats, and butterflies all have wings, but they are not closely related. Crows are birds, bats are mammals, and butterflies are insects. Their wings evolved independently as an adaptation to life in the air.

However, most scientists do think that birds and dinosaurs are related. They point to more than a hundred shared traits, including feathers, air filled skull bones, and wishbones. Says one scientist, "Dinosaurs are not extinct after all. They're alive and well and represented by more than 10,000 species of living birds."

Applying Knowledge to Other Contexts   Using the knowledge you gain in one situation and applying it to another can give you new insights about the world around you. For example, you just learned that birds, bats, and butterflies all have wings but are not closely related. Their traits converge because they each have adapted to their environment by taking up flight; and controlled flight requires wings.

Which of the following is another example of convergence?
a.   Sharks and dolphins have similarly shaped bodies and fins, but sharks are fish and dolphins are mammals.
b.   Humans and chimpanzees have thumbs that allow them to grasp objects, and both are mammals.

Check your answer on page 236.

Thinking About the Article

Practice Vocabulary

The terms below are in the passage in bold type. Study the way each term is used. Then complete each sentence by writing the correct term in the blank.

adaptation   **mutation**   **natural selection**

evolution   **convergence**

1 A(n) _____ is a change in a gene.

2 A trait that makes a plant or animal better able to live in its environment

is called a(n) _____.

3 _____ is the independent evolution of similar characteristics among unrelated organisms.

4 _____ means that organisms best suited to their environments are most likely to survive and reproduce.

5 The gradual change in a species over time is called

_____.

Understand the Article

Write or circle the answer to each question.

6 What was unusual about the dinosaur fossils found in northeastern China in the late 1990s?

_____

_____

7 What do scientists think dinosaurs might have used feathers for?

_____

_____

_____

8 How do species evolve?
   a.   Individuals with useful adaptations survive, reproduce, and pass the adaptations to their offspring.
   b.   Individuals may develop traits during their lifetime and teach them to their offspring.

Apply Your Skills

Circle the number of the best answer for each question.

9 You can infer that birds, bats, and butterflies are not closely related because they
  (1) have mutated.
  (2) are very different types of animals.
  (3) have wings.
  (4) can fly.
  (5) have feathers.

10 Antibiotics are drugs that fight disease-causing bacteria. After a few decades, the bacteria develop resistance to the antibiotic, and the drug no longer works. The resistance of bacteria to antibiotics is an example of a(n)
  (1) fossil.
  (2) convergence.
  (3) adaptation.
  (4) paleontologist.
  (5) evolution.

11 What might happen in the future if people did less standing, walking, and running?
  (1) Humans would develop bird-like wings.
  (2) Human legs would gradually become weaker.
  (3) Humans would gradually die out.
  (4) Humans would not reproduce.
  (5) Only humans with the strongest legs would survive.

Connect with the Article

Write your answer to each question.

12 Do you think that the theory that birds evolved from dinosaurs is correct? Or do you think, as some scientists do, that their similarities are the result of convergence? Cite evidence to support your opinion.

_____

_____

13 Did reading this article change the way you think of dinosaurs or birds? Explain your answer.

_____

_____

Check your answers on page 236.

Science at Work

Health: Fitness Instructor

Some Careers in Health and Fitness

Aerobics Instructor conducts fitness classes for groups of people

Assistant Aerobics Coordinator helps choose and schedule classes; selects instructors and conducts training sessions

Health Club Receptionist schedules appointments, greets members and visitors, and provides general information

Personal Trainer works individually with clients on fitness needs

A fitness instructor must understand the structure of the human body.

Health and fitness has become a huge industry in our country. People enjoy exercising because it helps them mentally and physically. Fitness instructors teach people to exercise safely and effectively. They design workout routines, demonstrate exercises and gym equipment, teach classes, and monitor clients' progress. Fitness instructors must be able to answer clients' questions clearly and correctly. Because they work closely with people most of the day, they should have excellent communication skills.

Fitness instructors need a good understanding of life science, especially the human body. They need to understand how the body and its systems work. They must know about human anatomy, or the parts of the body, and physiology—how the body parts work and how they interact. Fitness instructors must pay great attention to their clients' bones and muscles and cardiovascular and respiratory systems. They are responsible for helping their clients achieve their workout goals without the risk of injury.

Look at the chart showing some of the careers in health and fitness.

- Do any of the careers interest you? If so, which ones?

- What information would you need to find out more about those careers? On a separate piece of paper, write some questions that you would like answered. You can find more information about those careers in the *Occupational Outlook Handbook* at your local library.

Use the following memo to answer the questions below.

FROM: Fitness Instructor Diane

TO: Client Tom

Tom, I have designed an exercise program for you. To get your body in good shape, it is important that you complete all three parts. Only use this workout program 3–4 times a week. Give yourself a day of rest between each day of exercise to avoid injury or stress to your body. Be sure to start each workout session by stretching.

Part 1 – Cardiovascular Workout – to get your heart working more efficiently. Choose one of the following machines: step machine; treadmill; rowing machine; or stationary bicycle. These machines will strengthen lower body muscles. Do a 5-minute warm up, 10 minutes at peak working heart rate, and a 5-minute cool down.

Part 2 – Strength Training – to build muscle and bone density. Use either the weight machines, leg or hand weights. While using the weights, rotate between body parts to give each part time to rest. For example, first work on an arm muscle, then on a leg muscle. Start with light weights. Lift each weight 15 times. Do this twice. Work on at least 3 muscles in the leg and arm areas.

Part 3 – Stretching – to help your body cool down, relax, and resume its normal state. Stretch the same muscles you worked on in Part 2. Stretch and hold the position for 5–8 seconds. Do each muscle one time.

1 Which of the following will help Tom build muscle and bone density?
   (1) stretching
   (2) rowing machine
   (3) step machine
   (4) hand weights
   (5) stationary bicycle

2 Why is it important for Tom to rest between the days he works out?
   (1) He will get too tired at the gym.
   (2) He might get hurt from too much exercising.
   (3) Diane won't be there to help him.
   (4) Stretching is too difficult.
   (5) He must use all the machines.

3 Match the recommended exercise with its benefit.

   _____ treadmill   a. build muscle and bone density

   _____ weight machines   b. cool down

   _____ stretching   c. improve efficiency of the heart

How Cells Reproduce

The **nucleus** of a cell is the control center. In the nucleus are the chromosomes. They contain the genetic material, or **DNA.** This material has all the instructions the cell needs to live. When the cell reproduces, this information is passed on to the new cells.

A cell reproduces by dividing. This five-step process is called mitosis. In **mitosis,** one cell becomes two cells. Before a cell divides, it makes a copy of its DNA. Each new cell receives one copy of the DNA. These two new cells can then grow and divide.

Nucleus   Chromosomes

   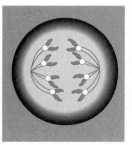 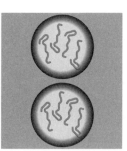

| DNA doubles in parent cell | Chromosomes shorten | Chromosomes line up | Chromosomes split | Two new cells form |

Fill in the blank with the word or words that best complete each statement.

1   The genetic material is called _____.

2   Cells reproduce by division, or _____.

Circle the number of the best answer.

3   The DNA in a cell is copied before the cell divides so that

   (1)   the parent cell won't run out of DNA.

   (2)   the parent cell will be able to grow.

   (3)   the two new cells will have all the information they need.

   (4)   the two new cells will be larger than the parent cell.

   (5)   the genetic material will be fatter and easier to see.

          Check your answers on page 236.

The Heart

Your heart is a large, muscular pump. As you read this, your heart is pumping blood to your lungs, where the blood absorbs oxygen. Your heart is also pumping blood throughout your body. The blood carries oxygen to the body. The parts of the heart are shown below.

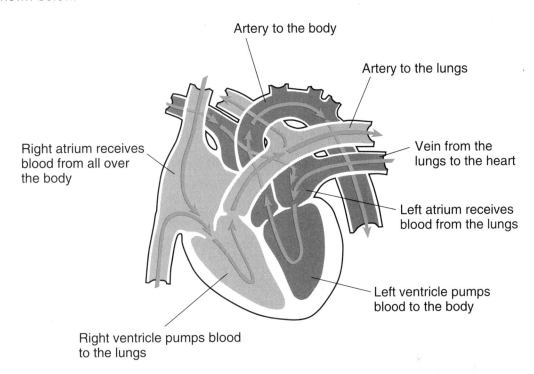

Artery to the body

Artery to the lungs

Right atrium receives blood from all over the body

Vein from the lungs to the heart

Left atrium receives blood from the lungs

Left ventricle pumps blood to the body

Right ventricle pumps blood to the lungs

Fill in the blank with the word or words that best complete each statement.

④ If blood is flowing away from the heart, it is in an

_____ .

⑤ Blood coming from the lungs flows through a vein to the

_____ of the heart.

Circle the number of the best answer.

⑥ Which structure has the thickest walls?

    (1) artery

    (2) vein

    (3) atrium

    (4) ventricle

    (5) They all have walls of the same thickness.

Immunity

We are surrounded by germs. Even though bacteria and viruses are all around us, they rarely make us ill. White blood cells protect the body against germs. Any germs that enter the body are seen as foreign substances. A foreign protein is called an **antigen.** When an antigen is in the body, the white blood cells begin to make antibodies. An **antibody** is a protein the body makes to defend itself. Antibodies attack and kill invading germs.

When you are **immune** to a disease, you have antibodies that protect you. One way to form antibodies is to get the disease. While you are sick, your body makes antibodies, which kill the germs. After the illness is over, you still have the antibodies. So the next time you come in contact with the germs, your body will fight them, and you will be immune to the disease. The antibodies you developed will protect you from getting sick again.

You can also become immune to a disease without becoming ill. Scientists have found that they can trick your body into making antibodies. A **vaccine** contains weakened or dead bacteria or viruses. These weakened or dead germs do not make you ill. But your white blood cells recognize them and make antibodies against them.

Some immunities last a lifetime. You may have been vaccinated for smallpox as a child. You will probably not need to have that done again. Other vaccinations have to be repeated. You have probably had more than one tetanus shot in your life. The booster shot reminds the white blood cells to make more antibodies.

Fill in the blank with the word or words that best complete each statement.

7 Proteins that protect the body from germs are called

_____ .

8 If you have had measles, you will not get them again. This is because you

are _____ to measles.

Circle the number of the best answer.

9 Scientists are working on a vaccine for the AIDS virus. The first step is

(1) making white blood cells attack the virus that causes AIDS.

(2) weakening the virus that causes AIDS.

(3) identifying the virus that causes AIDS.

(4) making antibodies against the virus that causes AIDS.

(5) killing the virus that causes AIDS.

Check your answers on page 237.

An Inherited Trait

Can you roll your tongue? Try it! Stick out your tongue and roll it into a tube. Some people can do this easily. Other people cannot do it at all. No matter how hard they try, they never will be able to roll their tongue. Like brown eyes or red hair, the ability to roll the tongue is an inherited trait.

Your characteristics are determined by the genetic material you inherited from your parents. Your genetic material for a particular trait comes in a pair. One type of genetic material in each pair came from each parent. The trait of tongue rolling is **recessive.** It shows up only if there is no dominant genetic material hiding it. The trait of not rolling the tongue is **dominant.** A dominant trait can hide a recessive trait. If you have any genetic material for the dominant trait, you cannot roll your tongue. You can roll your tongue only if each parent gave you the recessive genetic type for that trait.

What if you have one of each type of genetic material for tongue rolling? You will show the dominant form of the trait and will not be able to roll your tongue. However, the genetic material for the recessive trait is still there. It might be passed on to a child. In this way, recessive traits may be hidden for many generations in a family.

Fill in the blank with the word or words that best complete each statement.

10 Genetic material for a _____ trait can hide the presence of genetic material for another trait.

11 The ability to roll the tongue is a _____ trait.

12 Characteristics are determined by the _____ that is inherited from each parent.

Circle the number of the best answer.

13 Right-handedness is a dominant trait. If two right-handed parents have a left-handed child, it is because

(1) neither parent has the recessive genetic material for left-handedness.

(2) one parent has the recessive genetic material for left-handedness.

(3) both parents have the recessive genetic material for left-handedness.

(4) one parent has only the dominant genetic material for right-handedness.

(5) both parents have only the recessive genetic material for left-handedness.

The Nitrogen Cycle

All living things need nitrogen in some form. Nitrogen is an important part of proteins. Proteins make up much of the structure of living things. For example, muscles are made mostly of protein.

The air around you is 78 percent nitrogen. But your body cannot use it. Only a few kinds of bacteria can use nitrogen from the air. These nitrogen-fixing bacteria live in the soil. They change nitrogen into a form called **nitrates.** Plants take in the nitrates from the soil. Plants make protein, which animals get when they eat the plants. When plants and animals die, they decay. Some bacteria return the nitrogen to the soil. Other bacteria release nitrogen into the air.

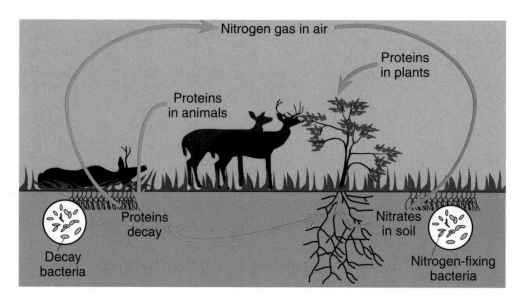

Match each organism with its source of nitrogen.

Organism

_____ 14 animals

_____ 15 plants

_____ 16 nitrogen-fixing bacteria

Nitrogen source

a.   air

b.   protein

c.   nitrates

Fill in the blank with the word or words that best complete the statement.

17 Lightning can cause a chemical reaction in which nitrogen from the air is changed into nitrates. This result is similar to the action of the

_____ .

The Ant and the Acacia

You have probably seen ants swarming all over a piece of candy dropped on the sidewalk. Cleaning up such bits of food and eating other dead animals is the role that most ants fill in nature. These ants are called scavengers.

Not all ant species are scavengers. Some species of ants live in a partnership with the acacia plant. Many partnerships in nature involve a give and take. Each partner gives the other something it needs. The need may be food, shelter, water, or protection from an enemy. In the case of the ant and the acacia tree, the trade is food and shelter for defense. A relationship in which two species help each other is called **mutualism.**

The acacia makes a sugary sweet nectar, which the ants eat. The ants also live in the thorns of the acacia plant. The ants protect the plant from animals that might eat it. If a deer starts nibbling on an acacia leaf, the ants swarm and sting it all over. The deer will probably avoid eating acacia leaves in the future. If any other plants start to grow near the acacia, the ants chew them down.

Fill in the blank with the word or words that best complete each statement.

18 In its relationship with the acacia plant, the ant gets

_____ and _____.

19 In its relationship with the ant, the acacia plant gets

_____.

20 Animals that eat other dead animals are called _____.

Circle the number of the best answer.

21 Which of the following is an example of mutualism?

  (1) A bird eats ticks that are on the back of an ox.

  (2) An ant cleans up a sidewalk by eating spilled food.

  (3) Ants carry bits of leaves back to the anthill.

  (4) A wild dog eats what is left of an antelope after lions have finished eating.

  (5) Two chimpanzees remove fleas from each other's fur.

Science Extension

Visit a drugstore or some other place that has a machine that takes blood pressure. Take your own blood pressure. Find out if it is normal. If it is too high or too low, find out what you can do to improve your blood pressure.

Science Connection: Life Sciences and Prose Information

The Newton Athletic Club advertisement below is an example of an advertorial. An advertorial looks like a typical magazine article and provides lots of important information. There is a major difference, though. After the information section of the advertorial, the reader receives a pitch. A pitch is used by the advertiser to sell the reader a specific product or service.

Can We Control the Aging Process?

Many scientists agree that the human body reaches its peak by age 30. By age 40, we begin experiencing noticeable changes in our bodies. By age 55, these changes become significant. Some of these changes include:

- **Bone and muscle mass decreases.** Since bones become more brittle, they break more easily. Injuries happen more frequently and they may take longer to heal.

- **Heart pumping function decreases significantly.** When the heart pumps less efficiently, less oxygen is carried throughout the body.

- **Breathing capacity decreases.** Age weighs heavily on the respiratory system. Our breathing ability declines by as much as 40% by the time we reach age 55.

- **Metabolism decreases.** A person's basic metabolic rate affects how his body breaks down, processes, and absorbs the nutrients in food.

Although many changes associated with aging are out of our control, some are not. Many can be controlled or improved through exercise. While we don't know for sure if exercise can extend a person's life, we do know it can slow down some of the impact of aging.

Regular exercise improves body strength. It slows down the loss of bone and muscle mass. It keeps the body flexible so it can do more. Exercise enables the heart and lungs to work better, bringing more oxygen into the body. It also helps control weight.

At Newton Athletic Club we help people of all ages improve and maintain their health. Good health in the early years is critical to good health in a person's later years. Come visit our state-of-the-art facilities or call us at (709)555-5555. We can set up a personal exercise program to fit your needs.

Use the material on the previous page to answer the questions below.

1 The reader of the advertorial would learn that regular exercise
(1) helps people run faster.
(2) decreases a person's metabolic rate.
(3) has a positive impact on an aging body.
(4) increases a person's appetite.
(5) is damaging after age 55.

2 What is the pitch of the advertorial on the previous page?
(1) Join the Newton Athletic Club to get the discounted rate.
(2) Get regular exercise now so you will have a healthy body.
(3) Begin a personal exercise program to strengthen your muscles.
(4) Join the Newton Athletic Club now to improve your health.
(5) Read more advertorials to buy more products.

3 From the information in the advertorial, identify three ways that aging affects the body.

_____

_____

_____

_____

4 List five positive effects of exercise on the body.

_____

_____

_____

_____

5 Today we find that young Americans are exercising less, while older Americans are exercising more. Many health professionals are worried about the trend among young people.

Do you get regular exercise? If so, what kind of exercise? Are you getting enough exercise or should you be getting more? Do you exercise more frequently now than you did a few years ago? Or do you feel that you don't have the time?

Use a separate piece of paper to write a paragraph about how exercise fits into your life. Your paragraph may answer some of the questions above, if they apply to you.

UNIT 2

Earth and Space Science

Imagine what it would be like to have a hurricane or blizzard hit your area without warning. Until the last few decades, people were surprised by severe storms. Today, thanks to weather satellites and global weather stations, meteorologists can predict bad storms and help us prepare for them.

Studying and forecasting the weather is just part of **Earth and space science.** This includes the study of Earth's interior and its surface—both land and water. Earth and space science is also the study of outer space. It covers topics as large as the universe and as small as a stone.

Studying Earth and space science helps you understand our universe, our solar system, and the planet on which we live. For example, learning about Earth's water supply helps us use its water resources wisely. Knowing about Earth and space science can help you take better care of yourself, your family, and your world.

◐ Have you ever experienced a natural disaster? How did you prepare for it?

◐ What are some things you could do to help improve your local environment?

SECTIONS

14 **Weather**

15 **The Atmosphere**

16 **Resources**

17 **The Solar System**

18 **Space Exploration**

14 Weather

Setting the Stage

Weather moves from one place to another. One day's snow in Kansas City may be the next day's snow in Cincinnati. Weather maps show the weather over large areas. Predictions about the coming weather are based in part on weather maps.

Sometimes the illustrations in an article give you an overview of what the article is about. Look at the illustrations on pages 105–107. What are some things you can expect to learn about the weather?

_____

_____

_____

RELATE TO THE TOPIC

This article is about weather and weather maps. It explains how air masses affect the weather and shows how to read a weather map. Describe an experience that you have had with really bad weather.

_____

_____

_____

VOCABULARY

air mass	front	stationary front	weather map
precipitation	meteorologists	forecast	

Check your answers on page 238.

Weather Systems

No doubt you've noticed that weather can change dramatically overnight. One day is hot, humid, and drizzling, and the next day is clear and dry. It feels as if the air has changed. In fact, the air *has* changed. One large body of air has replaced another.

Air Masses

Large areas of air near Earth's surface take on the same temperature and moisture as the surface. For example, the air over a tropical ocean becomes warm and humid. A large body of air with similar temperature and moisture is called an **air mass.** The term used to describe an air mass tells you where it came from. The word *continental* refers to a continent. The word *maritime* refers to the sea. There are four types of air masses:

- **Continental polar air masses** are cold and dry. They form over Canada and the northern United States.

- **Continental tropical air masses** are warm and dry. They form over the southwestern United States.

- **Maritime polar air masses** form over the northern Atlantic Ocean and the northern Pacific Ocean. These air masses are cold and moist.

- **Maritime tropical air masses** form over the Caribbean Sea, the middle of the Atlantic Ocean, and the middle of the Pacific Ocean. These air masses are warm and moist.

Air masses do not stay where they form. They may move thousands of miles. Think of a moving air mass as a large, flattened bubble of air. In the United States, air masses are usually pushed from west to east by winds. As the air mass moves, it may keep nearly the same temperature and moisture.

Fronts

The weather changes when one air mass moves out of an area and another moves in. The leading edge of a moving air mass is called a **front.** A cold front is at the front of a cold air mass. A warm front is at the front of a warm air mass. The weather can change quickly when a front passes through. A front often brings rain or snow to an area as it passes. When air masses stop moving for a while, the zone between them is called a **stationary front.**

Stormy weather often accompanies the passing of a front.

What Does a Weather Map Show?

Most newspapers print a **weather map** each day. A weather map shows where cold, warm, and stationary fronts are. It shows temperature and **precipitation,** such as rain, snow, and sleet.

Weather maps also show areas of high and low pressure. These areas of pressure are important because certain types of weather go with each. Most of the time, a high-pressure area means fair weather and no clouds. A low-pressure area is often cloudy with rain or snow.

High Temperatures and Precipitation for June 28

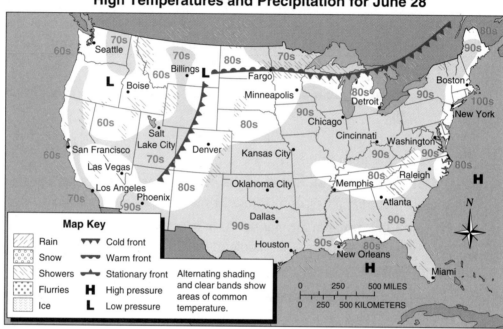

Map Key

Rain	Cold front
Snow	Warm front
Showers	Stationary front
Flurries	**H** High pressure
Ice	**L** Low pressure

Alternating shading and clear bands show areas of common temperature.

Reading a Map When you read a map, look at the title first. That gives you the main idea of the map. This map shows the weather for June 28, with high temperatures in degrees Fahrenheit, the temperature scale we usually use in the United States. It also shows precipitation. Next, look at the map key to see how information is shown. On this weather map, for example, cold fronts are shown by a line of triangles. The triangles point in the direction in which the front is moving. Finally, look at the map itself. Find details that will help you understand it. For example, look at Dallas. Dallas is in the shaded area that shows places with a high temperature in the 90s. There is no precipitation shading over Dallas. On this day Dallas is very hot and dry.

1 The symbol for a warm front looks like
    a.   a row of semicircles.   b.   a row of triangles.

2 The city closest to a warm front is   a.   Fargo.   b.   Chicago.

3 A cold air mass is behind a cold front. The high temperature in the cold air mass over the western United States is in the
    a.   80s and 90s.   b.   60s and 70s.

Weather Forecasts

Meteorologists are scientists who study the weather. Meteorologists study present weather conditions. Then they decide where the air masses and fronts will probably be the next day. From this data they **forecast,** or predict, the next day's weather. Suppose a meteorologist in Dallas studied the June 28 map. Her forecast for the next day might have said the high temperature would again be in the 90s and there would be no rain. Look at the map for June 29 below. Was the forecast correct?

High Temperatures and Precipitation for June 29

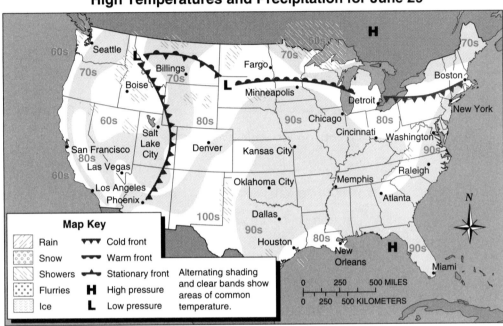

Making Predictions   Like a meteorologist, you can use what you know to predict what will happen to the weather. Look at the map for June 28. In the upper right, there is a cold front moving south toward the northeastern United States. Now look at the map for June 29. The cold front has reached Boston. You can predict that soon the high temperature in the Boston area will drop from the 80s to the 70s. Use the map to answer these questions.

1 What is the weather like in New York City on June 29?
   a. high temperature in the 70s, rain
   b. high temperature in the 90s, dry

2 What kind of weather would you predict for New York City on June 30?
   a. high temperature in the 70s, dry
   b. high temperature in the 90s, rain

People often make jokes about the accuracy of weather forecasts. Yet meteorologists are pretty good at predicting tomorrow's weather. However, their long-range forecasts are not so accurate. Many factors can affect the weather. So forecasting more than a few days in advance involves guessing as well as predicting.

Thinking About the Article

Practice Vocabulary

The words below are in the passage in bold type. Study the way each word is used. Then complete each sentence by writing the correct word in the blank.

air mass   **front**   **stationary front**   **weather map**

precipitation   **meteorologists**   **forecast**

1 A large body of air with similar temperature and moisture is called a(n) ——————————.

2 The edge of a moving air mass is called a(n) ——————————.

3 A(n) —————————— is a prediction about the weather.

4 Scientists who study weather are called ——————————.

5 A(n) —————————— can be used to help predict the coming weather.

6 The zone between air masses that have stopped moving is called a(n) ——————————.

7 Rain and snow are the most common forms of ——————————.

Understand the Article

Match the air mass with its characteristics. You may have more than one answer for each air mass.

Air Mass		Characteristic
———— **8** continental polar		a. cold
———— **9** continental tropical		b. warm
———— **10** maritime polar		c. dry
———— **11** maritime tropical		d. moist

Write the answer to each question.

12 In what direction does weather in the United States generally move?

——————————————————————————

13 Why are long-range weather forecasts often inaccurate?

——————————————————————————

Apply Your Skills

Circle the number of the best answer for each question.

14 On a weather map, there is a line of alternating triangles and half circles pointing in opposite directions. Look at the map key. What does this symbol indicate?
(1) cold front
(2) warm front
(3) stationary front
(4) high-pressure area
(5) precipitation

15 Refer to the map for June 28 on page 106. In which city are people most likely to be going to the beach to get relief from the heat?
(1) Seattle
(2) San Francisco
(3) Los Angeles
(4) New York
(5) Detroit

16 Refer to the map for June 29 on page 107. What do you predict the next day's weather forecast for Salt Lake City is likely to be?
(1) occasional showers, high temperature in the 60s
(2) occasional showers, high temperature in the 90s
(3) clear, high temperature in the 90s
(4) clear, high temperature in the 50s
(5) heavy rain, high temperature in the 80s

Connect with the Article

Write your answer to each question.

17 Refer to the map for June 28 on page 106. Which of the four types of air mass do you think is covering the western states? Give reasons for your answer.

_____

_____

_____

18 Describe today's weather in your area. What kind of air mass is in your area now?

_____

_____

15

The Atmosphere

Setting the Stage

The air that surrounds Earth does more than provide oxygen for us to breathe. It acts like a blanket that helps keep Earth warm. Some scientists think that the air is getting warmer. They think Earth's climate may change.

PREVIEW THE ARTICLE

Reading the headings in an article can tell you the main ideas. Knowing the main ideas before you actually read helps improve your understanding. Look at the headings on pages 111–113. What are some things you can expect to learn about the atmosphere?

_____

_____

_____

RELATE TO THE TOPIC

This article explains how the atmosphere keeps Earth warm. It also describes global warming, a trend that many scientists think is caused in part by the burning of fuels like oil, coal, and gas. Describe what you and your family use such fuels for.

_____

_____

_____

VOCABULARY

atmosphere   infrared radiation   greenhouse effect

fossil fuels   global warming

    Check your answers on page 238.

The Greenhouse Effect

The last 25 years have been unusually warm. Since the mid 1970s the average global temperature has risen by almost one degree Fahrenheit (abbreviated 1°F). This is about 0.5 degrees Celsius (0.5°C) as measured on the scale used by scientists. Is the recent heat wave part of a long-term rise in Earth's temperature? Or were the warm years just a matter of chance? Whatever caused this trend, the heat has focused people's attention on global, or worldwide, warming.

How Earth is Warmed

The air around us, called the **atmosphere,** plays a large role in the warming of Earth. When the gases in the atmosphere absorb energy, they become warmer. But from where does the energy come? It comes from two places, the sun and Earth.

Energy from the sun is called **radiant energy.** When you are outside on a bright day, the radiant energy of sunlight warms you. The atmosphere absorbs about 20 percent of the sun's radiant energy and reflects about 30 percent back into space. The remaining 50 percent of the sun's radiant energy is absorbed by Earth.

Earth radiates energy back into the atmosphere as **infrared radiation.** We feel infrared radiation as heat. You can feel heat rising from the pavement or from sand on a beach. These are examples of infrared radiation.

The infrared radiation reflected from Earth's surface does not escape into space. Instead, water vapor, carbon dioxide, and other gases in the atmosphere trap the heat. This is called the **greenhouse effect** because it is similar to what happens in a greenhouse. The gases that trap heat are called greenhouse gases.

Greenhouses use radiant energy from the sun to foster plants' growth.

Are People's Activities Increasing the Greenhouse Effect?

The greenhouse effect is a normal effect of the atmosphere. Without it, Earth would be much colder. But scientists say that the greenhouse gases in the atmosphere are increasing. This may cause Earth to become warmer, a trend called **global warming.** Such a change would be the result, or effect, of human activity.

In the last hundred years, people have burned more and more **fossil fuels.** Fossil fuels include coal, oil, gasoline, and wood. When these fuels burn, they increase the amount of carbon dioxide, a greenhouse gas, in the air. Also, people have destroyed many forests throughout the world. Plants absorb carbon dioxide during **photosynthesis.** Fewer plants means that more carbon dioxide remains in the atmosphere. More carbon dioxide in the atmosphere means that more heat is trapped close to Earth.

Carbon dioxide is the main greenhouse gas, but there are several others. Ozone, chlorofluorocarbons (CFCs), methane, and nitrogen oxide all absorb infrared radiation, trapping heat close to Earth. These greenhouse gases have increased as a result of pollution from cars, factories, and farms.

If greenhouse gas emissions continue at their present level, some scientists think that Earth's temperature will increase 0.9° to 3.6°F (0.5° to 2°C) by 2050. Since emissions are likely to increase, the rise in temperature may be even higher than this estimate. Global warming could melt the ice caps at the North and South poles, flooding coastal areas and low-lying islands around the world. It could reduce the amount of land suitable for farming and change weather patterns, affecting crops.

Understanding the Relationships Among Ideas   When you read, you are thinking all the time. Your mind is busy linking facts and ideas to one another and to things you already know. Reread the section of the article under the heading *Are People's Activities Increasing the Greenhouse Effect?* The main ideas are: (1) People are burning more fossil fuels. (2) People are destroying forests. (3) People are producing more air pollution. (4) Carbon dioxide and other greenhouse gases are increasing. (5) Global temperature is increasing. The first three main ideas are related. They are all things people do that affect the atmosphere.

❶   How are Ideas 4 (increased greenhouse gases) and
    5 (increased global temperature) related to one another?
    a.   Idea 5 may be the result of Idea 4.
    b.   Idea 4 may be the result of Idea 5.

❷   What is the relationship of Ideas 1, 2, and 3 to Ideas 4 and 5?
    a.   Ideas 1, 2, and 3 are the causes of Ideas 4 and 5.
    b.   Ideas 4 and 5 are parts of Ideas 1, 2, and 3.

   Check your answers on page 238.

What Can Be Done About Global Warming?

The problem of global warming may seem so large that no one can do anything about it. Still, many nations have agreed on a plan to cut the global emissions of greenhouse gases. Industrial nations have committed themselves to reducing their production of these gases. Individuals also can do many things that will help. Almost anything a person does that saves energy means that less fossil fuels are burned. If less fossil fuels are burned, there is less air pollution and less greenhouse gases are put into the air.

Reducing air pollution might help slow global warming.

People can save energy at home by adding insulation and turning down the thermostat in the winter and turning it up in the summer. Conserving electricity, which is usually produced by burning fossil fuels, will also help. Driving a car that gets many miles per gallon of gasoline saves energy. Driving only when necessary will help, too. If your car is old, make sure its air conditioner is in good working order. The air conditioners of older model cars can leak CFCs into the air.

Recycling also saves energy. When recycled materials are used in manufacturing, less energy is used. Also, recycling can help reduce the amount of garbage in landfills and incinerators. Landfills produce methane gas when garbage breaks down. Garbage burned in incinerators produces carbon dioxide.

In addition, each person can plant a tree. A single tree may not do much, but it will help, especially if many people each plant one. Some cities, such as Los Angeles, even sponsor tree plantings.

Understanding Compound Words Science books are full of long words. Most of these words are compound words: long words that are made of smaller parts. Some familiar compound words are *baseball, sunshine,* and *supermarket.* Often you can figure out what a compound word means if you know what each part means. There are several compound words in the article you just read. *Sunlight* is light energy from the sun. A *landfill* is a place to bury trash (fill) in the ground (land).

❶ What does *worldwide* mean (page 111, first paragraph)?

_____

❷ What does *greenhouse* mean (page 111, last paragraph)?

_____

Thinking About the Article

Practice Vocabulary

The words below are in the passage in bold type. Study the way each word is used. Then complete each sentence by writing the correct word in the blank.

fossil fuels   **atmosphere**   **greenhouse effect**

infrared radiation   **global warming**

1 The air that surrounds Earth is called the _____.

2 The trend toward higher average temperatures worldwide is called _____.

3 The heat you feel rising from hot pavement is called _____.

4 Gases in the atmosphere absorb heat energy radiated from Earth. This is known as the _____.

5 Some scientists think that burning _____ contributes to the warming trend.

Understand the Article

Write the answer to each question.

6 What kind of energy warms you when you sit out in the sun?

_____

7 How is the greenhouse effect like a blanket?

_____

_____

8 List the major greenhouse gases.

_____

_____

9 What did many nations agree to do to help slow global warming?

_____

Check your answers on pages 238–239.

Apply Your Skills

Circle the number of the best answer.

⑩ The word *photosynthesis* has two parts. *Photo-* means light, and *synthesis* means combining parts into a whole. The word *photosynthesis* means
  (1) combining hydrogen and oxygen to make water.
  (2) using light to combine substances into food.
  (3) artificial light.
  (4) artificial food made from light.
  (5) the release of light.

⑪ Which idea links the following ideas? (a) Carbon dioxide is a greenhouse gas. (b) Planting trees may help reduce emissions of greenhouse gases.
  (1) Trees take in carbon dioxide during the process of photosynthesis.
  (2) The emissions of greenhouse gases are on the rise.
  (3) Burning fossil fuels releases carbon dioxide.
  (4) Cutting down trees may reduce the amount of carbon dioxide in the atmosphere.
  (5) Recycling saves energy.

⑫ Why would the sea level rise if the temperature on Earth becomes several degrees warmer?
  (1) Less ocean water would evaporate.
  (2) Some land would no longer be suitable for farming.
  (3) The ice caps at the North and South poles would melt.
  (4) There would be more waves.
  (5) The pull of Earth's gravity would decrease.

Connect with the Article

Write your answer to each question.

⑬ Why do industrialized nations produce more greenhouse gases than nonindustrialized nations?

_____

_____

⑭ What specific things can you do to help slow global warming?

_____

_____

_____

Setting the Stage

Most of us just turn on the faucet to get fresh water. We usually take an endless supply of water for granted. But if you lived in a place where you had to haul water every day from a distant well, you would soon come to value it more. Fresh water is one of Earth's most precious resources.

PREVIEW THE ARTICLE

Sometimes the illustrations in an article give you an overview of what the article is about. Look at the illustrations on pages 117–119. What are some things you can expect to learn about the water as a resource?

_____

_____

_____

RELATE TO THE TOPIC

This article is about the supply of fresh water. It describes what a water-poor area like California does to ensure fresh water for its cities and farms. Describe where your water comes from. Do you pay for your water? How much does it cost?

_____

_____

_____

VOCABULARY

glaciers   resource   groundwater

water cycle   renewable resource

Supplying Fresh Water

California is well known for its extreme weather and natural disasters. Storms, earthquakes, and mud slides there often make the national news. But these are single events lasting a few days at most. In contrast, one of California's major everyday problems—its water supply—gets much less attention.

California, like many areas of the West, is mostly desert. But you would never guess this when touring the state. In the Central Valley, a low-lying area that runs more than half the length of the state, green orchards and crops are planted in neat rows, mile after mile. In the Los Angeles area, sprinklers water lush lawns and gardens, and swimming pools dot the backyards. Yet normal rainfall in Los Angeles is just 14 inches per year—about the same as Tripoli, Libya, another desert city.

Most of the precipitation that falls in California falls in the northern mountains. Yet most of the people and agriculture are in the southern part of the state. A complex system of trapping and moving water from the north and from other states allows California to supply water to its farm industry and more than 30 million people.

Dams create lakes by slowing the flow of water in a river.

Water as a Resource

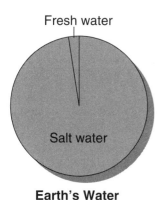

Earth's Water Resources

Astronauts often call Earth the blue planet because it is covered by water. Earth has plenty of water, but most of it is in the oceans. Ocean water is salty, and you cannot drink it. Less than 3 percent of Earth's water is fresh water. Most of this fresh water is frozen in ice at the poles and in **glaciers,** which are large masses of ice that form where more snow falls than melts. Only about one percent of all Earth's water is available as a resource. A **resource** is a substance that is needed for human life and activities. Usable fresh water is a resource that is found in rivers, lakes, and the atmosphere. It is also found underground in **groundwater.**

The supply of fresh water is constantly being renewed in an endless **water cycle.** Water that evaporates from lakes, rivers, and the salty oceans falls as saltless precipitation. In this way, water can be considered a **renewable resource.** However, the amount of fresh water used worldwide continues to grow. As the population expands, more people need more water for drinking, cooking, sanitation, crops and livestock, and factories and power plants. At the same time more human activity means more water pollution. And last, the water is often not present where it is most needed. Like California, some regions are water-poor; others are water-rich.

Drawing Conclusions A conclusion is an idea that follows logically from the information you have. Conclusions must be supported by facts. For example, from the facts in the previous paragraph you can conclude that the fresh water supply may eventually be too small to meet the world's needs.

You can conclude that water pollution cuts the supply of fresh water because
   a.   less of the available water is fit for drinking and cooking.
   b.   rivers with polluted water eventually dry up.

Water Supplies

The United States as a whole has more than enough water for everyone. Moving the water where it is needed is the problem. For example, most precipitation in the West falls in the mountains, such as the Rockies, the Cascades, and the Sierra Nevada. It flows as surface water in rivers, such as the Sacramento and Colorado. **Reservoirs,** lakes created by dams, store water. Large pipes called **aqueducts** carry the water to Southern California, Arizona, and other dry areas of the West.

California's Water Supply System

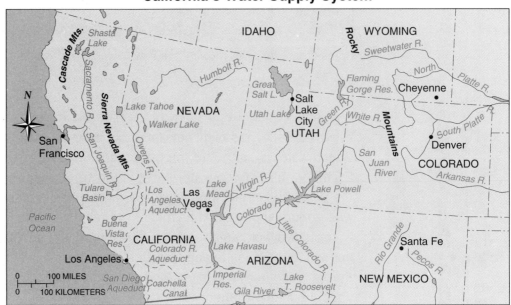

Check your answer on page 239.

Another problem is that supplies of surface water depend on precipitation. If less than the normal amount of rain or snow falls over a long period of time, a drought occurs in that area. Groundwater, rivers, lakes, and reservoirs become low. During a drought, water use may have to be restricted.

Groundwater supplies are threatened by overuse and pollution. When a lot of water is taken from wells, the groundwater levels may go down. In West Texas, water for irrigating crops has been pumped for a hundred years. In that time the level of the groundwater has dropped almost one hundred feet. In other areas polluted wells have been shut down.

Finally, as the population of an area grows, competition for water increases. Southern California's population has been growing since the early 1900s. More and more people are moving to California's cities. Some people in California feel that the state has enough water. But they think that farms are getting more than their fair share. The farmers and their supporters argue that California supplies most of the country with food products. These people feel that irrigated open land adds to the quality of life for everyone in the country. While California tries to solve its long-term water problems, all Californians must conserve water.

Distinguishing Fact from Opinion   Remember that facts can be proved true. Opinions are beliefs that may or may not be true. To decide whether a statement is an opinion, ask yourself: Can this statement be proved true? If the answer is no, it is an opinion. In the previous paragraph, you read different opinions about California's water problems. One opinion is that open irrigated land benefits everyone.

In the space beside each statement, write whether it is a fact or an opinion.

1 Agriculture gets more than its fair share of water in California. _____

2 Southern California's population has been growing since the early 1900s. _____

Conserving Water

Many areas, not just California, have problems with their water supply. That is why it's important to get into the habit of conserving water. Here are some things you can do.

- Take shorter showers and install a water-saving shower head.

- Fix leaks. A dripping faucet can waste 300 to 600 gallons of water per month.

- Put a brick in the toilet's tank to cut the amount used for each flush. Or install a new low-flow toilet: they use 1.6 gallons per flush as opposed to 3.5 to 7 gallons for older toilets.

- Run the washing machine and dishwasher only with full loads.

- If you're doing dishes in the sink, don't run the water. Use one basin to wash and another to rinse.

- Turn off the water when you're brushing your teeth or shaving. A bathroom faucet uses up to five gallons of water per minute.

Thinking About the Article

Practice Vocabulary

The words below are in the passage in bold type. Study the way each word is used. Then complete each sentence by writing the correct word in the blank.

glaciers	resource	groundwater
water cycle	renewable resource	

1 A _____ is one for which there is a replaceable supply.

2 Water that is found underground is called _____.

3 Water is a _____ that most of us take for granted.

4 _____ are large masses of ice that form where more snow falls than melts.

5 The endless movement of water from oceans to atmosphere to land is called the _____.

Understand the Article

Write the answer to each question.

6 Where does most of the water used in California come from?

_____

7 Where is the world's supply of usable fresh water found?

_____

_____

8 What causes a drought?

_____

_____

9 List two ways to conserve water.

_____

_____

_____

Check your answers on page 239.

Apply Your Skills

Circle the number of the best answer.

10 When there is a drought in California, you can conclude that
   (1) there was not enough precipitation in the northern part of the state.
   (2) the reservoir levels were high all over the state.
   (3) there was not enough precipitation in the southern part of the state.
   (4) the system of aqueducts failed to transport water as needed.
   (5) farm crops will not be affected by the lack of water.

11 Why are there water shortages in parts of the United States?
   (1) Not enough rain falls in the United States each year.
   (2) Most of the water in the United States is polluted.
   (3) Much of the water in the United States is groundwater.
   (4) Some areas get too much precipitation, while others do not get enough.
   (5) The United States does not have many glaciers.

12 Which of the following is an opinion rather than a fact?
   (1) People should not live in areas that do not have an adequate supply of water.
   (2) A drought is a period of abnormally dry weather in a particular place.
   (3) Aqueducts, dams, and reservoirs are parts of water supply systems.
   (4) Much of the Earth's fresh water is trapped in the polar ice caps and glaciers.
   (5) The world's water supply is poorly distributed and often polluted.

Connect with the Article

Write your answer to each question.

13 If the world's supply of drinkable fresh water were running low, what alternative source of water can you think of to tap?

_____

_____

14 Describe ways in which you or someone you know has conserved water.

_____

_____

The Solar System

Setting the Stage

Several unmanned space probes have explored the far reaches of the solar system. By sending photos and data back to Earth, these space probes gave us a closer look at Jupiter, Saturn, Uranus, and Neptune, as well as their moons. Among the exciting discoveries was that several of these moons may have water, a necessity for human life.

PREVIEW THE ARTICLE

The headings of an article provide an outline of its content. Read the headings on pages 123–125. What are some things you can expect to learn about the solar system?

_____

_____

_____

RELATE TO THE TOPIC

This article is about the outer planets. It describes some of the unmanned space missions that provided us with most of the information we have about these planets. If you had the opportunity to visit one of the outer planets, would you go? Explain your answer.

_____

_____

_____

VOCABULARY

solar system   inner planets   outer planets

space probe

Check your answers on page 240.

The Outer Planets

The first spacecraft to visit planets were launched in the 1960s. Since then, scientists have been learning new things about the solar system. The **solar system** is made up of the sun and the objects that revolve around the sun. These objects include the planets and their moons. Mercury, Venus, Earth, and Mars are called the **inner planets** because they are fairly close to the sun. They are all rocky planets. Jupiter, Saturn, Uranus, Neptune, and Pluto are called the **outer planets.** Except for rocky Pluto, the outer planets are huge balls of gas. They are much farther from the sun than the inner planets. They are so far away that only unmanned spacecraft, often called **space probes,** have been sent to explore them. It takes these spacecraft years to reach the outer planets.

Missions to the Outer Planets

Pioneer 10 was the first space probe to visit an outer planet. It was launched in 1972 and provided the first close-up pictures of Jupiter and its moons. The following year *Pioneer 11* sent back photos of Saturn and its rings.

Like *Pioneer 10* and *11,* most space probes are designed to visit only one planet. But scientists got a bonus with *Voyager 1* and *Voyager 2.* When these probes were launched in 1977, four of the outer planets were on the same side of the sun. These planets would not be in this position again for 175 years. So after reaching Jupiter, the *Voyager* space probes were able to fly on to Saturn, Uranus, and Neptune. They used the gravity of one planet to speed on to the next. Despite problems with radio reception, cameras, and computers, scientists on Earth guided *Voyager 1* and *Voyager 2* through an almost perfect grand tour.

Each *Voyager* had three computers, scientific instruments, and cameras mounted on a movable platform.

The *Pioneer* and *Voyager* probes flew by the outer planets and then continued out of the solar system. But the *Galileo* spacecraft was designed to orbit its target planet, Jupiter. Launched in 1989, *Galileo* took pictures of the 1994 collision of comet Shoemaker-Levy and Jupiter. It reached Jupiter in 1995 and began orbiting the planet. *Galileo* lowered a separate probe into the atmosphere. Then it continued to circle Jupiter, sending back data about the planet and its moons.

All the space probes sent back spectacular photos. They also sent back data about Jupiter, Saturn, Uranus, Neptune, and their moons. Some basic data about these four planets and Earth are shown here.

Earth and Four Outer Planets

	Earth	Jupiter	Saturn	Uranus	Neptune
Diameter (miles)	8,000	89,000	75,000	32,000	30,000
Mass (compared to the mass of Earth)	1	318	95	15	17
Distance from the sun (millions of miles)	93.5	486.4	892	1,790	2,810
Time of one revolution around sun (years)	1	12	29	84	165
Time of one rotation (length of day in hours)	24	10	11	17	16
Number of known moons	1	16	18	17	8

Reading a Table One way to present a set of facts is to organize them in a table or chart. When you read a table, start with the title to get the main idea. From the title of this table, you know you will find information about Earth and four outer planets. The column headings ("Earth," "Jupiter," and so on) tell you which planet's information is in that column. The entries in each row of the left-hand column tell you what information appears in that row. For example, the first row of the table gives you information about diameter in miles. To find Saturn's diameter, you look along that row until you reach the Saturn column. Its diameter is 75,000 miles.

❶ How many moons does Jupiter have? _____

❷ How long does it take Uranus to revolve around the sun? _____

Jupiter and Saturn

Photos sent back by the spacecraft showed that Jupiter has rings. Jupiter also has a swirling, stormy atmosphere into which *Galileo*'s probe parachuted. It is made mostly of hydrogen and helium gases. The Great Red Spot of Jupiter is a storm several times larger than Earth.

 Check your answers on page 240.

Saturn's rings photographed by *Voyager 2* when it was 27 million miles away

Jupiter's four largest moons were first seen by the astronomer Galileo with a telescope in 1610. Ganymede, the largest moon in the solar system, looks similar to our moon. Io has active volcanoes, and its surface looks like pizza. Europa has a smooth surface of ice with a network of grooves. Callisto also has ice, but its surface has many deep craters.

Like Jupiter, Saturn is made mostly of hydrogen and helium. Saturn rotates quickly, causing bands of clouds to form in its atmosphere. Wind speeds of three hundred miles per hour have been measured.

The biggest surprise for scientists was Saturn's rings. Instead of there being a few rings, it was discovered that the planet has thousands of rings. Saturn's rings are made of particles ranging from specks of dust to large rocks. Some rings have "spokes" that appear and disappear. This new information has raised many questions about Saturn's rings.

Uranus and Neptune

It took almost five years for *Voyager 2* to travel the distance between Saturn and Uranus. Uranus is made mostly of hydrogen and helium. The temperature in the atmosphere is about −330°F. At Uranus, *Voyager 2* found ten new moons.

The last planet *Voyager 2* flew by was Neptune. Neptune, made mostly of hydrogen, also has a stormy atmosphere. One feature seen by *Voyager 2* is the Great Dark Spot. This spot is a storm almost as big as Earth. Data sent back to Earth suggests that Neptune's winds, moving over 1,200 miles per hour, might be the fastest in the solar system. *Voyager 2* also discovered six new moons orbiting Neptune, bringing the total number of known moons to eight.

Drawing Conclusions Conclusions are ideas that are based on facts. They follow logically from the facts. This article describes four of the outer planets and some of their moons. From the fact that the author refers to the number of "known" moons of Uranus and Neptune, you can reach the conclusion that further exploration may lead to the discovery of more moons.

Refer to the table on page 124. What can you conclude about a planet's distance from the sun and the time it takes to revolve around the sun?

   a.   The farther away it is from the sun, the longer a planet takes to revolve around the sun.

   b.   The closer it is to the sun, the longer a planet takes to revolve around the sun.

The Missions Continue

A new space probe called *Cassini,* launched in 1997, is scheduled to reach Saturn and its largest moon, Titan, in 2004. *Galileo's* data continues to be analyzed by scientists. And *Voyager 1* and *Voyager 2* are still speeding out of the solar system. Some *Voyager* instruments will continue to send data until about 2015. If aliens ever come across one of the *Voyager* space probes, they will find a recording aboard. It has greetings from Earth in sixty languages.

Thinking About the Article

Practice Vocabulary

The words below are in the passage in bold type. Study the way the words are used. Then complete each sentence by writing the correct words in the blank.

solar system   inner planets   outer planets   space probes

1   All of the _____ except Pluto are balls of gas.

2   _____ like *Pioneer, Voyager,* and *Galileo* send data about the planets and moons back to Earth.

3   The _____ consists of the sun and all the objects revolving around it.

4   Earth is one of the _____, which are small and rocky.

Understand the Article

Match each planet with its description. Write the letter of the planet in the space provided.

Description

_____   **5**   Largest planet in the solar system

_____   **6**   Planet with the most rings

_____   **7**   Has longest time of revolution

_____   **8**   Rotates in 24 hours

_____   **9**   Has 17 known moons

Planet

a.   Earth

b.   Saturn

c.   Jupiter

d.   Uranus

e.   Neptune

Write the answer to each question.

10   Name all of the planets in the solar system.

_____

_____

11   What was the mission of the *Pioneer, Voyager,* and *Galileo* spacecraft?

_____

_____

12   What is the most distinctive characteristic of Saturn?

_____

Apply Your Skills

Circle the number of the best answer.

⓭ According to the table on page 124, which planet is about twice as far from the sun as Saturn?
  (1) Earth
  (2) Jupiter
  (3) Uranus
  (4) Neptune
  (5) Pluto

⓮ According to the table on page 124, which planet has the <u>most</u> known moons?
  (1) Earth
  (2) Jupiter
  (3) Saturn
  (4) Uranus
  (5) Neptune

⓯ Which of the following can be concluded from the fact that the *Voyager* probes had a movable camera platform?
  (1) The camera lenses could be switched from the control center on Earth.
  (2) The cameras took color photographs and radioed them to Earth.
  (3) The cameras were mounted on tripods on the platform.
  (4) The platform was used to steady the cameras.
  (5) The cameras could be pointed at specific objects.

Connect with the Article

Write your answer to each question.

⓰ Why do you think that it is not practical to send astronauts on missions to the outer planets at this time?

_____

_____

⓱ Do you think it is a good idea to spend tax dollars on missions to explore the solar system? Explain your answer.

_____

_____

_____

18 Space Exploration

Setting the Stage

What comes to mind when you hear the word Martian? Perhaps you think of the aliens who catch colds in *The War of the Worlds.* Or you might think of TV's *My Favorite Martian* or the sci-fi comedy movie *Mars Attacks!* It's a tribute to our fascination with the planet Mars that so many Martians appear in science fiction. Now we have a real chance of finding out whether there have ever been Martians on Mars. Space missions to Mars are sending information about the planet back to Earth.

PREVIEW THE ARTICLE

Reading the first sentence of each paragraph of an article can tell you the main ideas that will be in the article. Read the first sentence of each paragraph on pages 129–131. What are some things you can expect to learn about Mars?

_____

_____

_____

RELATE TO THE TOPIC

This article is about a space mission to Mars. It describes some of the similarities and differences between Mars and Earth. Describe something you have seen or read about the planet Mars.

_____

_____

_____

VOCABULARY

spectrometer   silicon   crust

eroded   conglomerates

Pathfinder on Mars

The planet Mars has appealed to the human imagination for thousands of years. Because of its blood-red color, the ancient Babylonians called it the Star of Death. The ancient Romans named the planet Mars after their god of war. Many centuries later, astronomers using telescopes claimed to see canals and other structures not made by nature. Could there be intelligent life on Mars? Even today, after several spacecraft have visited Mars, we still do not know whether life has ever existed there. But we have learned a great deal about the planet, especially from the *Pathfinder* mission.

Pathfinder Lands

The main goal of the *Pathfinder* mission was to gather information by landing something safely—and cheaply—on Mars. No spacecraft had landed on Mars since 1976, when *Vikings 1* and *2* landed there at a cost of more than $3 billion. In 1997, *Pathfinder* made a safe landing for less than $265 million. It also did some great, and very entertaining, science.

For a landing site, project scientists picked a rocky plain that looked as though it had been formed by floods. As it descended through the thin Martian atmosphere, *Pathfinder* was slowed by rockets and a parachute. Ten seconds before landing, air bags inflated, enclosing the craft inside a huge cushion. Looking like a giant beach ball, *Pathfinder* bounced across the surface more than 15 times until it rolled to a stop. The air bags were deflated and pulled back. Then the panels covering the payload opened, revealing the star of the mission, *Sojourner,* the robotic rover that could be controlled from Earth by the scientists.

The rover *Sojourner* rolled cautiously over the rocky Martian surface at a speed of two feet a minute.

Sojourner Explores

While the lander *Pathfinder* took pictures and collected data on the atmosphere, *Sojourner* explored the surrounding area. Using cameras on its front and back, *Sojourner* took pictures of the rocky landscape. Since the rover was so small and close to the ground, its view of the rocks was very detailed. Following the mission on TV and on the Internet, millions of people watched as *Sojourner* checked out rocks that the scientists named Barnacle Bill, Yogi, and Scooby Doo.

Sojourner's **spectrometer** studied eight rocks to analyze what they were made of. Barnacle Bill has a lot of silicon. **Silicon** is a substance also common in Earth's **crust,** the top rocky layer of our planet. Yogi is like Barnacle Bill, but it is covered with a thick layer of dust and has a more rounded shape. Its shape suggests that it was **eroded,** or worn away, by water. In contrast, Scooby Doo seems to be similar to conglomerate. **Conglomerates** form when water rounds pebbles and larger stones and deposits them in sand and clay, which eventually cement them together. From the evidence gathered by *Sojourner*, scientists concluded that the landing area had been formed ages ago by a huge flood.

Evaluating Support for Conclusions   Conclusions are ideas that flow logically from a set of facts. In science, before you can draw a conclusion, you must have evidence, or data, to support it. When you read about science, you are often reading about the data scientists find and the conclusions they draw from this data. In the previous paragraph, for example, you read about data that *Sojourner* collected. Round-shaped rocks, the presence of a rock similar to conglomerate, and the fact that the rocks contain lots of silicon are all bits of data. But not all this data supports the scientists' conclusion that the landing area had been formed by flooding water. Only the rounded rock and the conglomerate-like rock support this conclusion. That some rocks contain a lot of silicon is true, but it does not have anything to do with the shaping force of water.

Reread the first paragraph on this page. Circle the letter next to any data supporting the conclusion that the *Pathfinder* mission was popular with the public.

    a.   Project scientists named some of the rocks Barnacle Bill, Yogi, and Scooby Doo.

    b.   Millions of people watched the mission on TV or followed it on the Internet.

    c.   *Sojourner*'s small size meant it had a close-up look at the landscape.

In about two-and-a-half months, *Sojourner* explored about 240 square yards of the Martian surface. The rover and the lander sent back more than 17,000 images. *Sojourner* took 16 spectrometer readings of the planet's rocks and soil. There was lots of evidence that water had once flowed on Mars. However, despite the possible ancient presence of water, there was no evidence that life had ever existed on the planet. Mars still looked rocky, dusty, and dead.

What Is Mars Like?

In some ways Mars is a lot like Earth. It is a small rocky planet. A day on Mars is just 37 minutes longer than a day on Earth. Thin wispy clouds of carbon dioxide drift through its atmosphere. Like Earth, Mars has ice caps at its poles, although they are mostly frozen carbon dioxide. Mars has seasons, too. During the summer, the polar ice caps shrink, just as they do on Earth.

Despite the similarities, Mars is very different from Earth. It is much colder, with extremely wide temperature swings. The thin Martian atmosphere is mostly carbon dioxide. It has little oxygen, so people couldn't breathe. Most oxygen on Mars is trapped in the rusty soil, giving the planet its red color.

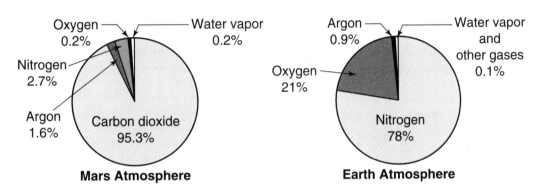

Mars Atmosphere

Oxygen 0.2%
Water vapor 0.2%
Nitrogen 2.7%
Argon 1.6%
Carbon dioxide 95.3%

Earth Atmosphere

Argon 0.9%
Water vapor and other gases 0.1%
Oxygen 21%
Nitrogen 78%

The lack of water is another way Mars is different from Earth. On Earth about 70 percent of the surface is covered by water. On Mars, there is a little water vapor in the atmosphere and a little water frozen in the polar ice caps. However, there may be lots of frozen water below the surface.

Comparing and Contrasting   When you compare things, you are noting their similarities. In the first paragraph above, the author compares Mars and Earth, telling how they are alike. For example, Mars and Earth have days of about the same length. When you contrast things, you are noting their differences. In the second and third paragraphs, some differences between the planets are pointed out. For example, Mars has much less surface water than Earth does.

Compare and contrast the ice caps of Mars with those of Earth.

a.   Both planets have ice caps at the poles but those on Mars are mainly frozen carbon dioxide.

b.   Both planets have water ice caps but those on Earth are at the poles.

Future Missions to Mars

Despite its differences from Earth, Mars is the planet most likely to be settled by humans. More than a dozen unmanned spacecraft are scheduled to explore Mars in the next two decades. These include the *Global Surveyors,* the *Climate Orbiter,* and the *Polar Lander.* By adding to our knowledge of the red planet, these missions will help us prepare for the first human visit to Mars.

Check your answer on page 240.

Thinking About the Article

Practice Vocabulary

The words below are in the passage in bold type. Study the way each word is used. Then match each word to its meaning by writing the correct letter in the blank.

_____ **1** crust

_____ **2** eroded

_____ **3** conglomerate

_____ **4** spectrometer

_____ **5** silicon

a. a rock that forms when smaller rocks are cemented together

b. a very common substance found in Earth's rocks and soil

c. the top rocky layer of Earth

d. a device used to analyze what substances are made of

e. worn away

Understand the Article

Write or circle the answer to each question.

6 What was the main goal of the *Pathfinder* mission?

_____

7 List two characteristics of the rocks that *Sojourner* examined.

_____

_____

8 What is the atmosphere of Mars like?
    a.   It is thin and consists mostly of carbon dioxide.
    b.   It has heavy clouds consisting of carbon monoxide gas.

9 Circle the letter beside each phrase that correctly describes Mars.
    a.   rocky planet
    b.   thick, cloudy atmosphere
    c.   polar ice caps
    d.   rusty soil
    e.   water vapor clouds
    f.   has seasons

10 What are the most serious problems humans would have to overcome to settle Mars?

_____

_____

Apply Your Skills

Circle the number of the best answer.

11 All of the following support the conclusion that the first human settlers on Mars would need to live inside a protected environment <u>except</u>
  (1) the lack of oxygen in the atmosphere.
  (2) the lack of surface water.
  (3) an environment that would not support growing food.
  (4) temperatures that can get 100° colder than Earth's coldest places.
  (5) the rocky surface that would make getting around difficult.

12 Mars and Earth are similar in that both have
  (1) the same average temperature.
  (2) atmospheres made mostly of nitrogen.
  (3) thick atmospheres with water vapor clouds.
  (4) days about 24 hours long.
  (5) lots of surface water.

13 Mars and Earth are different in that Mars
  (1) is a gas planet and Earth is a rocky planet.
  (2) has no atmosphere and Earth has a thick atmosphere.
  (3) has little surface water and Earth has a lot of surface water.
  (4) has little variation in temperature and Earth has lots of variation in temperature.
  (5) has no seasons and Earth has seasons.

Connect with the Article

Write your answer to each question.

14 Compare and contrast how automobile air bags work with how those on the *Pathfinder* lander worked.

_____

_____

_____

15 Most people pay little or no attention to space shuttle missions, yet the *Pathfinder* mission caught the attention of millions. In your opinion, why was this mission of such general interest?

_____

_____

_____

Science at Work

Building Trades: Construction Worker

Some Careers in Building Trades

Carpet Installer removes any existing carpet and lays new padding and carpeting

Electrician installs, repairs, and rewires buildings for electricity

Painter prepares walls for painting, selects color, and applies paint to surface

Tilesetter prepares floor for new tile; lays tiles in specific pattern

Construction workers on the job

As you walk or drive around your city or town, you will see construction workers. Construction workers work on a variety of projects. Some help build highways and roads. Others work on huge projects like skyscrapers or smaller projects like houses. Regardless of the size of the project, construction workers must be **in good physical shape,** have a good working **knowledge of Earth's forces and materials,** be able to **read blueprints,** and have **strong measurement and visual skills.**

Construction workers learn to use a wide variety of tools and machines. The equipment must be operated safely and correctly. Workers must also be concerned with the safety of others working at the job site. Working with Earth's materials such as sand, dirt, rock, and water and the forces of nature can be dangerous. Depending on the type of project on which they are working, construction workers must wear protective clothing such as hard hats, goggles, boots, and durable pants and shirts.

Look at the Some Careers in Building Trades chart.

- Do any of the careers interest you? If so, which ones?

- What information would you need to find out more about those careers? On a separate piece of paper, write some questions that you would like answered. You can find more information about those careers in the *Occupational Outlook Handbook* at your local library.

Construction workers must be able to follow directions to ensure that a project is done safely and correctly. They also need to use their knowledge about different forces and materials in the earth.

Read the directions below for constructing a swimming pool. Then answer the questions that follow.

Building an In-ground Swimming Pool

1 **Pick and Prepare the Pool Site.** Pick a level area a good distance away from any structures. The pool site should be a little higher than the surrounding area to allow for drainage. Make sure the area directly around the pool is sloped downward from the pool itself. Too much rain and splash water around the pool causes slipperiness and is a safety hazard.

2 **Dig the Hole.** Plot out the area for the pool by connecting stakes one foot wider and one foot longer than the actual size of the pool itself. Dig the hole 2–4 inches deeper than the pool itself. Dig another 4-ft. x 6-ft. hole in the middle of the deep end of the pool. Make it one foot deep. This is where the pool's drain equipment will be placed.

3 **Prepare the Hole to Receive the Pool Shell.** Fill and level the base of the hole with 2–4 inches of sand or rock dust, as they do not absorb water. This sand bed will support the pool. A sand bed is needed for consistent, unchanging support and drainage underneath the pool. Do not use dirt because it absorbs too much water. If too much water collects beneath the pool, the shell may crack or shift.

1 Which materials are acceptable for making the pool shell's support base?
(1) dirt and sand
(2) dirt and rock dust
(3) stakes and water
(4) sand and rock dust
(5) sand and water

2 Why is it important to grade the area around the pool?
(1) to make the pool look attractive and expensive
(2) to make sure the water stays in the pool and not on the land
(3) to make sure rain and splash water don't collect around the pool
(4) to make sure the construction worker does his or her job correctly
(5) to make sure that the pool can be drained for the winter

3 Have you seen construction workers on the job? Use a separate piece of paper to describe the job they were doing. What safety, weather, or pollution issues did they need to consider?

Weather Maps

Most daily newspapers print a weather map. The heavy lines show fronts. The symbols point in the direction in which the front is moving. The terms *warm front* and *cold front* describe the kind of temperatures that are behind the front. Temperatures on U.S. weather maps are shown in degrees Fahrenheit. A stationary front is the area between two air masses that have stopped moving for awhile.

High Temperatures and Precipitation

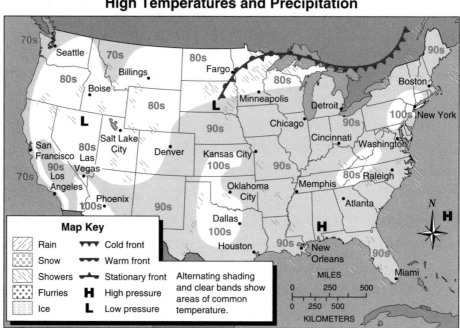

Map Key

Rain	Cold front
Snow	Warm front
Showers	Stationary front
Flurries	**H** High pressure
Ice	**L** Low pressure

Alternating shading and clear bands show areas of common temperature.

Fill in the blank with the word or words that best complete each statement.

1 According to the map, the high temperature in degrees Fahrenheit for Oklahoma City is in the ———————————.

2 The type of precipitation falling in the United States is ———————————.

Circle the number of the best answer.

3 What is the weather like along the stationary front?
(1) hot, with sunshine
(2) hot, with showers
(3) cold, with sunshine
(4) cold, with snow flurries
(5) moderate temperatures, with high winds

Check your answers on page 241.

The Ozone Layer

You may have noticed that many products that used to be sold in aerosol spray cans are now sold in pump sprays. The reason for this is that many of the gases used in aerosols harm the environment. These gases are called chlorofluorocarbons (CFCs). CFCs escape into the air when products containing them are used. Once in the atmosphere, CFCs can damage the ozone layer.

Ozone is a form of oxygen. A layer of ozone is found ten to fifty miles above Earth's surface. The ozone layer absorbs ultraviolet rays from the sun. **Ultraviolet rays** cause sunburn and skin cancer. The ozone layer protects plants and animals from the effects of these harmful ultraviolet rays.

The ozone layer has become thinner in the last thirty years. There is now a hole in the ozone layer. It is over Antarctica and seems to be getting larger. Many people are concerned about the damage that has been done to the ozone layer. Without a protective layer of ozone, ultraviolet rays may cause increases in the cases of skin cancer throughout the world.

Fill in the blank with the word or words that best complete each statement.

4 Ozone is a form of _____ .

5 _____ rays are dangerous rays from the sun.

Circle the number of the best answer.

6 Which of the following statements does <u>not</u> describe the ozone layer?
   (1) It has a hole in it.
   (2) It is ten to fifty miles above Earth's surface.
   (3) It is getting thinner.
   (4) It absorbs ultraviolet rays.
   (5) It is made up of CFCs.

7 If the use of CFCs were to increase, more people would probably die of
   (1) oxygen poisoning.
   (2) CFC poisoning.
   (3) skin cancer.
   (4) sunburn.
   (5) all of the above.

8 CFCs
   (1) are still used extensively in aerosol cans.
   (2) are used extensively in pump sprays.
   (3) are trapped by the ozone layer.
   (4) have been found to cause damage to the ozone layer.
   (5) cause skin cancer.

The Oceans

Oceans cover nearly three-fourths of Earth's surface. The water is shallow where the oceans meet the continents. The bottom of the ocean has a gentle slope in this area. It is called the **continental shelf** because the ocean bottom is almost flat. Since the water is shallow, sunlight can reach the bottom. There are many plants here. There are also many animals. We get shellfish, such as clams and lobsters, from the continental shelf. This is also the richest part of the sea for fishing.

Along the world's coastlines, the continental shelf can extend from just a few miles to as much as a thousand miles from the shore. Then the bottom slopes more steeply. This is the **continental slope.** The slope levels out to form the **ocean basin,** the bottom of the sea. The resources from these regions come mostly from the upper layers of the water in the open ocean. Large fish, such as tuna, are caught here.

The ocean gives us more than food resources. The rock layers of the continental shelf are sources of oil and natural gas. On the ocean basin are lumps of minerals, called nodules. They consist mostly of manganese. They also contain some iron, copper, and nickel.

Fill in the blank with the word or words that best complete the statement.

9 The part of the ocean where the water meets the land is the

_____.

Circle the number of the best answer.

10 The best food resources in the ocean are in
(1) nodules on the ocean basin.
(2) nodules on the continental shelf.
(3) waters of the open ocean.
(4) waters of the continental-shelf region.
(5) waters of the continental-slope region.

11 All of the following are resources from the ocean except
(1) oil.
(2) manganese.
(3) iron.
(4) natural gas.
(5) coal.

12 The continental shelf
(1) extends for hundreds of miles along the U.S. coastline.
(2) levels out to form the ocean basin.
(3) is shallow enough for sunlight to reach its bottom.
(4) is where tuna are caught.
(5) is the source of rich mineral nodules.

Check your answers on page 242.

The Sun

The sun is the nearest star to Earth. The sun appears very large and bright. However, it is not especially large or bright when compared to other stars. The sun appears large and bright because it is so much closer to Earth than any other star. The next nearest star is more than 250,000 times farther away.

Huge amounts of heat energy and light energy are given off by the sun. The energy comes from nuclear reactions in the sun. These reactions take place in the **core,** which is the center of the sun. The temperature there is believed to be about 27 million degrees Fahrenheit. A large portion of the heat energy is changed into light energy on the surface of the sun. As a result, the temperature of the surface is only about 10,000 degrees F.

Even at this temperature, the sun is very hot. Earth is about 93 million miles from the sun. This is just the right distance for people to live on Earth. If Earth were closer to the sun, it would be too hot to support most forms of life. If Earth were much farther from the sun, it would be too cold.

Fill in the blank with the word or words that best complete each statement.

⓭ The nearest star to Earth is the _____.

⓮ The hottest part of the sun is the _____.

Circle the number of the best answer.

⓯ Many people have solar-powered calculators. What kind of energy from the sun do these devices use?
- (1) heat
- (2) light
- (3) nuclear
- (4) wind
- (5) chemical

Science Extension

Select one natural disaster or type of bad weather that your area sometimes experiences. For example, you could pick earthquakes or tornadoes. Then make a list of things you could do to prepare yourself and your family for such an event.

Science Connection: Earth and Space Science and Geography

The International Space Station

DATELINE 2000: How would you like to live in space? In the early twenty-first century, an international team of three astronauts will find out what it is like. They will be launched from Earth in a Russian spacecraft and headed for their destination—the International Space Station (ISS). In 1996, the team of Russian and American astronauts began preparing for their journey.

This historic scientific effort involves the participation of 16 countries. It will take a total of 45 missions, conducted by the United States and Russia, to carry and construct the 100 elements needed to complete the ISS. While ISS components are being designed and built on Earth, they will be assembled in space.

Astronauts in charge of building the ISS will be putting together these elements "in the blind." They will use computers and robotics to construct the station. It will take at least until the year 2004 to complete the assembly. When finished, the ISS will weigh over 450 tons and measure 361 feet in length. The scientists and engineers living in the ISS will use solar, electric, and battery power.

The ISS will be a scientific laboratory where astronauts can better control challenging environmental factors like gravity, temperature, and pressure. Countries participating in the ISS project hope to learn more about Earth science, technology, and space from experiments conducted aboard the ISS.

Geography:
Continents and Countries

Earth, the planet on which we live, is covered by water and land masses. The extremely large land masses completely or mostly surrounded by water are called **continents.** While there are only seven continents in the world, these continents are home to 260 **countries.** Very few of the world's countries are stable enough, both politically and financially, to support space exploration programs. In fact, the ISS program was too expensive for any single country to develop on its own. The 16-nation partnership allowed many countries scattered across the globe to learn about the regions beyond Earth's surface.

Countries Participating in Creation of the International Space Station

Country	Continent	Country	Continent
Belgium	Europe	Netherlands	Europe
Brazil	South America	Norway	Europe
Canada	North America	Russia	Europe/Asia
Denmark	Europe	Spain	Europe
France	Europe	Sweden	Europe
Germany	Europe	Switzerland	Europe
Italy	Europe	United Kingdom	Europe
Japan	Asia	United States	North America

Use the material on the previous page and the map below to answer the questions that follow.

Earth's Seven Continents

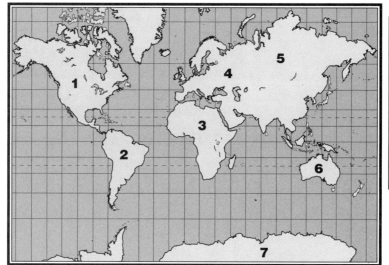

Key
1 North America
2 South America
3 Africa
4 Europe
5 Asia
6 Australia
7 Antarctica

1 On which continent is Belgium located?
   (1) 1
   (2) 2
   (3) 4
   (4) 5
   (5) None of the above.

2 How many missions will it take to complete the International Space Station?
   (1)   16
   (2)   45
   (3) 100
   (4) 361
   (5) 450

3 You could conclude that scientists are excited about using the ISS for experiments because
   (1) gravity, temperature, and pressure do not exist on Earth.
   (2) gravity, temperature, and pressure are more difficult to control on Earth.
   (3) gravity, temperature, and pressure are stronger in space.
   (4) gravity, temperature, and pressure are stronger on Earth.
   (5) There is not enough information to answer this question.

4 Use a separate piece of paper to list all 16 nations participating in the ISS program. Using the map above, write the number of the continent on which each nation is located next to the country's name.

UNIT 3

Chemistry

A fire raging out of control is terrifying. But when it is controlled, fire is a powerful tool. Fire is actually a chemical reaction called combustion. Since people first used fire thousands of years ago, they have been fascinated by **chemistry**, the study of matter and its changes. Chemistry involves studying physical properties of matter. What are the building blocks of matter? How does matter change from a solid to a liquid? At what temperature will a substance burn? Answers to these questions help us understand ordinary things like ice, wood, and salt.

Changes in energy take place during chemical reactions. Reactions such as combustion release energy. Learning about such reactions helps us understand heaters and engines. It also helps us recognize different sources of air pollution.

Knowing about chemistry can help you understand many of the ordinary things and processes in the world around you.

How can learning chemistry help you with household chores?

Is the air in your home dangerous? How can knowing about chemistry help keep your home's air healthful?

SECTIONS

19   Matter

20   Changes in Matter

21   Mixtures and Solutions

22   Combustion

23   Nuclear Fission

Matter

Setting the Stage

Supermarkets usually have a whole aisle full of cleaning products. There are cleaners for the kitchen and cleaners for the bathroom. There are cleaners for white laundry and cleaners for colored laundry. Many of these cleaners contain the same few chemicals in different combinations. It's interesting to look at some basic facts about matter, using cleaning products and processes as examples.

PREVIEW THE ARTICLE

Reading the headings of an article is a good way to preview its contents. Read the headings on pages 145–147. What are some things you can expect to learn about matter?

_____

_____

_____

RELATE TO THE TOPIC

This article is about types of matter, the symbols and formulas that chemists use to represent matter, and chemical reactions. It describes the types of matter contained in some common cleaning products. List some household cleaning products that you and your family use.

_____

_____

_____

VOCABULARY

substance	mixture	element
compound	atom	chemical reaction

Check your answers on page 242.

The Chemistry of Cleaning

Almost everyone has run into the laundry problems of "ring around the collar" or stubborn yellow stains. Makers of detergents and bleaches claim their products can remove the toughest stains. Detergents can remove many stains. But recently scientists figured out why some oily yellow stains won't go away.

If the clothing is washed right away, the oily stain can be removed. But what happens if the stain sets for a week? The aging oil can combine with oxygen from the air. This process changes the colorless oil to a yellow substance. The yellow substance reacts with the fabric. In effect, the clothing is dyed yellow.

The sooner this stained clothing is washed, the easier it will be to get it clean.

Substances and Mixtures

Solving laundry problems is just one practical application of chemistry. Knowing about chemistry can help you make better use of the products you buy for cleaning and other jobs around the house.

Everything is made up of matter. Matter can be divided into two groups—substances and mixtures. All the matter in a **substance** is the same. A **mixture** is a combination of two or more substances that can be separated by physical means.

There are two kinds of substances. An **element** is a substance that cannot be broken into other substances by ordinary means. Two or more elements can combine chemically to form a **compound,** another type of substance. The smallest particle of an element is an **atom.** The smallest particle of a compound is a **molecule.** Each molecule in a compound is made up of atoms from each of the elements in the compound.

Forms of Matter

| Mixtures | Substances | |
	Compounds	Elements
lemonade	salt	oxygen
coffee	sugar	carbon
salad	water	iron
soil	ammonia	gold
cement	bleach	nitrogen

Symbols of Common Elements

Element	Symbol
Hydrogen	H
Carbon	C
Nitrogen	N
Oxygen	O
Sodium	Na
Magnesium	Mg
Sulfur	S
Chlorine	Cl
Iron	Fe
Calcium	Ca

Chemical Symbols and Formulas

When they write about matter and its changes, chemists use a kind of shorthand. A **chemical symbol** of one or two letters stands for each element. The symbols for some common elements are shown in the table on this page. When elements combine to form a compound, the symbols are grouped together in a **chemical formula.** For example, H_2O is the chemical formula for water. The formula shows that the elements hydrogen (H) and oxygen (O) make up the compound water. The formula also shows there are two atoms of hydrogen for each atom of oxygen in the compound. Another chemical formula is NH_3. It is the formula for ammonia.

Understanding Chemical Formulas   Chemical formulas can tell you a great deal if you know how to decode them. They tell what elements are in a compound. Formulas also show how many atoms of each element make up each molecule of the compound. For example, the formula for sugar is $C_{12}H_{22}O_{11}$. This means that each molecule of sugar has 12 atoms of carbon, 22 atoms of hydrogen, and 11 atoms of oxygen. Reread the first paragraph on this page, and refer to the table above to answer these questions.

1   Name the elements in NH_3 (the compound ammonia).

_____

2   How many atoms of each element are in each molecule of ammonia?

_____

Chemical Reactions

In a **chemical reaction,** elements are combined into compounds or compounds are changed into other substances. For example, iron is a gray solid. Oxygen is a colorless gas. When iron and oxygen combine, they form a new substance. This substance is iron oxide, or rust. It is a brownish red or orange solid. In a chemical reaction, the substances that you start with are called the **reactants.** In this example, iron and oxygen are the reactants. The substances that result from the reaction are called the **products.** In this example, there is only one product, iron oxide.

Scientists use equations to describe reactions. A **chemical equation** shows the reactants and products of a reaction. This equation shows how rust forms:

$$\text{iron} + \text{oxygen} \rightarrow \text{iron oxide } (Fe + O \rightarrow FeO_2)$$

Rust stains are hard to remove from clothing. However, you can remove the stain if you reverse the chemical reaction. The acid in lemon juice can remove the oxygen from iron oxide. The remaining iron rinses away.

Check your answers on page 242.

Compounds in Household Cleaners

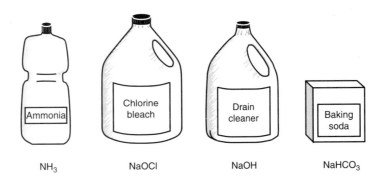

Ammonia
NH₃

Chlorine bleach
NaOCl

Drain cleaner
NaOH

Baking soda
NaHCO₃

Another example of a chemical reaction is the effect of bleach on clothing. The formula for chlorine bleach is NaOCl. In water, this compound produces salt and oxygen. The release of oxygen causes the whitening of the fabric. Nonchlorine bleaches use other sources of oxygen. One source is hydrogen peroxide, H_2O_2. Another source is calcium carbonate, $CaCO_3$.

Understanding Chemistry Roots, Suffixes, and Prefixes   The name of a compound tells you what's in it. The root names of the elements are in the name of the compound. For example, table salt, NaCl, is called sodium chloride. It consists of sodium (Na) and chlorine (Cl). But why is it called sodium chlor*ide* and not sodium chlorine? When the suffix *-ide* is added to the end of the root name of the second element of a compound, it has a special meaning. It means the compound consists of just two elements. Another special suffix in chemistry is *-ate*. For example, calcium carbon*ate* is $CaCO_3$. The suffix *-ate* is used when the second element of a compound has the element oxygen with it.

❶ What elements are in the compound barium chloride? Circle the letters of all correct answers.

   a. barium   b. calcium   c. chlorine   d. oxygen

❷ What elements are in the compound calcium chlorate? Circle the letters of all correct answers.

   a. barium   b. calcium   c. chlorine   d. oxygen

Prefixes are used when more than one compound can be made from the same elements. For example, CO and CO_2 are both made from carbon and oxygen. Prefixes are used to distinguish the two compounds. So CO is carbon *monoxide. Mon-* means "one," and it tells you there is one atom of oxygen in each molecule of carbon monoxide. CO_2 is carbon *dioxide. Di-* means "two," and it tells you there are two atoms of oxygen in each molecule of carbon dioxide. Some common prefixes are shown in the table at the right.

Prefix	Meaning
mono-	one
di-	two
tri-	three
tetra-	four

❸ How many chlorine atoms are in the compound carbon tetrachloride?

_____

❹ What is the name of the compound that has one aluminum atom and three oxygen atoms? Circle the letter of the correct answer.

   a. aluminum monoxide   b. aluminum dioxide   c. aluminum trioxide

Check your answers on page 242.

Thinking About the Article

Practice Vocabulary

The terms below are in the passage in bold type. Study the way each term is used. Then complete each sentence by writing the correct term in the blank.

mixture	substance	element
compound	atom	chemical reaction

1 A(n) _____ such as iron or oxygen is a pure substance that cannot be broken down into other substances by ordinary means.

2 Salad dressing is a(n) _____, a combination of two or more kinds of matter that can be separated by physical means.

3 When elements or compounds change into one or more different substances, a(n) _____ takes place.

4 All the matter in a(n) _____ is the same.

5 The smallest particle of an element is a(n) _____.

6 The elements sodium and chlorine combine chemically to form a(n) _____ commonly called table salt.

Understand the Article

Circle the letter of the correct answer.

7 The chemical symbol for the element calcium is
a. C   b. Ca

8 The chemical formula for the compound called chlorine bleach is
a. NaOCl   b. Cl

9 Chemists show the reactants and products in a chemical reaction by writing a
a. chemical symbol.
b. chemical equation.

10 Which two elements combine to form rust?
a. oxygen and iron
b. hydrogen and oxygen
c. iron and calcium

11 The products of a chemical reaction have
a. the same characteristics as the reactants.
b. different characteristics than the reactants.

Check your answers on pages 242–243.

Apply Your Skills

Circle the number of the best answer for each question.

12. What elements are in hydrogen peroxide (H_2O_2)?
    (1) helium and potassium
    (2) helium and boron
    (3) hydrogen and chlorine
    (4) hydrogen and oxygen
    (5) hydrogen and phosphorus

13. What is the name of the compound MgS?
    (1) magnesium sulfur
    (2) magnesium sulfide
    (3) magnesium disulfide
    (4) sulfur magnesiate
    (5) magnesium sulfate

14. The compound calcium carbonate has the elements calcium and carbon. The suffix -*ate* tells you that the compound also has the element
    (1) iron.
    (2) chlorine.
    (3) nitrogen.
    (4) oxygen.
    (5) hydrogen.

Connect with the Article

Write your answer to each question.

15. The body of an automobile is made mostly of steel, which contains iron. Paint protects these steel parts from rusting. If the paint wears away, the auto body will start to rust. Why does painting the steel help prevent it from rusting?

    _____

    _____

16. Name a common household cleaning compound and describe how you or someone you know uses it.

    _____

    _____

    _____

Changes in Matter

Setting the Stage

All cooks use chemistry, even cooks who can only boil water or fry an egg. When you cook, you often change matter from one state to another. For example, heating water changes it from a liquid to a gas—steam—if you leave it boiling long enough. You also make chemical changes when you cook. One example is frying an egg. Adding heat to an egg makes chemical changes in the proteins the egg contains.

PREVIEW THE ARTICLE

Sometimes the illustrations in an article give you an overview of what the article is about. Look at the illustrations on pages 151 and 153. What are some things you can expect to learn about changes in matter?

_____

_____

_____

RELATE TO THE TOPIC

This article is about changes in matter. It tells the difference between physical and chemical changes. It explains changes in matter by using examples from cooking. Describe your favorite cooked food. What is it like when it is raw? What is it like when it is cooked?

_____

_____

_____

VOCABULARY

solid   liquid   gas

physical change   chemical change

Cooking with Chemistry

Ice cubes, water, and steam are used by cooks. Ice cubes are used to chill liquids. Water is used to boil food and as an ingredient in many recipes. Steam, which is actually water vapor, is used to cook vegetables. What do ice, water, and steam have in common? They are three forms, or states, of the same compound, H_2O.

Each state of matter has its own properties, or characteristics. A **solid** has a definite shape and takes up a definite amount of space. A **liquid** takes up a definite amount of space, but it doesn't have a definite shape. A liquid flows and takes the shape of its container. A **gas** does not have a definite size or shape. It expands to fill its container. If you remove the lid from a pot of steaming vegetables, water vapor escapes and spreads throughout the kitchen.

Changes of State

Matter changes state when energy, in the form of heat, is added to or removed from a substance. When you leave an ice cube tray on the counter, the ice absorbs heat from the air. Eventually the ice cubes melt. **Melting** is the change from a solid to a liquid. If you put the tray back in the freezer, the water will change back into ice. **Freezing** changes a liquid to a solid by removing the heat from it.

When you heat water, bubbles of gas form. They rise and burst on the surface of the water. **Boiling** is the rapid change from a liquid to a gas. A liquid can also change to a gas slowly through **evaporation.** If a glass of water is left out for a long time, the water evaporates from its surface. The reverse of boiling or evaporation is **condensation.** This is the change from a gas to a liquid. If a soft drink bottle is taken from the refrigerator, water vapor in the air will condense on the cold surface of the bottle.

Melting and boiling are two changes in state.

Physical Changes and Chemical Changes

A **physical change** is one in which the appearance of matter changes but its make-up and most of its properties stay the same. The boiling of water, the melting of butter, the dissolving of sugar in tea, and the smashing of a plate are physical changes. No new substances are formed. Matter is changed from one state to another in boiling and melting. When sugar dissolves, matter is mixed. When a plate breaks, it changes size and shape.

Unlike a physical change, a **chemical change** causes new substances to form. Some people make a beverage called a lemon fizz with baking soda and lemonade. This involves a chemical change. Baking soda mixed with an acid, like lemonade, gives off the gas carbon dioxide. This is a new product.

Many activities involve both physical and chemical changes. Making an omelet is an example. Breaking and beating the eggs cause physical changes. The chemical make-up of the eggs has not changed. You have just mixed the parts together. Cooking the eggs causes a chemical change. The heat changes the chemical make-up of the proteins in the eggs and makes them harden.

Finding the Main Idea   The **main idea** of a paragraph tells what the paragraph is about in general. It is often stated in a topic sentence. The main idea of the first paragraph on this page is that the chemical make-up of matter stays the same during physical change. The main idea is stated in the first sentence of the paragraph, the topic sentence. Reread the second paragraph on this page. Look for the main idea and topic sentence.

What is the main idea of the second paragraph on this page?
a.   A chemical change causes new substances to form.
b.   Making a lemon fizz involves a chemical change.

Cooking a Hamburger

Cooking and eating a hamburger involves both physical and chemical changes. When the butcher grinds beef to make hamburger meat, the meat is ground into small pieces. No new substances are made, so grinding beef is a physical change.

Until the meat is packaged in plastic, the surface of the meat reacts with oxygen in the air. Myoglobin, a chemical in the beef, combines with oxygen. This chemical change is called **oxidation.** This change turns the surface of the meat bright red.

The next step is to form hamburger patties. In this step, you are changing the shape of the ground beef. There aren't any chemical changes, just a physical change.

Check your answer on page 243.

Cooking hamburgers involves both physical and chemical changes.

Now the hamburgers are ready for cooking. Many cooks quickly sear one side and then the other on a very hot surface. Searing causes a chemical change in the surface proteins, and they form a crust. The crust keeps too much water from evaporating. It also keeps some of the fat from melting and seeping out of the hamburger. By preventing these physical changes, the crust keeps the hamburger from becoming dry.

Applying Knowledge to Other Contexts   Information becomes more valuable when you use it. This article describes the physical and chemical changes in a hamburger as it is prepared and cooked. You can apply your knowledge of physical and chemical changes to other foods. For example, baking brownies causes a chemical change. The proteins in the liquid batter undergo chemical changes and it becomes firm. On the other hand, cutting up brownies is a physical change. You are just changing the shape of the brownies when you cut them. Label each of the following as a *chemical change* or a *physical change*.

❶   A piece of apple turns brown when it is exposed to the oxygen in air.

❷   A tray of ice cubes melts when left outside of the freezer.

As a hamburger cooks, the inside loses its red color. This is caused by another chemical change in myoglobin. At the same time, chemical changes in the proteins make the meat become firmer.

When you eat the hamburger, more physical and chemical changes occur. Your teeth cut and grind the hamburger. This is a physical change. The hamburger is broken down chemically by substances in your digestive system. Digestion is another series of physical and chemical changes.

Check your answers on page 243.

Thinking About the Article

Practice Vocabulary

The terms below are in the passage in bold type. Study the way each term is used. Then complete each sentence by writing the correct term in the blank.

gas   chemical change   solid

physical change   liquid

① A _____ is a state of matter that has a definite shape and takes up a definite amount of space.

② A _____ is a state of matter that takes up a definite amount of space but doesn't have a definite shape.

③ A _____ is a state of matter that will spread out to fill all the available space.

④ A _____ is one in which the appearance of matter changes, but its make-up and most of its properties remain the same.

⑤ A _____ causes new substances to form that were not present before the change.

Understand the Article

Write the answer to the question.

⑥ Name the three states of matter of H_2O.

_____

Match the process with its description.

_____ **⑦** boiling	a.	change from liquid to solid
_____ **⑧** evaporation	b.	rapid change from liquid to gas
_____ **⑨** freezing	c.	change from gas to liquid
_____ **⑩** condensation	d.	slow change from liquid to gas

Identify each of the following as a *chemical change* or *physical change.*

⑪ Chopping onions _____

⑫ Baking cookies _____

Check your answers on page 243.

Apply Your Skills

Circle the number of the best answer for each question.

13 Which title best describes the main idea of this article?
(1) Chemical Changes
(2) Physical Changes
(3) Chemical Changes in Cooking
(4) Chemical and Physical Changes in Cooking
(5) Cooking a Hamburger

14 Jason leaves a bar of chocolate on the dashboard of his car. When he comes back, he finds it has melted in the sun. This is an example of
(1) a chemical reaction.
(2) condensation.
(3) a chemical change.
(4) a physical change.
(5) oxidation.

15 All of the following are physical changes except
(1) melting a bowl of ice cream.
(2) freezing a popsicle.
(3) mixing a milk shake.
(4) baking a cake.
(5) bringing soup to a boil.

Connect with the Article

Write your answer to each question.

16 Choose one of the changes of state, such as freezing or evaporating, and give an example of it from everyday life.

____

____

____

17 Describe an experience you or someone you know has had while cooking a meal or snack. Identify any physical or chemical changes that occurred in the food as it was cooked.

____

____

____

Check your answers on page 243.

Mixtures and Solutions

Setting the Stage

What do orange soda, brass, and a cup of instant coffee have in common? All are solutions, mixtures in which one substance is dissolved in another. We use many mixtures and solutions in our daily lives.

PREVIEW THE ARTICLE

One way to preview an article is by reading the first sentence of every paragraph. This gives you some of the main ideas in the article. Read the first sentence of each paragraph on pages 157–159. What are some things you can expect to learn about mixtures and solutions?

_____

_____

_____

RELATE TO THE TOPIC

This article is about common types of substances called mixtures and solutions. It describes some properties of mixtures and solutions and gives examples of them. Most of the beverages we drink are either mixtures or solutions. What is your favorite beverage?

_____

VOCABULARY

distillation   solution   solvent

solute   solubility

Check your answers on page 244.

Mixing It Up

Mixtures are all around you. The paper in this book is a mixture of fibers. The inks with which it is printed are mixtures of colored substances. Even the air around you is a mixture. It contains nitrogen, oxygen, carbon dioxide, and other gases.

What is a mixture? A **mixture** is made up of two or more substances that can be separated by physical means. The properties of a mixture are the properties of its ingredients. That is why sugar water is sweet and wet. Neither the sugar nor the water loses its properties when they are mixed together. Another characteristic of a mixture is that the amounts of its ingredients can vary.

Mixtures can be solids, liquids, or gases. A penny is a solid mixture of the elements copper and zinc. Blood is a mixture of liquids, such as water; solids, such as cells, sugar, and proteins; and gases, such as oxygen and carbon dioxide. A soft drink is a mixture of flavored liquid and the gas carbon dioxide.

The substances in a mixture can be separated by physical means. A mixture of red and blue blocks can be sorted by hand. A filter can be used to separate sand from water. A magnet can separate a mixture of steel and plastic paper clips. Liquid mixtures can be separated by distillation. **Distillation** is the process of boiling a mixture of liquids so that they will separate from one another. Since the different liquids boil at different temperatures, the gases formed can be condensed and the condensed liquids collected as they boil out of the mixture one at a time. That's how alcohol is obtained from fermented juices and brewed grains.

Sterling silver is a mixture of silver and copper.

Milk is a mixture of water, proteins, fat, and sugar.

What Is a Solution?

A solution is a special type of mixture. In a **solution,** the ingredients are distributed evenly throughout. All samples taken from a solution have the same amount of each substance. That's why the first and last sip from a soft drink taste the same. Solutions can be made of solids, liquids, or gases. Brass is a solid solution. Tea is a liquid solution. Seltzer is a solution of carbon dioxide gas in water.

In a solution, the substance that is present in the greater amount is called the **solvent.** Water is the most common solvent. The substance present in the smaller amount is called the **solute.** The solvent and solute may be in different states before the solution is formed. However, the final state of the solution will be that of the solvent. So a solution of water and powdered fruit drink is a liquid, not a solid.

Comparing and Contrasting   When learning about things that are related, it is helpful to compare and contrast them. **Comparing** is pointing out how two things are alike. **Contrasting** is showing how two things are different. This article compares solutions and other mixtures. They are alike in that both can be separated by physical means. This article also contrasts solutions and other mixtures. One way they are different is that the ingredients of a solution are distributed evenly throughout. In other mixtures the ingredients can be mixed unevenly.

1   How are mixtures and solutions alike?
   a.   Both are only liquids or gases.
   b.   Both consist of two or more substances mixed together.

2   How are mixtures and solutions different?
   a.   A solution is always liquid, and a mixture can be solid, liquid, or gas.
   b.   A mixture can be in any state of matter, but a solution is always in the state of matter of the solvent.

How Solutions Form

When a solute dissolves, its particles spread evenly throughout the solution. How quickly the solute dissolves depends on several things. The smaller the particles of solute, the more quickly they dissolve. That's why instant coffee is made of small grains, not large chunks.

Stirring or shaking make a solute dissolve faster. The movement brings the solvent in contact with more of the solute. Stirring a cup of instant coffee makes the coffee dissolve more quickly.

Heat also makes a solute dissolve faster. Molecules move more quickly when they are hot. You can make instant coffee more quickly with boiling water than with cold water.

Check your answers on page 244.

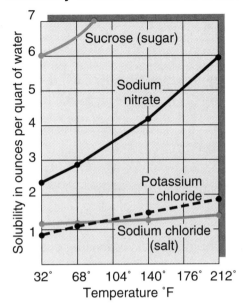

Solubility of Some Solids in Water

Solubility in ounces per quart of water (y-axis)

7
Sucrose (sugar)
6
Sodium nitrate
5
4
3
Potassium chloride
2
Sodium chloride (salt)
1

32° 68° 104° 140° 176° 212°
Temperature °F

Solubility

The amount of a solute that will dissolve in a given amount of solvent at a given temperature is called its **solubility.** The effect of temperature on solubility is shown in the graph on this page. Each line on the graph is called a solubility curve. You can use this graph to find the solubility of substances in water at various temperatures.

The solubility of solids and liquids usually increases as the temperature rises. However, the opposite is true of gases. As the temperature rises, dissolved gas particles gain energy. They escape from the surface of the solution. That's why an opened bottle of soda goes flat more quickly at room temperature than in the refrigerator.

Reading a Line Graph Line graphs show information instead of presenting it in words. The title tells you the main idea of the graph. This graph shows the solubility of some solids in water. The labels along the side show how many ounces of the solid will dissolve in one quart of water. The labels along the bottom show the temperature of the water. To find out how much sodium nitrate will dissolve in a quart of water heated to 176°F, first find the line that shows sodium nitrate. Then find the point on that line that intersects with the grid line for 176°F on the bottom temperature scale. From that point on the sodium nitrate line, look along the horizontal grid line to the left-hand scale. There you will see that 5 ounces of sodium nitrate will dissolve in 1 quart of water heated to 176°F.

1 How many ounces of salt will dissolve in one quart of boiling water (212°F)?
   a.   about 1.5   b.   about 6

2 Which of the following substances is more soluble in water?
   a.   potassium chloride   b.   sugar

What happens if you add more solute than the solvent can hold? Extra solute settles to the bottom. That is why there is a limit to how sweet you can make iced tea. Once you reach the solubility limit of sugar, no more dissolves. The sugar on the bottom doesn't make the tea sweeter.

If the temperature of a sugar solution changes, the solubility of sugar changes. Suppose you dissolve all the sugar you can in hot water. Then you let the water cool. Sugar crystals will come out of the solution. If you let the water evaporate, the sugar crystals will be left behind. This is how rock candy is made.

Thinking About the Article

Practice Vocabulary

The terms below are in the passage in bold type. Study the way each term is used. Then complete each sentence by writing the correct term in the blank.

distillation   solution   solvent

solute   solubility

① A mixture in which the substances are distributed evenly throughout is

called a _____ .

② _____ is a process of boiling and condensing that is
used to separate liquids in a mixture.

③ The _____ of liquids and solids usually increases with
increases in temperature.

④ The substance present in the smaller amount in a solution is called the

_____ .

⑤ Because so many substances dissolve in it, water is often called the
universal _____ .

Understand the Article

Identify each of the following as a *mixture* or a *solution*.

⑥ Instant coffee _____

⑦ Chocolate chip cookie dough _____

⑧ Milk _____

Circle the letter of the correct answer.

⑨ Refer to the line graph on page 159. The solubility of which of the
following solids is <u>less</u> affected by changes in temperature?
   a.   sodium chloride   b.   sodium nitrate

⑩ Why does adding heat make a solid or liquid solute dissolve more quickly?
   a.   The heat melts the solute.
   b.   The heat makes the molecules move more quickly so they mix
       together faster.

Check your answers on page 244.

Apply Your Skills

Circle the number of the best answer for each question.

11 What is the difference between a solvent and a solute?
    (1) A solvent is part of a mixture, and a solute is part of a solution.
    (2) A solvent is always a liquid, and a solute is always a solid.
    (3) A solvent is always a gas, and a solute is always a liquid.
    (4) A solvent is present in a greater amount in a solution, and a solute in a lesser amount.
    (5) A solvent can be separated out by chemical means, and a solute can be separated out by physical means.

12 How are soil, cement, and air alike?
    (1) They are all in the same state of matter.
    (2) They are all solutions.
    (3) They are all mixtures.
    (4) They are all elements.
    (5) They are all compounds.

13 Refer to the line graph on page 159. Approximately how much sugar will dissolve in 1 quart of water at 32°F?
    (1) 1 ounce
    (2) 2 ounces
    (3) 4 ounces
    (4) 6 ounces
    (5) 7 ounces

Connect with the Article

Write your answer to each question.

14 Suppose you mixed a fruit drink from grape-flavored powder, sugar, and water. Identify the solvent and the solutes, and describe what happens when you combine them.

    _____

    _____

    _____

15 Describe an experience you or someone you know has had with a mixture or solution.

    _____

    _____

    _____

Combustion

Setting the Stage

For two of our most basic needs—food and shelter—people need heat. We use heat to cook our food and warm our homes. To produce heat, we burn fuels like gas and oil. The burning of fuel is a chemical reaction called combustion.

PREVIEW THE ARTICLE

The headings in an article give you an overview of what the article is about. They provide an outline of its contents. Look at the headings on pages 163–165. What are some things you can expect to learn about combustion?

_____

_____

_____

RELATE TO THE TOPIC

This article is about combustion. It describes how combustion produces heat in a small space heater. It explains how burning fuel produces other products, some of which are harmful pollutants. Describe an experience that you have had with fire.

_____

_____

_____

VOCABULARY

combustion   hydrocarbons

activation energy   kindling temperature

The By-Products of Burning

Humans first used fire in prehistoric times. Ever since then, people have been burning fuels to produce heat. At first, people burned wood for warmth and then for cooking. During the 1700s, the first engines were invented. In an engine, a fuel is burned and heat energy is produced. This energy is then captured and used to produce motion. Today, fuels are used to provide heat and to power engines.

Combustion Reactions

Burning is a chemical change that chemists call **combustion.** In combustion, oxygen reacts with a fuel. Heat and light energy are released. An example of combustion is the burning of a fuel such as kerosene, oil, or gas. These fuels are **hydrocarbons,** or compounds made only of hydrogen and carbon. When they burn, the hydrogen and carbon combine with oxygen from the air. Carbon dioxide and water vapor are produced.

Combustion reactions need a little energy to get them started. This energy is called **activation energy.** To start a twig burning, you must light a match to it. Once combustion starts, no additional energy is needed.

Each substance has its own **kindling temperature.** That's the temperature to which the substance must be heated before it will burn. The form of a substance affects its kindling temperature. For example, sawdust catches fire faster than a log. Vaporized gasoline ignites more easily than liquid gasoline.

The burning of gasoline in this motorcycle engine is an example of combustion.

How a Combustion Heater Works

A small kerosene or natural gas heater can be used to warm one or two rooms. A kerosene heater has a small built-in fuel tank. Some natural gas heaters have fuel tanks, too. Other gas heaters are connected to the gas lines of the house. The fuel is piped to the burners. Most heaters use an electric spark to start the combustion reaction. Cool air from the room enters at the base of the heater. The heat from combustion warms the air. Warmed air flows into the room. With a gas heater, the waste products of combustion leave the house through a vent. With a kerosene heater, all of the hot air flows into the room.

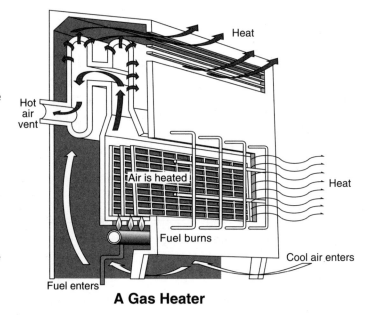

A Gas Heater

Kerosene heaters have many advantages. A kerosene heater is not very expensive. It does not have to be attached to a chimney, so it can be moved from room to room. These heaters warm up quickly and provide heat for up to thirty hours without refueling.

Kerosene heaters also have some disadvantages. If not used properly, they can be unsafe. If the heater is close to drapes, they may catch fire. The outside of the heater is very hot and can cause burns. The heater may tip over, causing injury or a fire. These are all obvious hazards. Less obvious is the hazard caused by the release of pollutants into the air.

Making Predictions   Active readers think about what they read. They make predictions about what will come next. Sometimes the predictions are based only on what they have just read. Sometimes they look ahead for clues about what's coming. Reread the second and third paragraphs above. The second paragraph discusses the *advantages* of kerosene heaters. When you read that, you can predict that the next paragraph will discuss the *disadvantages* of kerosene heaters. Based on what you have read about the advantages and disadvantages of kerosene heaters, which of the following topics is more likely to come next? Circle the letter of your prediction.

a.   The low cost of running combustion heaters.

b.   The hazards of pollutants produced by combustion heaters.

Check your answer on page 244.

Indoor Air Pollution

Complete combustion produces carbon dioxide and water vapor. Combustion is complete only if the fuel is pure and there is plenty of oxygen. Often the fuel is not pure. Also, there may be too little oxygen. Then combustion is incomplete. When combustion is incomplete, other substances are released along with carbon dioxide and water vapor. These substances pollute the air.

If the room is airtight, a high level of pollutants can develop in the air. The air may contain carbon monoxide, nitric oxide, nitrogen dioxide, or sulfur dioxide. These substances can harm the eyes, throat, and lungs. Carbon monoxide is especially dangerous. You can't smell it or see it. Yet high levels of carbon monoxide can cause death.

Understanding the Implied Main Idea   Sometimes a writer does not actually state the main idea of a paragraph in a topic sentence. You have to "read between the lines" and add up the details to figure out the main idea. The first paragraph above has no topic sentence. Instead, it describes complete combustion and incomplete combustion. The main idea is that complete combustion produces harmless products, and incomplete combustion produces pollutants. Reread the second paragraph on this page. Circle the letter of its implied main idea.

    a.   Indoor air pollutants can be harmful to health and can even cause death.

    b.   Indoor air pollutants can collect even when a room is not airtight.

Both natural gas and kerosene heaters can give off pollutants. Natural gas burns more cleanly than kerosene. But makers of kerosene heaters claim that these heaters can burn cleanly, too. If high-quality kerosene is used, the combustion reaction is 99.5 percent complete. This means that only 0.5 percent of the reaction is incomplete.

Kerosene and natural gas heaters are not the only producers of indoor air pollution. Wood stoves, fireplaces, gas stoves, and tobacco smoke are other sources. Leaking chimneys and furnaces also produce indoor air pollution.

Safety Precautions

People using kerosene heaters or other types of combustion devices indoors should always follow the manufacturer's instructions. The heater should always be in a safe place. It should be placed away from materials that might burn and away from places where children play.

To reduce indoor pollution, use only high-quality kerosene in a kerosene heater. Keep the doors to other rooms open for ventilation. Remember that combustion uses oxygen from the air. It is a good idea to open a window slightly to let more oxygen in and allow pollutants to escape.

Check your answer on page 244.

Thinking About the Article

Practice Vocabulary

The terms below are in the passage in bold type. Study the way each term is used. Then complete each sentence by writing the correct term in the blank.

combustion	kindling temperature
activation energy	hydrocarbon

1 Chemists call burning _____.

2 A(n) _____ is a compound, such as kerosene or natural gas, made only of hydrogen and carbon.

3 The energy required to start a combustion reaction is called

_____.

4 Before it will burn, a substance must be heated to its

_____.

Understand the Article

Write or circle the answer to each question.

5 Which gas from the air is needed for combustion?

_____

6 What happens during a combustion reaction?
   a. Oxygen reacts with a fuel, producing heat, light, carbon dioxide, and water vapor.
   b. Carbon dioxide, water vapor, and carbon monoxide combine to form heat, oxygen, and carbon by-products.

7 These pollutants can be produced when combustion is incomplete:
   a. oxygen   d. kerosene
   b. sulfur dioxide   e. nitrogen dioxide
   c. carbon monoxide f. nitric oxide

8 Why is it important to provide oxygen to a kerosene or gas heater?
   a. Without enough oxygen, combustion is incomplete, producing pollutants.
   b. Without enough oxygen, the heater costs more to run.

Check your answers on page 244.

Apply Your Skills

Circle the number of the best answer for each question.

9 On the basis of the information in the article, which of the following can you predict about small kerosene and gas heaters?
   (1) Wood-burning stoves produce more air pollution than do small heaters.
   (2) Sales of small heaters have increased since the fuel shortages of the 1970s.
   (3) High-quality kerosene produces more pollutants than low-quality kerosene.
   (4) More fires are caused by small heaters than by built-in heating systems.
   (5) A shortage of kerosene and natural gas makes small heaters too expensive.

10 Which of the following would you predict might happen if kerosene were used in a small heater in an airtight room?
   (1) Only carbon dioxide and water vapor would be produced, making the room warm and damp.
   (2) The pollutants released by incomplete combustion would eventually overcome the people in the room.
   (3) Oxygen from outdoors would be used to keep the combustion reaction going to heat the room.
   (4) The combustion reaction would speed up, eventually causing the heater to explode.
   (5) The heater would become so hot that the drapes would ignite, causing a fire in the home.

11 What is the implied main idea of the first paragraph on page 163?
   (1) The first fuel was wood, used to provide heat.
   (2) Over time, people have burned fuels for many purposes.
   (3) Engines change heat energy into the energy of motion.
   (4) Fire was discovered in prehistoric times.
   (5) Air pollution is caused by burning fuels.

Connect with the Article

Write your answer to each question.

12 How can the hazards of using a kerosene or gas heater be reduced?

_____

13 Describe something you have that uses combustion. What type of fuel is used? Do you think it is producing any air pollutants? Explain.

_____

_____

23 Nuclear Fission

Setting the Stage

Nuclear power usually doesn't get much attention unless something goes wrong. Then, a power plant accident leads the news. When accidents occurred in nuclear power plants at Three Mile Island and Chernobyl, people all over the world worried about explosions and radioactive fallout. Still, nuclear power plants usually operate safely and have few emergencies.

PREVIEW THE ARTICLE

The illustrations in an article can give you an overview of what the article is about. Look at the illustrations on pages 169–171. Read the captions and titles. What are some things you can expect to learn about nuclear power?

_____

_____

_____

RELATE TO THE TOPIC

This article is about using nuclear fission, a type of reaction, to heat water to produce electricity. It explains how nuclear power plants work. Describe something you have seen or read about nuclear fission or nuclear power.

_____

_____

_____

_____

VOCABULARY

nuclear energy	nuclear reactions	radioactive decay
fission	chain reaction	

Check your answers on page 245.

Using Nuclear Power

There's something eerie about a visit to a nuclear power plant. The many power lines let you know that huge amounts of electricity are being sent out. Yet, oddly enough, the power plant is quiet. You expect a power plant to give off smoke. But there aren't any smokestacks. What goes on inside this silent giant?

A Modern Energy Source

In the early 1900s, scientists predicted that atoms could produce huge amounts of energy. But this wasn't proved until 1939. In that year, a group of scientists split an atom for the first time. Atoms must be split to produce nuclear energy. Since then, people have been finding different uses for nuclear energy.

Nuclear energy comes from inside the atom. The reactions that release this energy are more powerful than ordinary chemical reactions. As a result, nuclear power plants produce a lot of electricity from very little fuel. Some countries, such as France, depend on nuclear power for more than three-quarters of their electricity. In the United States, about one-fifth of the electricity comes from nuclear power plants.

A nuclear power plant

Nuclear Reactions

Nuclear reactions are changes in the **nucleus,** or center, of an atom. The nucleus of an atom contains two kinds of particles. **Protons** are particles with a positive electrical charge. All atoms of a substance have the same number of protons. **Neutrons** are particles that have no charge. The number of neutrons in a nucleus can vary.

The atoms of many elements have about the same number of protons and neutrons. The atoms of some elements have an unbalanced number of these particles. This causes the nucleus to be unstable. An unstable nucleus gives off particles until it becomes stable. This change is called **radioactive decay.** When an atom of an element decays, it becomes another element. For example, when uranium decays it becomes lead. This is a natural nuclear reaction. Atoms that decay are **radioactive.** They give off particles and energy in the form of radiation.

Using a Glossary or Dictionary   The glossary at the end of this book is a good source of information. If you don't understand a word, look it up in the glossary. If the word is not in the glossary, look it up in a dictionary. As an example, look up the word *radioactive* in the glossary. It means "the state of atoms in the process of decay, in which the nuclei are giving off particles and energy in the form of radiation." Look up *neutron* in the glossary. What does the word *neutron* mean? Circle the letter of the correct answer.

    a.   a change in the nucleus, or center, of an atom

    b.   a particle that has no charge, found in the nucleus of an atom

Some radioactive atoms can be split. The splitting of an atom's nucleus is called **fission.** This reaction releases both energy and radiation. It also gives off more neutrons. Fission does not occur in nature. It occurs when neutrons are shot at an unstable nucleus. The nucleus splits, and two new nuclei are formed.

The neutrons released during one fission reaction strike other atoms, producing more fission reactions. This is called a chain reaction. A **chain reaction** is one that keeps itself going. Toppling a row of dominoes by knocking over the first one is similar to a chain reaction.

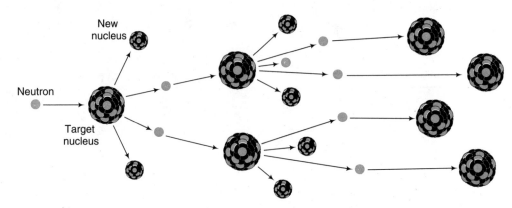

A Fission Chain Reaction

Check your answer on page 245.

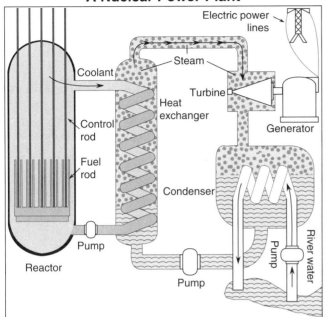

A Nuclear Power Plant

Electric power lines

Steam

Coolant

Turbine

Heat exchanger

Generator

Control rod

Fuel rod

Condenser

Pump

Reactor

Pump

Pump

River water

How a Nuclear Power Plant Works

The fission reactions at a nuclear power plant occur in a structure called a **reactor.** The core of the reactor holds the fuel rods and control rods. The fuel rods contain the element plutonium. The control rods keep the chain reaction going at a steady rate. These rods are made of a substance that absorbs neutrons. If the reaction is too slow, the control rods are pulled out a bit. This makes more neutrons available to split more atoms. The control rods are pushed back in if the reaction speeds up too much.

The fission reaction gives off heat. A coolant, usually water, absorbs this heat. The coolant carries the heat away from the core into a heat exchanger. There the heat is used to boil water. The resulting steam turns a turbine, which operates a generator that produces electricity.

Understanding Sequence   The order in which things happen is very important. If the steps in a process, such as generating electricity, are out of sequence, the process doesn't work. Review the diagram and the two paragraphs above. The first step in making electricity using nuclear power is to start a fission chain reaction that produces heat. The second is that the coolant absorbs this heat. Put the remaining steps of the process in the correct sequence by placing the numbers 3 through 5 in the spaces provided. The first and second steps have been done for you.

___1___   Fission reaction produces heat.   _____ Steam turns a turbine, making electricity.

___2___   Coolant absorbs heat.   _____ Coolant carries heat into a heat exchanger.

_____ Heat from the coolant boils water, producing steam.

The reactor is housed in a containment building, which has thick concrete walls that can absorb radiation. If the core gets too hot, safety systems provide emergency cooling. The reaction can be shut down quickly by pushing the control rods all the way into the core.

Accidents at nuclear power plants can be deadly. In 1979, a reactor at Three Mile Island in Pennsylvania overheated. Luckily, only a small amount of radioactive material escaped and no one died. In 1986, a reactor at Chernobyl in Ukraine exploded and burned. There was no containment building, so radioactive material spread. More than thirty people were killed and thousands were exposed to radioactivity, which spread all over the world. These accidents highlighted the need for better design and construction of nuclear power plants. In addition, it became clear that plant operators must be trained to handle emergencies as well as routine tasks.

Check your answers on page 245.

Thinking About the Article

Practice Vocabulary

The terms below are in the passage in bold type. Study the way each term is used. Then complete each sentence by writing the correct term in the blank.

nuclear energy   **nuclear reaction**   **radioactive decay**

fission   **chain reaction**

1. _____ occurs naturally in the nucleus of unstable atoms.

2. In nuclear _____, a type of reaction, an atom's nucleus is split, giving off energy and radiation.

3. _____ is energy released from inside an atom.

4. A change in the nucleus of an atom is a _____.

5. In a _____, the neutrons produced by one fission reaction strike other atoms, producing more fission reactions, and so on.

Understand the Article

Write or circle the answer to each question.

6. What two types of particles does the nucleus of an atom contain?

   _____

   _____

7. Which of the following is a nuclear reaction that occurs in nature?
   a. uranium, in the process of decay, becomes lead
   b. a chain reaction of plutonium produces huge amounts of energy in a short time

8. In a nuclear power plant, the control rods
   a. control the amount of coolant flowing into the heat exchanger.
   b. keep the chain reaction going at a steady, safe speed.

9. The main purpose of the coolant in a nuclear power plant is to
   a. absorb and transfer heat.
   b. turn turbines that produce electricity.

Check your answers on page 245.

Apply Your Skills

Circle the number of the best answer for each question.

10 Use the glossary to help you find the meaning of the word *fission*.
    (1) a negatively charged particle orbiting the nucleus of an atom
    (2) a neutral particle in the nucleus of an atom
    (3) the splitting of an atom's nucleus
    (4) the combining of two atomic nuclei into one
    (5) the weight of the protons and neutrons in the nucleus of an atom

11 According to the diagram on page 171, after the coolant reaches the heat exchanger, it
    (1) cools the steam, condensing it to water.
    (2) cools the fuel rods.
    (3) turns the turbine.
    (4) boils water, producing steam.
    (5) cleans the control rods.

12 Which is the first step of a chain reaction?
    (1) A neutron splits a target nucleus.
    (2) A proton is emitted by a nucleus.
    (3) Many nuclei split at the same time.
    (4) Uranium decays, turning to lead.
    (5) An unstable nucleus decays.

Connect with the Article

Write your answer to each question.

13 Describe one safety feature in the design of a nuclear power plant.

_____

_____

_____

14 Is any of the electricity in your area produced by a nuclear power plant? If so, what do you and the people in your area think about having a nuclear power plant close by? If not, what would you think about having a nuclear power plant built in your area?

_____

_____

Science at Work

Service: Beautician/Cosmetologist

Some Careers in Service

Barber
cuts and styles men's and children's hair

Cosmetology Instructor
trains students in the use of beauty aids and products

Make-up Consultant
works with customers to select colors and facial care products

Manicurist
treats customers' cuticles and nails by shaping, polishing, and applying decorations

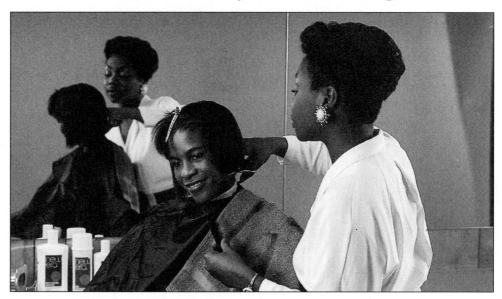

Beauticians work with clients' hair, nails, and skin.

Do you like to help people look their best? Do you have a good sense of style? If so, you may be interested in becoming a beautician or cosmetologist.

Helping people look their best involves careful analysis of their individual physical traits. It also involves a strong working knowledge of chemicals and how to use them safely and effectively.

Beauticians shampoo, cut, style, and treat hair. This often involves the use of chemicals to curl, straighten, or color hair. If not used properly, these chemical products may prove harmful. Treating clients' skin with chemical products must also be done with great care. Leaving a product on too long or using it in sensitive areas may result in burns or infection.

Beauticians and cosmetologists need excellent oral communication skills and pleasant personalities. Because they often are on their feet for long periods of time, beauticians should be in good physical health.

Look at the chart showing some of the careers in service.

- Do any of the careers interest you? If so, which ones?

- What information would you need to find out more about those careers? On a separate piece of paper, write some questions that you would like answered. You can find out more information about those careers in the *Occupational Outlook Handbook* at your local library.

Use the following information to answer the questions below.

When Ramon's customers ask about how to care for their hair, he tells them about pH values. He explains the pH scale ranges from 0–14. Products with a pH value under 7 are called acids. Products on the acidic side of the scale make hair look shinier but not as thick. Distilled water has a value of 7 and is neutral. Those products with a pH value above 7 are called bases or alkaline products. They make hair thicker, but they are also harder on hair because they dry it out and make it swell.

Ramon's Shampoo Choices

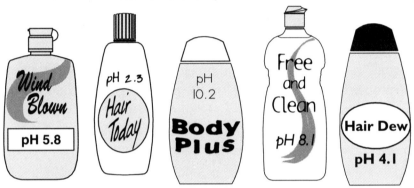

① Ramon's customer Renee wants her hair to look thicker. The shampoo that will make her hair look the thickest is
   (1) Wind Blown.
   (2) Hair Today.
   (3) Body Plus.
   (4) Free and Clean.
   (5) Hair Dew.

② Which shampoo is closest to neutral in pH value?
   (1) Wind Blown
   (2) Hair Today
   (3) Body Plus
   (4) Free and Clean
   (5) Hair Dew

③ A sequence is an ordered list. Which sequence below ranks the shampoos from most acidic to most alkaline?
   (1) Wind Blown; Hair Today; Body Plus; Free and Clean; Hair Dew
   (2) Hair Dew; Free and Clean; Body Plus; Hair Today; Wind Blown
   (3) Hair Today; Hair Dew; Free and Clean; Wind Blown; Body Plus
   (4) Body Plus; Free and Clean; Wind Blown; Hair Today; Hair Dew
   (5) Hair Today; Hair Dew; Wind Blown; Free and Clean; Body Plus

Mixtures

The "lead" in your pencil is not actually made of the metal lead. It is made mostly of a form of carbon called graphite. Graphite is very soft. As a result, anything you write with graphite will easily smudge. To solve this problem, graphite is mixed with something else.

A **mixture** is a combination of two or more substances, in which the proportions may vary. A mixture has the properties of the substances in the mixture. These properties vary depending on the make-up of the mixture. For example, salt is salty and water is not. A mixture of salt and water is salty but not as salty as salt alone. If you keep adding water to the mixture, the taste gets less salty. The property of saltiness is still there, but the amount of saltiness varies.

In a pencil, the "lead" is a mixture of graphite and clay. Graphite is very soft, but clay is hard. The mixture of the two is harder than graphite but softer than clay. You may have noticed a number stamped on a pencil. The number tells how hard the pencil is. Number 2 pencils are fairly soft and are the most common. These pencils make dark lines, but the lines can smudge. As the amount of clay in the mixture increases, the hardness increases. A number 9 pencil is very hard. It makes fine lines that do not smudge.

Fill in the blank with the word or words that best complete each statement.

❶ A(n) _____ is a combination of two or more substances that are combined in varying proportions.

❷ The lead in a pencil is a mixture of _____ and

_____ .

Circle the number of the best answer.

❸ As the amount of clay in a pencil increases,
  (1) the number of the pencil increases.
  (2) the lines it makes become finer.
  (3) the lines it makes smudge less.
  (4) the pencil lead becomes harder.
  (5) all of the above

Energy and Chemical Reactions

In a **chemical reaction**, one substance or set of substances is changed into another substance or set of substances. In this process, energy may be given off or taken in. An **exothermic reaction** gives off energy. Burning, or **combustion**, is an example of an exothermic reaction. When wood is burned, energy is given off in the form of light and heat.

Photosynthesis is a chemical reaction that takes place in plants. In this reaction, plants use the energy in sunlight to turn carbon dioxide and water into glucose, a type of sugar, and oxygen. This is an example of an **endothermic reaction**, or one that takes in energy.

You may have used an instant hot pack for first aid. These plastic pouches contain chemicals. When you break the seal inside the pouch, the chemicals come together and react. The reaction is exothermic and gives off heat. Once the reaction is finished, no additional heat is given off.

There are also instant cold packs used for first aid. When the chemicals in these pouches react, they do not give off heat. Instead, they take in heat. The reaction is endothermic. Because the reaction absorbs heat, the pouch feels cold when placed against the skin.

Fill in the blank with the word or words that best complete each statement.

4 A(n) _____ gives off energy.

5 A(n) _____ takes in energy.

6 In a(n) _____ , substances are changed into other substances.

7 One type of exothermic reaction that gives off heat and light energy is

_____ , or burning.

Circle the number of the best answer.

8 Which of the following is an example of an endothermic reaction?
   (1) burning a candle
   (2) combustion of wood
   (3) exploding dynamite
   (4) photosynthesis in a plant
   (5) production of light by a firefly

Putting Out Fires

Fire, or **combustion,** is a useful chemical reaction. However, sometimes a fire gets out of control and must be put out. There are several ways to do this. All methods of putting out a fire work by removing something the reaction needs in order to continue.

One way of putting out a fire is to take away one of the substances that is used in the reaction. The simplest way to do this is to remove the **fuel,** or the material that is burning. You do this when you turn off the gas on the stove.

In a raging fire, it is hard to remove the fuel. It is easier to remove the oxygen that is needed to keep the reaction going. A small fire can be smothered. Baking soda can be poured on a small grease fire on a stovetop. The layer of baking soda keeps oxygen away from the grease, which is the fuel. Smothering a campfire with dirt works the same way.

Another way to put out a fire is to take away some of its heat. Materials do not burn until they are heated to the **kindling temperature.** Once a fire is burning, it continues to heat its fuel to the kindling temperature. If you can take enough heat away from the fuel, it will be below the kindling temperature and will not burn. This is how water puts out a fire.

A carbon-dioxide fire extinguisher uses two methods at once. The carbon dioxide is heavier than oxygen. It makes a layer below the oxygen but above the fuel, smothering the fire. As the carbon dioxide comes out of the extinguisher, it expands rapidly. This process absorbs heat. So the carbon dioxide also cools the burning material.

Circle the number of the best answer.

9 If a fire is to continue burning, it must have enough
(1) carbon dioxide.
(2) oxygen and carbon dioxide.
(3) fuel and heat.
(4) oxygen and heat.
(5) oxygen, fuel, and heat.

10 A heavy blanket thrown on a small fire puts out the fire by
(1) adding carbon dioxide.
(2) removing oxygen.
(3) removing fuel.
(4) removing heat.
(5) removing carbon dioxide.

Check your answers on page 246.

Fusion Reactions

Nuclear reactions are changes in the nucleus, or center, of an atom. One kind of nuclear reaction that is being studied by many scientists is fusion. **Nuclear fusion** is the reaction in which two nuclei combine. In the process, the nucleus of a larger atom is formed.

In nuclear fusion, hydrogen nuclei fuse, or join, and form a helium nucleus. A huge amount of energy is released. This reaction takes place only under conditions of great pressure and high temperature. These conditions are found on the sun. Fusion reactions are the source of the energy that the sun gives off.

Hydrogen nucleus

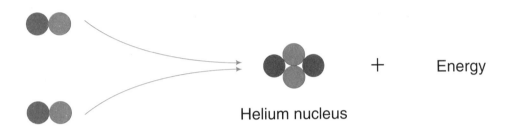

Helium nucleus

Hydrogen nucleus

Fusion reactions do not take place naturally on Earth. There is no place on the planet as hot as the sun. Scientists are looking for ways to make fusion occur at lower temperatures. If scientists could make such "cold fusion" reactions work, they would have a powerful energy source.

Fill in the blank with the word or words that best complete each statement.

⑪ A nuclear reaction in which two nuclei combine is called

_____ .

⑫ Fusion reactions take place naturally on the _____ .

⑬ In a nuclear fusion reaction, hydrogen nuclei combine to form the

nucleus of a(n) _____ atom.

Science Extension

Check your refrigerator and make a list of the mixtures and solutions you find there. Remember, mixtures and solutions can be solid, liquid, or gas, or a combination of these.

Science Connection: Chemistry and World History

Toxins in the Environment

Toxins are harmful chemicals or materials. Some are man-made, others are found in nature. Toxins are present in the air, land, and water. Toxins can also be found in our food and homes. They can be mildly harmful or extremely poisonous to living things.

Some toxins have come from natural events like erupting volcanoes. Others have developed from the estimated 75,000 man-made chemicals that have been created over the past 50 years. Whatever the source, these toxins have polluted Earth's oceans, lakes, rivers, streams, and ponds.

Toxins can be introduced into the food we eat through the water supply. Simple plant and animal life in the water absorb the toxins. As larger animals eat these simple organisms, the toxins are passed along. The toxins begin to build up in the body fat of these larger animals. When we eat these animals, the toxins can enter our bodies. Some toxins can cause cancer, respiratory illnesses, and damage to the nervous and reproductive systems.

Among the most common toxins are pesticides. Pesticides are toxins used to keep away or kill insects and other pests. Pesticides are sprayed on many of the fruits and vegetables we eat. Pesticides are also used in our homes to get rid of unwanted insects. Eventually these pesticides make their way into the food we eat and the air we breathe. Over the past 25 years, use of some pesticides like DDT has been made illegal in some nations.

World History: Toxins—A Global Concern

Many nations control the use of toxic chemicals by making laws. As we gather increasing evidence that Earth's environmental state is becoming more fragile, nations have begun working together to control the use of dangerous chemicals.

One of the first international agreements related to the use of toxic chemicals was made in 1979. Thirty-four European and North American countries agreed to reduce the amount of toxins released into the air. These toxins are called **emissions.** The agreement affected how factories produced and disposed of their waste. It also affected the kind of gasoline we could use in our cars.

In June 1998, representatives from 100 nations came together for the first of five meetings. The meetings are being held to discuss the worldwide ban of the 12 most dangerous toxins. These chemicals, called "The Dirty Dozen," include DDT and PCBs.

Use the material on the previous page and the timeline below to answer the questions that follow.

Toxin Timeline

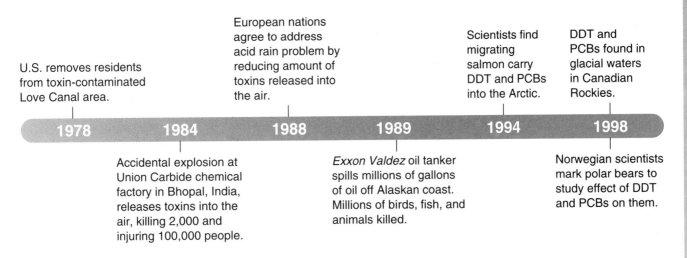

1. Man-made toxins are introduced into the food supply through
   (1) the action of foreign countries.
   (2) larger animals eating smaller animals and plants.
   (3) international agreements.
   (4) erupting volcanoes.
   (5) unwanted insects.

2. Which of the following statements about toxins is not true?
   (1) All toxins in the environment are man-made.
   (2) Humans and plants are responsible for spreading toxins.
   (3) Many governments control the use of toxins.
   (4) Simple organisms transfer toxins to larger animals.
   (5) Toxins are a threat to the environment.

3. According to the timeline above, which country experienced the toxic event that resulted in the most human deaths?
   (1) Norway
   (2) United States
   (3) India
   (4) Canada
   (5) Kenya

4. On a separate sheet of paper, make two lists. Title one list, *Toxin-Related Disasters.* Title the other, *Progress Against Toxins.* Use the timeline to write the lists.

U N I T

4 Physics

Beams of colored light play across the walls of a dance hall while the music pounds. Together, light and sound are energizing the crowd. Both are forms of energy, which is part of physics. **Physics** is the study of the basic things that make up the universe, including energy and forces.

Learning about energy can help you understand why forms of energy, such as light, sound, and electricity, behave as they do. It can help you better understand lasers and computers. Forces, including gravity and electrical forces, make machines work. Understanding forces can help you move heavy objects and understand what happens when objects collide.

Knowing about physics can help you understand the world. It can help you take better care of yourself, your family, and your things.

◖ Machines make life easier by helping us get things done. How can learning about how machines work help you?

◖ We use many forms of energy every day. How can learning about forms of energy help you use them in everyday life?

SECTIONS

24 Machines

Setting the Stage

Walk into a bicycle store and you'll see an amazing assortment of bikes. There are bikes with training wheels, racing bikes, and mountain bikes. There are one-speed bikes and 21-speed bikes. But despite their differences, all bicycles contain the same simple machines.

PREVIEW THE ARTICLE

Before you read, scan the headings of the article. That will give you an overview of the contents. Read the headings on pages 185–187. What are some things you can expect to learn about machines?

_____

_____

_____

RELATE TO THE TOPIC

This article is about force and work, two important ideas in physics. It explains that machines are devices that help us do work. It describes some simple machines, as well as a compound machine—the bicycle. Think about the last time you or someone you know rode a bicycle. Describe the bicycle you used.

_____

_____

VOCABULARY

force   work   simple machine

mechanical advantage   compound machine

Check your answers on page 247.

How a Bicycle Works

In many large cities, businesses use messengers to carry documents across town. These messengers can be seen speeding past clogged traffic. Are they running? Are they driving? No, they're riding bicycles.

A bicycle is a good way to get around. You don't have to be very strong to go at a moderate speed. If you have a bicycle with 3, 10, or 21 speeds, it can help you ride easily up most hills. By riding a bicycle, you can get your exercise on the way to work.

A bicycle is a good means of transportation.

Force and Work

When you push down on the pedal of a bicycle, you are applying a force to it. A **force** is a push or a pull. There are many kinds of forces. The pull of one magnet on another is a force. The pull that Earth has on you and all other objects is the force of **gravity.** A force between surfaces that touch each other is known as **friction.** Friction between the brake pads and the wheel of a bicycle or automobile stops the wheel from turning.

Work is done when a force causes an object to move. Lifting a bag of groceries is work. Your upward force of lifting overcomes the downward force of gravity. The force you exert is called the **effort.** The force you overcome is the **resistance.**

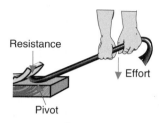

Lever

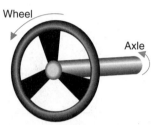

Wheel and Axle

Gears

Simple Machines

Sometimes your effort cannot overcome the resistance. Then you need the help of a machine. If you have ever used a screwdriver to pry the lid off a paint can, you have used a machine. A **simple machine** is a device used to do work. There are several kinds of simple machines. A bicycle has three of them: a lever, a wheel and axle, and gears.

A **lever** is a bar that turns on a pivot. A **pivot** is an object on which another object turns. When you open the paint can, you are using the screwdriver as a lever. The lever transfers the force from your hand to the lid. The lever also multiplies your effort. The greater force overcomes the friction holding the lid on the can.

The number of times a machine multiplies your effort is the **mechanical advantage** of the machine. You may have noticed that a longer screwdriver is a better lever than a shorter screwdriver. That is because a longer lever gives a greater mechanical advantage.

A **wheel and axle** is another type of simple machine. It is made of two objects that turn in a circular motion on the same center. A wheel and axle doesn't always look like a wheel. A crank handle is a wheel and axle. Pencil sharpeners work this way. You turn the handle through a big circle. This turns the blades inside the sharpener in a small circle. As a result, some wood is cut away, and the pencil gets sharper.

Gears are wheels with teeth. Unlike a wheel and axle, gears do not turn on the same center. The gears are arranged so that the teeth meet, and each gear turns on its own center. If you turn one gear, you cause any gear it touches to turn.

Recognizing Cause and Effect   Situations in which one thing makes another thing happen are *cause-and-effect relationships*. For example, when you turn a crank handle, the blades inside a pencil sharpener turn. Your action is the **cause**. The turning of the blades is the **effect**. Watch for words and phrases that can signal cause-and-effect relationships, such as *because, for this reason,* and *as a result.*

What is the effect of turning one gear on the other gears that touch it?
a.   The other gears turn on their own centers.
b.   The other gears turn on the same center as the first gear.

A Compound Machine

Sometimes it takes more than one machine to get a job done. A **compound machine** is made up of several simple machines. A bicycle is a compound machine. The brake handles and gearshifts are levers. The wheels and pedals are wheel and axle machines. Bicycles also contain gears. The number of "speeds" a bicycle has equals the number of front gears multiplied by the number of back gears. If a bike has many "speeds," you can get the mechanical advantage you need for any situation.

Check your answer on page 247.

A bicycle is a compound machine.

A machine can multiply your effort. It can also multiply your speed. However, it cannot do both at once. Riding a bicycle on a level path, you use the higher "speeds." The highest "speed" on a bicycle combines the largest front gear—at the pedals, which are a crank—with the smallest gear on the rear wheel. You have to pedal hard but not very quickly. Yet the bicycle moves quickly. The only resistance is friction, which is a small force. The bicycle is not multiplying your force. Instead, it is using your force to multiply your speed.

You use the lower "speeds" to climb hills. In the lowest "speed," you combine the smallest front gear at the pedals with the largest rear gear. You don't need to pedal hard. However, you do have to pedal quickly, even though the bike moves slowly. The bicycle is multiplying your effort to move you against a large force—gravity.

Drawing Conclusions **Conclusions** are ideas that are based on facts. They follow logically from the facts. The previous paragraph describes pedaling a bicycle on a hill at the lowest gear speed. The low gear speed multiplies your effort. From the facts in the paragraph you can conclude that pedaling uphill is easier on a 21-speed bike than on a one-speed bike, because the 21-speed bike multiplies your effort much more.

From the information in the first two paragraphs on this page, you can conclude that

a. gravity exerts a larger force when you ride up a hill than friction does on level ground.

b. higher gear speeds result in more friction on a level path than lower gear speeds do.

Check your answer on page 247.

Thinking About the Article

Practice Vocabulary

The terms below are in the passage in bold type. Study the way each term is used. Then complete each sentence by writing the correct term in the blank.

force   **work**   **simple machine**

mechanical advantage   **compound machine**

1 A _____ is a push or a pull.

2 A basic device used to do work is called a _____.

3 A _____ like a bicycle contains several simple machines.

4 The number of times a machine multiplies your effort is the

_____ of the machine.

5 In physics, _____ is done when a force causes an object to move.

Understand the Article

Circle the letter of the answer to each question.

6 Gravity, magnetism, and friction are all examples of
a.   forces   b.   energy

7 When effort force is greater than resistance force, what happens?
a.   movement, or work   b.   nothing

8 Why does it take less effort to pry up the lid of a paint can with a longer screwdriver than with a shorter screwdriver?
a.   The longer screwdriver provides a greater mechanical advantage.
b.   The longer screwdriver fits better under the lid of the can.

Match each simple machine with its example.

_____ **9** lever   a.   a doorknob

_____ **10** wheel and axle   b.   a crowbar

_____ **11** gears   c.   the wheels that turn the blade of a can opener

Check your answers on page 247.

Apply Your Skills

Circle the number of the best answer for each question.

12. The effect of increasing the mechanical advantage of a machine is to
    (1) make the machine more difficult to use.
    (2) make work easier.
    (3) make work harder.
    (4) increase the effort required to use the machine.
    (5) decrease the force of friction.

13. When gears turn, the teeth rub on each other. This adds extra resistance, which is because of the force of
    (1) friction.
    (2) gravity.
    (3) magnetism.
    (4) electricity.
    (5) advantage.

14. If the resistance force is larger than the effort force, you can conclude that
    (1) the effort force will overcome the resistance force.
    (2) the effort force will stop.
    (3) the effort force will continue.
    (4) the resistance force will decrease.
    (5) no work will be done.

Connect with the Article

Write your answer to each question.

15. When you ride a bicycle up a hill, you can stand up as you pedal. How would this help you get up a hill?

____

____

____

16. Describe an experience you or someone you know has had riding or repairing a bicycle. Discuss simple machines, effort, resistance, or work in your description.

____

____

____

Check your answers on page 247.

Momentum

Setting the Stage

At a baseball game, the sound of the bat making contact with the ball is unmistakable. This collision sends the ball flying. If the ball takes the right path and has enough momentum, there could be a home run. Some players are willing to bend the rules to make this happen.

PREVIEW THE ARTICLE

One way to preview an article is to read the first sentence of each paragraph. That will give you an idea of what the article is about. Read the first sentence of each paragraph on pages 191–193. What are some things you can expect to learn about momentum?

_____

_____

_____

RELATE TO THE TOPIC

This article is about momentum. It explains how momentum is transferred from one object to another, for example, when a bat hits a ball. It describes how some baseball players change their bats to improve their hitting. What other sports do you or someone you know play that also involve the transfer of momentum?

_____

_____

VOCABULARY

energy   **collision**   **momentum**   **elastic**

Check your answers on page 247.

Breaking the Rules

A major league pitcher can throw a fastball at more than ninety miles per hour. At this speed, the ball reaches the batter in less than half a second. The batter has only a bit more than one tenth of a second to decide if the pitch looks good. The batter must swing quickly. The swing cannot be early or late by more than a few thousandths of a second. If it is, what might have been a home run becomes a foul ball.

Even good batters get hits only about three out of ten times at bat. So batters are always looking for ways to improve their averages. Practice helps. Physical conditioning is also important. However, some batters look for ways that are outside the rules. Most of these ways involve changing the bat.

Collisions

A moving baseball has **energy,** the ability of matter to do work. A catcher can feel this energy as the pitched baseball slams into the mitt. In a **collision,** a moving object strikes another object. The second object may or may not be moving. A catcher's mitt is not moving at the time the ball collides with it. A bat, on the other hand, is moving as the ball collides with it.

These players have just collided.

All moving objects have momentum. **Momentum** is a measure of the motion of an object, and it depends on the object's weight and speed. When two objects collide, momentum is transferred from one object to the other. Suppose you stand still with your arm extended to the side. If someone throws a baseball into your hand, this collision will push your hand back. The ball transfers some of its momentum to your hand. The effect of the ball on your hand would be greater if the ball had more momentum. This would be true if the ball were heavier or moving faster.

The transfer of momentum is more complicated when both objects are moving. When the moving bat hits the moving ball, they are traveling in opposite directions. The bat is not moving as fast as the ball, but it is much heavier. Therefore, the bat has more momentum than the ball. When the two collide, the ball moves off in the direction in which the bat was swinging.

The transfer of momentum also depends on how elastic the objects are. Something that is **elastic** can be stretched or compressed and will return to its original shape. In many collisions much of the momentum is lost. If the colliding objects are very elastic, only a little momentum is lost. If you drop a golf ball and a Super Ball, the Super Ball will bounce higher. This is because the Super Ball is more elastic than the golf ball and so it loses much less momentum.

Drawing Conclusions   A **conclusion** is an idea that follows logically from the information you have. Conclusions must be supported by facts. You have just read that a baseball moves in the direction in which the bat is swinging. You have also read that the bat has more momentum than the ball. From these facts, you can conclude that two colliding objects will move in the direction of the object that has more momentum.

Reread the third paragraph on this page. What can you conclude about the materials that Super Balls are made of?

a. Super Balls are made of materials that when compressed return to their original shape.

b. Super Balls are made of materials that when compressed do not return to their original shape.

Corking Bats

Some baseball players "cork" their bats. They cut off the top of the bat and hollow it out. They fill the space with cork, sawdust, or even Super Balls. Then they glue the top back on. Baseball players feel that this kind of change makes a bat springy. They think the bat becomes more elastic.

Corking bats is against the rules of professional baseball. If a player who hasn't been hitting well suddenly hits a string of home runs, the bat may be taken by the umpires. The bat is x-rayed or cut open. If the bat is corked, the player may be suspended from playing.

Check your answer on page 247.

When Howard Johnson's hitting suddenly improved, he was accused of corking his bat. The bat was x-rayed and found to be solid wood.

Players who cork their bats are cheating. Yet there is so much money in professional baseball that some players are willing to cheat in order to play better. After retiring, one player admitted to using a corked bat for years. He believed that it enabled him to hit a lot of home runs. The player who used Super Balls got caught when his bat cracked. The balls bounced out right in front of the umpire!

What Does Corking a Bat Do?

Scientists have analyzed what happens when a bat is corked. They have found that the bat gets lighter. A batter can swing a lighter bat more quickly. In the opinion of some scientists, this is the reason that the corked bat is better. If the batter can swing more quickly, the swing can be started a bit later. This gives the batter a little more time to decide whether or not to swing at the ball.

Distinguishing Fact from Opinion **Facts** can be proven true. **Opinions**, on the other hand, are what someone believes, thinks, or feels. They may or may not be true. When reading about science topics, it is important to distinguish fact from opinion. Reread the previous paragraph. One fact in the paragraph is that a corked bat is lighter than a solid wood bat. One opinion is that a corked bat results in more home runs because a lighter bat requires less time to swing, giving the player extra time to decide whether to swing.

Reread the first paragraph on this page. Write fact or opinion next to each statement.

1 The player who used Super Balls got caught when his bat cracked. _____

2 Using a corked bat is the best way to hit more home runs. _____

There may be one more advantage to the corked bat. This one is in the player's mind. If the batter thinks that the bat gives him an advantage, it may improve the batter's confidence. The batter steps up to the plate believing that he is about to hit a home run.

Thinking About the Article

Practice Vocabulary

The terms below are in the passage in bold type. Study the way each term is used. Then complete each sentence by writing the correct term in the blank.

energy   **collision**   **momentum**   **elastic**

1. In a(n) _____, a moving object strikes another object.

2. An object's _____ depends on its weight and speed.

3. An object that is _____ returns to its original shape after being stretched or compressed.

4. _____ is the ability of matter to do work.

Understand the Article

Circle the letter of the best answer.

5. Why does a moving baseball bat have more momentum than the ball?
   a. The bat is much heavier than the ball.
   b. The bat is moving much faster than the ball.

6. How can you increase an object's momentum? Circle the letters of all correct answers.
   a. increase its weight
   b. make it more elastic
   c. increase its speed
   d. decrease its speed

7. Why do some baseball players cork their bats?
   a. They think it makes the bat more elastic, giving a hit ball more momentum.
   b. They think solid wood bats are too heavy to swing properly.

8. Which of the following items is more elastic?
   a. a golf ball
   b. a Super Ball

9. When a moving object collides with a standing one, what decides if the standing object will be moved? Circle the letter of all correct answers.
   a. the speed of the moving object
   b. the weight of the moving object
   c. the weight of the standing object

Check your answers on page 247.

Apply Your Skills

Circle the number of the best answer for each question.

10 From the information about collisions in the article, you can conclude that
   (1) collisions occur only when two objects are moving.
   (2) collisions occur only when one object is moving.
   (3) all momentum is lost in collisions.
   (4) the momentum of a moving object increases after a collision.
   (5) a standing object will move if enough momentum is transferred.

11 Which of the following statements describes a <u>fact</u>?
   (1) A corked bat helps batters hit the ball better.
   (2) A corked bat can make a poor hitter into a good hitter.
   (3) A corked bat is lighter than a solid bat.
   (4) A corked bat will help a player hit more home runs.
   (5) A corked bat is better than a solid bat.

12 From the appearance of a car after a collision, you can conclude that cars
   (1) have little momentum.
   (2) have more momentum than trucks.
   (3) usually collide with moving objects.
   (4) are not very elastic.
   (5) return to their original shapes.

Connect with the Article

Write your answer to each question.

13 Your friend is in a compact car and you are in a sport utility vehicle. Both vehicles are moving at the same speed along a highway. Which has more momentum? Explain your answer.

_____

_____

14 Think about a time when you collided with something while in a car, walking, or playing a sport. Describe the collision and the transfer of momentum.

_____

_____

_____

SECTION 26 Electricity

Setting the Stage

The contest between man and machine dates back to John Henry, who according to legend died trying to outperform a steam engine. The modern version of that contest took place between a chess master and a masterpiece of electronics—a computer named Deep Blue.

PREVIEW THE ARTICLE

One way to preview an article is to read the headings. That will give you an idea of what the article is about. Read the headings on pages 197–199. What are some things you can expect to learn about electricity?

_____

_____

_____

RELATE TO THE TOPIC

This article is about electronic devices—machines that use electricity to perform various tasks. It describes some of these devices. It also tells the story of a contest between the human world chess champion and an electronic computer. Think about a time you or someone you know played a game against a computer. Describe the game and what happened.

_____

_____

_____

VOCABULARY

electronics   transistor   diode

integrated circuits   microprocessors

Check your answers on page 248.

Computers and Electronics

It was a dramatic battle between man and machine—the world's greatest chess player against a computer. The battleground was a chessboard. Garry Kasparov represented humankind. IBM's Deep Blue supercomputer was the challenger. Chess is a game with clear and strict rules, yet it is complex enough to challenge some of the finest human minds. Until Deep Blue, no machine had been able to beat a reigning chess champion.

In 1996 Deep Blue and Kasparov met for their first six-game match. Much to his surprise, Kasparov lost the first game. But he was able to adjust his playing style to take advantage of Deep Blue's weaknesses. Kasparov went on to win the match. For the time being, at least, the human race had prevailed.

How Deep Blue Plays Chess

Deep Blue's approach to chess is very different from that of a human being. A chess master like Kasparov plays by recognizing patterns, forming concepts, and creating plans based on past experience. In contrast, Deep Blue relies primarily on its ability to calculate fast. It can analyze the consequences of 200 million chess positions per second. This speed is made possible by advances in **electronics,** a branch of engineering. Electronics is concerned with controlling the motion of electrons in order to generate, transmit, receive, and store information. **Electrons** are tiny particles of matter with a negative electrical charge.

Garry Kasparov used his wits to defeat Deep Blue's calculating power in their first match.

A printed circuit board.

Electronic Components

When electrons flow, they create an electric current. This current can be controlled by devices called electronic components. There are many types of electronic components, and each affects electric current in different ways. For example, a **transistor** is a device that can be used to amplify, detect, or switch electric current on and off. A **diode** allows current to flow in one direction only.

When components are linked together to form a circuit, they can be designed to perform tasks. For example, the circuits in a remote control unit allow you to change channels and turn the TV on and off. Today **integrated circuits** are so tiny they fit on a small silicon chip. Each chip can contain several hundred thousand components. Many chips can be connected to form even more complex circuits. Electronic components, including integrated circuits, are attached to a **printed circuit board.** They are connected by a pattern of metal tracks along which electrons flow. Printed circuit boards are found in all types of machines, from digital watches to cars to computers like Deep Blue.

Making Inferences An **inference** is a fact or an idea that follows logically from what has been said. It is not actually stated by the author. Instead, the reader makes inferences based on what the author writes. Reread the previous paragraph. Based on the facts in that paragraph, you can infer that the components of an electronic circuit can be linked in different ways to perform different tasks. From the information in the second paragraph on this page, you can infer that the electronic components of a machine like a digital watch are

    a.   simpler than those of a computer

    b.   more complex than those of a computer

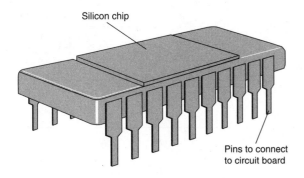

Silicon chip

Pins to connect to circuit board

Microprocessor

Diagram shown adapted from *The Kingfisher Science Encyclopedia,* "Microprocessor," Kingfisher Press, New York 1991, page 456.

Microprocessors

The most complex and advanced integrated circuits are the **microprocessors** of computers. These devices function as the computer's central processing unit, controlling the computer and performing calculations. First developed by Intel in the early 1970s, the microprocessor made small personal computers possible. Before the microprocessor, computers were very large, often taking up several rooms.

The central processing unit of a personal computer is usually on one microprocessor. In contrast, Deep Blue has 32 microprocessors, all working at the same time. Each coordinates the work of 16 special-purpose "chess chips." This combination of microprocessors and special chips designed for a particular use is the basis for superior problem-solving computers.

Kasparov Versus Deep Blue, Round Two

After Kasparov's 1996 win, the computer scientists and chess experts on IBM's Deep Blue team went back to work to improve its performance. They doubled Deep Blue's speed by adding new microprocessors to its central processing unit. They doubled the number of special-purpose chess chips. These changes increased Deep Blue's calculation power tremendously.

The team made Deep Blue approach chess more as a human being does. They gave it more chess knowledge by redesigning the chess chips. And they gave it a limited ability to adjust to Kasparov's playing. They did this by designing **software,** instructions to the computer, that enabled them to change Deep Blue's playing between games.

Recognizing Cause and Effect   Situations in which one thing makes another thing happen are *cause-and-effect relationships.* For example, the IBM team gave Deep Blue more chess knowledge and software that enabled them to adjust its playing. These causes led to an effect—Deep Blue was able to play chess more like a human being. What was the effect of adding new microprocessors to Deep Blue's central processing unit?
  a.   Deep Blue's speed doubled.
  b.   Deep Blue had better decision-making capabilities.

Kasparov also prepared for the 1997 rematch. He decided to use unusual opening moves, hoping that Deep Blue would not be prepared for them. He also decided to use odd playing styles. By doing this he hoped to confuse Deep Blue's ability to evaluate the positions of pieces on the chess board.

Kasparov's strategy worked for the first game, and he won. But Deep Blue's team changed the computer's strategy for the second game. Instead of trying to take Kasparov's pieces, it began to "crowd" him, limiting the moves he could make. Kasparov was so rattled by Deep Blue's change in strategy that he lost the second game. By the sixth game, Kasparov gave in to the pressure. He resigned the game after just 19 moves, making Deep Blue the match winner. It was the first time a computer had won a chess match against a reigning world champion.

To most people, Kasparov's battle with Deep Blue was mainly a contest between a man and a machine. But to the people at IBM who designed Deep Blue, it was an opportunity to test a complex computer system. The knowledge gained from these two chess matches can be applied to a variety of complex tasks, including analyzing financial data and predicting the behavior of molecules.

Thinking About the Article

Practice Vocabulary

The terms below are in the passage in bold type. Study the way each term is used. Then match each term to its meaning by writing the correct letter in the blank.

_____ **1** electronics

_____ **2** transistor

_____ **3** diode

_____ **4** integrated circuit

_____ **5** microprocessor

a. an electronic circuit that fits on a small silicon chip

b. an electronic device that allows current to flow in only one direction

c. a complex integrated circuit that serves as a computer's central processing unit

d. an electronic component that can be used as an amplifier, detector, or switch

e. a branch of engineering concerned with devices that control the flow of electric current

Understand the Article

Write or circle the answer to each question.

6 When playing chess, Deep Blue relies primarily on its ability to
   a. make calculations fast.   b. imitate its human opponent.

7 What is an electronic component? Give one example.

_____

_____

8 What is the purpose of the metal tracks on a printed circuit board?
   a. They connect the electronic components on the board, allowing electrons to flow along them.
   b. They prevent the board from cracking after heavy use.

9 What development in electronics made personal computers possible?
   a. transistors   b. microprocessors

10 What is the chief difference between an ordinary personal computer and IBM's Deep Blue?
   a. An ordinary personal computer has transistors and diodes, and Deep Blue does not.
   b. An ordinary personal computer has one microprocessor, and Deep Blue has 32.

Check your answers on page 248.

Apply Your Skills

Circle the number of the best answer for each question.

11 From the information about the second match between Kasparov and Deep Blue, you can infer that Kasparov lost mainly because
(1) Deep Blue played each game without mistakes.
(2) Deep Blue was able to calculate faster than Kasparov.
(3) Deep Blue had a winning strategy that it used in each game.
(4) Kasparov's human emotions interfered with his ability to play.
(5) Kasparov's strategy of using unusual moves had not worked in the first game.

12 As a result of the development of the microprocessor, computers
(1) were able to make calculations.
(2) had central processing units that took up several rooms.
(3) were able to play chess.
(4) no longer needed printed circuit boards.
(5) became much smaller.

13 What was the effect of the new software that Deep Blue's designers developed before the second chess match?
(1) It increased Deep Blue's ability to evaluate chess positions.
(2) It gave Deep Blue more chess knowledge.
(3) It enabled Deep Blue's playing to be adjusted between games.
(4) It enabled Deep Blue to remember previous moves.
(5) It cut the time between games in half.

Connect with the Article

Write your answer to each question.

14 List at least three machines that you or your family own that have electronic components.

_____

_____

_____

15 After Kasparov lost to Deep Blue, some people concluded that computers were smarter than people. Do you agree? Why or why not?

_____

_____

_____

Light and Lasers

Setting the Stage

What do you think of when you hear the word *laser?* Perhaps you think of science fiction characters fighting with laser weapons. You may not think of medical tools. Yet lasers and the light that they produce are being used as tools in surgery. Lasers are ideal for the delicate skin treatments needed in some types of cosmetic surgery.

PREVIEW THE ARTICLE

One way to preview an article is to look at the illustrations and read the captions. That will give you an idea of what the article is about. Scan the illustrations and captions on pages 203–205. What are some things you can expect to learn about light and lasers?

_____

_____

_____

RELATE TO THE TOPIC

This article is about the use of lasers in cosmetic surgery. It describes how cosmetic surgeons use lasers to perform delicate operations. It explains how laser light is different from ordinary light. If you could improve just one feature with cosmetic surgery, which would it be? Why?

_____

_____

_____

VOCABULARY

laser   light   frequency   wavelength

Check your answers on page 249.

Laser Surgery

On the morning of her 44th birthday, Paulette examined her face in the mirror. The bags under her eyes were dark and huge. A few age spots clustered on her cheeks. Wrinkles and frown lines were everywhere. Paulette thought about getting a chemical peel to improve her skin, but she didn't like the idea of putting strong chemicals on her face. She briefly considered a face lift, but it was too expensive. Finally, Paulette decided to go for the latest treatment—a laser peel.

Cosmetic surgeons perform laser peels, also called laser resurfacing, using a new type of laser. A **laser** produces a narrow beam of light that is strong and hot. Older lasers produced a continuous beam of intense light, making them ideal for cutting. The new lasers used for most cosmetic surgery produce short bursts of light. They pulse on and off in less than a thousandth of a second. These fast pulses are strong enough to burn off surface skin cells. Yet the pulsing prevents the heat from burning deep into the skin. So the laser doesn't hurt the deeper layers of skin that produce new cells and healthy looking skin. The pulsing laser has another benefit. It shrinks the skin, making sagging skin look tight and young.

Paulette's laser peel took about half an hour. Her surgeon had a computerized system that allowed him to map areas of her face and adjust the laser's energy. He used less energy near her eyes, where the skin is thin. He used more energy near her mouth, where the skin is thicker.

The surgery was short, but the recovery was long. Paulette had to treat her face to keep it moist and free from infection. Her skin was swollen, red, and tender for four weeks. Yet Paulette thinks the treatment was worth it. Six months after her laser peel, she loves the way her face looks—young, clear, and smooth.

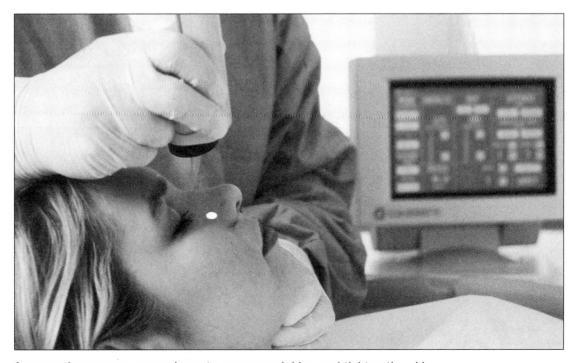

A cosmetic surgeon uses a laser to remove wrinkles and tighten the skin.

Removing wrinkles and age spots is not the only use of lasers in cosmetic surgery. Lasers can remove birthmarks, warts, scars, and tattoos. They are also used in other types of surgery in which precise, delicate control is needed. For example, they are used by eye surgeons to correct vision. Different kinds of lasers are used for each purpose. However, they all have the same basic design.

Getting in Step

Light is a form of energy that travels in waves. Other kinds of waves include sound waves, radio waves, and X rays. A wave has a regular pattern. It is usually drawn as a curved line that goes up and down. If you drop a stone into a pond, ripples of water move out in a circle. Each ripple is a wave. The energy of the wave makes the water move up and down. The **frequency** is the number of waves that pass a point in a certain amount of time. The **wavelength** is the distance from the top of one wave to the top of the next wave.

What we see as ordinary white light is made up of all the colors of a rainbow. Each color of light has its own frequency and wavelength. Imagine a crowd of people moving forward at the same speed. The people are not trying to walk in step. This is what ordinary light is like. Now imagine the crowd all marching in step. This is what laser light is like. All the waves have the same frequency and wavelength.

Ordinary Light

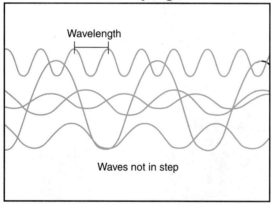

Waves not in step

Laser Light

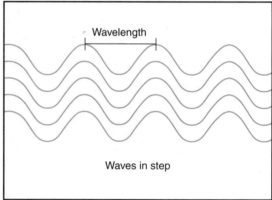

Waves in step

Reading a Diagram   A **diagram** can help you see how something looks or works. This helps you follow what the author is describing. The diagrams above show how ordinary light waves differ from laser light waves. The labels are words that point out things you should look at closely.

❶ Which is a good description of the wavelengths of ordinary light?
   a.   waves in step, all of the same wavelength
   b.   irregular waves, of different wavelengths

❷ What is an important characteristic of laser light?
   a.   Its wavelengths are all the same.   b.   Its waves are irregular.

How a Laser Works

A laser contains a material that will give off light waves that are all in step. A burst of electrical or light energy is applied to the tube. This energy is absorbed by the atoms in the tube. The atoms then give off the energy in the form of light. All the light given off has the same wavelength and frequency. A mirror at one end of the tube reflects light completely. A mirror at the other end reflects only some light. The light is reflected back and forth between the mirrors. The light gets stronger and stronger as this happens. When the light becomes strong enough, it passes through the partially reflecting mirror. This light is the laser beam.

How a Laser Produces Light

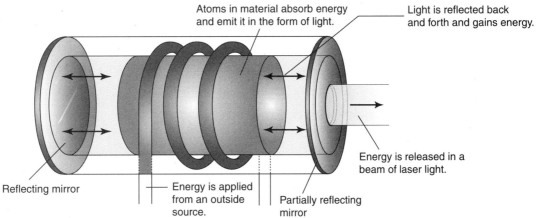

Atoms in material absorb energy and emit it in the form of light.

Light is reflected back and forth and gains energy.

Reflecting mirror

Energy is applied from an outside source.

Partially reflecting mirror

Energy is released in a beam of laser light.

Understanding Sequence   The order in which things happen is called **sequence**. Understanding sequence helps you understand how things like lasers work. For example, the paragraph above explains the sequence of events that leads to the production of the laser beam. The diagram helps you visualize this sequence. The first step in producing a laser beam is applying energy to the laser. What happens after the light reflects back and forth between the mirrors?

    a.   The light is strong enough to pass through the partially reflecting mirror.

    b.   Energy is absorbed by the atoms in the tube.

Lasers with Different Wavelengths

What makes one kind of laser different from another is the material in the tube. Each type of material gives off a different wavelength of laser light. And different substances in the body absorb different wavelengths of light. Thus lasers of different wavelengths can be used on different types of tissue in laser surgery.

For example, removing a tattoo is similar to removing wrinkles and spots, but the wavelength of the laser must be matched to the wavelength absorbed by the tattoo, which depends on its color. If a tattoo has more than one color, more than one laser treatment is needed. Removing some professional tattoos requires six to ten treatments. This is a good reason to think twice about getting a tattoo!

Check your answer on page 249.

Thinking About the Article

Practice Vocabulary

The terms below are in the passage in bold type. Study the way each term is used. Then complete each sentence by writing the correct term in the blank.

laser	light	frequency	wavelength

1 _____ is a form of visible energy that travels in waves.

2 The _____ is the number of waves that pass a point in a certain amount of time.

3 The _____ is the distance from the top of one wave to the top of the next wave.

4 A _____ produces a narrow, intense beam of light.

Understand the Article

Write or circle the answer to each question.

5 How can a laser be used to correct skin problems?
   a. The laser is used to make an incision, and then the surgeon uses other tools to correct the problem.
   b. The laser burns off the thin upper layer of skin, allowing new skin to form from the healthy layers below.

6 How are light, sound, and X rays similar?

_____

7 In laser light, all the waves are
   a. in step with one another.
   b. of different frequencies.

8 The type of light produced by a laser depends on
   a. the material inside the laser tube.
   b. the length of the laser tube.

9 Lasers of different wavelengths are useful in surgery because
   a. different substances absorb different wavelengths of laser light, meaning that a particular substance can be targeted, leaving other nearby substances alone.
   b. the different wavelengths are absorbed by many layers of skin, enabling surgeons to make deeper incisions.

Check your answers on page 249.

Apply Your Skills

Circle the number of the best answer for each question.

10 According to the diagrams on page 204, a wavelength is the
   (1) time it takes for one wave to pass a given point.
   (2) number of waves that pass a given point in a given time.
   (3) distance between the highest and lowest part of a wave.
   (4) distance between the top of one wave and the top of the next.
   (5) midpoint of a wave.

11 What is the first thing that happens when energy is applied to a laser tube?
   (1) The atoms in the tube absorb the energy.
   (2) The atoms in the tube give off the energy in the form of light.
   (3) Mirrors reflect the light back and forth to increase its energy.
   (4) The material in the tube changes state.
   (5) The laser light passes through one end of the tube.

12 According to the diagram on page 205, the mirrors in a laser
   (1) provide technicians with a way to see what is happening inside.
   (2) direct a beam of light at the targeted object.
   (3) reflect the light back and forth.
   (4) change the angle at which light hits the sides of the tube.
   (5) focus the light on the energy source inside the laser.

Connect with the Article

Write your answer to each question.

13 When he was 18, Jim had his arm tattooed with his girlfriend's name in blue inside a dark red heart. Now Jim is getting married to another woman and his fiancee wants him to have the tattoo removed. How many treatments will he need? Explain your answer.

_____

_____

_____

14 Suppose you had a skin spot that could be removed either by applying a chemical or by laser. Would you try the laser? Explain your answer.

_____

_____

_____

Science at Work

Construction: Insulation Contractor

Some Careers in Construction

Carpenter
frames, finishes, and remodels buildings and furniture

Drywall Installer
measures, installs, and finishes drywall or sheetrock surfaces in homes and buildings

Plumber
installs and repairs water pipes and drains

Roofer
repairs leaks and problems in roofs; removes old material and installs new roofs

Good insulation helps conserve energy.

Have you ever wondered what helps keep your home warm in the winter and cool in the summer? Through the use of insulation materials, homes and workplaces are kept at appropriate temperatures all year round. Selecting and installing the proper insulation materials are the responsibility of insulation contractors.

Insulation contractors pick the type of insulation material best suited for specific places in a building. Basements, walls, attics, water heaters, and ceilings are just some of the places where they apply their knowledge of insulation material selection and installation.

Insulation contractors must understand basic physics principles such as energy and heat transfer, condensation, and evaporation. They must also have good math and measurement skills and be able to read blueprints and other diagrams. The consistent introduction of new building materials and building safety codes requires insulation contractors to keep up to date about new developments in their field.

Look at the Some Careers in Construction chart.

● Do any of the careers interest you? If so, which ones?

● What information would you need to find out more about those careers? On a separate piece of paper, write some questions that you would like answered. You can find more information about those careers in the *Occupational Outlook Handbook* at your local library.

Use these guidelines to answer the questions that follow.

Insulation Installation Guidelines

1. Before installing any insulation material, check for and seal any air leaks in the structure.

2. Check for sufficient ventilation and circulation of air in the building. Sufficient ventilation must be present to control moisture from condensation in heated areas of the building and to allow for circulation of clean air.

3. Select appropriate insulation material.

   a. Insulation blankets—laid in unfinished attic spaces, walls, and floors. Trim blanket to fit snugly in space.

   b. Loose-fill particles—blown into attic spaces or other unfinished, accessible building openings. Adhesive solutions may also be applied to help particles hold together if necessary.

   c. Spray foams—sprayed into hard-to-reach areas or between framing timbers. Must be applied with care, as the foam will be 30 times the original amount applied when it dries.

   d. Rigid insulation—used as exterior or interior protection. Some types may include foil layer to prevent moisture buildup.

   e. Foil insulation—applied before finishing ceilings, walls or floors. Good at shielding against extreme summer heat and preventing winter heat loss.

① The best insulation behind an existing interior brick wall would be
   (1) insulation blanket.
   (2) loose-fill particles.
   (3) spray foam.
   (4) rigid insulation.
   (5) foil insulation.

② Which of the following would be an effective insulation material for homes in desert environments?
   (1) insulation blanket
   (2) loose-fill particles
   (3) spray foam
   (4) rigid insulation
   (5) foil insulation

③ Heat loss occurs when warm air moves from heated sections of the home to unheated sections. Using a separate piece of paper, explain why it would be important for the contractor to install insulation material under the floor of a room located above the home's garage.

The Inclined Plane

A **simple machine** is a device used to do work. An inclined plane is one type of simple machine. An **inclined plane** is a long, sloping surface that helps raise an object that cannot be easily lifted. A ramp is an example of an inclined plane. Imagine trying to get a person in a wheelchair onto a porch that is one foot above the ground. Lifting the person and the wheelchair would be difficult. You may not be able to exert a large enough force to do this. If the porch had a four-foot-long ramp, you could easily get the person and the wheelchair onto the porch.

The amount of work done depends on the force needed and the distance moved. You would need less force to move the person up the ramp than to lift her straight up. However, you would have to move the person a longer distance, four feet instead of one. It takes about the same amount of work to push the person up the ramp as it does to lift the person.

Friction is a force between surfaces that rub against each other. Friction makes it harder to use an inclined plane. It is easy to use an inclined plane to move the person in a wheelchair because the wheels have little friction. But if you had to push a box up the same ramp, you would need a large force just to overcome the friction.

Fill in the blank with the word or words that best complete each statement.

1 A(n) _____ is a long, sloping surface that helps raise an object that cannot be lifted.

2 _____ is a force between surfaces that rub against each other.

Circle the number of the best answer.

3 In which situation would you need to exert the least force?
   (1) lifting a 75-pound box to a height of one foot
   (2) lifting a 120-pound box to a height of one foot
   (3) pushing a 75-pound box up a ramp three feet long
   (4) pushing a wheeled 75-pound cart up a ramp three feet long
   (5) lifting a wheeled 75-pound cart up to a height of one foot

Check your answers on page 249.

Momentum

If an object is moving, it has momentum. The object's **momentum** depends on its weight and speed. The faster an object moves and the heavier it is, the more momentum it has. If an object is not moving, it has no momentum.

Momentum is transferred between objects when they collide. Pool players make use of the transfer of momentum. A good player knows how to set up collisions between the balls on the table. The player uses a long stick, the cue, to hit one of the balls. The ball that is hit is called the cue ball. In the collision between the cue and the cue ball, momentum is transferred to the ball. The cue ball rolls along the table until it strikes one of the numbered balls. The momentum of the cue ball is transferred to the numbered ball. The cue ball stops moving and the numbered ball moves. If the player has aimed correctly, the numbered ball will go into a pocket.

A good pool player knows how to set up collisions between more than two balls. If the cue ball strikes two numbered balls at the same time, the two balls move away from the cue ball. Each of the numbered balls gets only some of the momentum of the cue ball. Because of this, neither of the numbered balls moves as fast as the cue ball was moving.

Players also make bank shots, in which a ball collides with the side of the table. In this collision, the ball keeps its momentum and bounces off the side of the table, moving in a new direction.

Circle the number of the best answer.

4 What factors determine an object's momentum?
   (1) speed and direction of motion
   (2) weight and direction of motion
   (3) weight and speed
   (4) weight and how far the object has moved
   (5) speed and how far the object has moved

5 What happens to a rock as it rolls down a hill, picking up speed?
   (1) Its momentum increases as the speed increases.
   (2) Its momentum decreases as the speed increases.
   (3) Its momentum increases, making the rock heavier.
   (4) Its momentum decreases because the rock gets heavier.
   (5) Its momentum does not change.

Check your answers on page 250.

Sound Waves

Sound is caused by vibrations. If you pluck a stretched rubber band, you can see it vibrate, or move back and forth. The rubber band makes the air near it vibrate. These vibrations move through the air like ripples in a pond. Each ripple is a wave.

If you look at water waves, you can see the distance from the top of one wave to the top of the next. This distance is the **wavelength.** Each wavelength makes a sound of a different pitch. Short wavelengths are high sounds, like a flute. Long wavelengths are low sounds, like a tuba.

The height of a wave is the **amplitude.** The amplitude of a sound wave is the loudness of the sound. The higher the amplitude, the louder the sound.

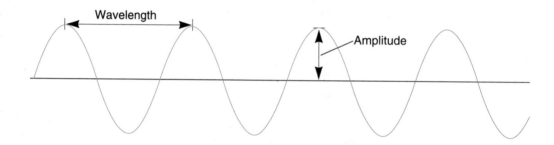

Fill in the blank with the word that best completes each statement.

6 _____ is caused by vibrations.

7 The height of a wave is the _____ .

Circle the number of the best answer.

8 A loud, high-pitched sound has a wave with a
   (1) high amplitude and long wavelength.
   (2) high amplitude and short wavelength.
   (3) low amplitude and long wavelength.
   (4) low amplitude and short wavelength.
   (5) low amplitude and medium wavelength.

9 What will happen to the wave in the diagram if the sound gets softer and lower in pitch?
   (1) The wavelength will be longer and the amplitude higher.
   (2) The wavelength will be shorter and the amplitude higher.
   (3) The wavelength will be longer and the amplitude lower.
   (4) The wavelength will be shorter and the amplitude lower.
   (5) Nothing will happen to the wave.

Check your answers on page 250.

Electromagnetic Fields

Any device that uses electricity has an energy field around it. The field caused by an electric current is called an **electromagnetic field,** or **EM field.** The EM field has properties of electricity and magnetism. For example, the EM field of a TV can turn the needle of a compass, just as a magnet can. An EM field is produced only while the electric current is flowing. When the TV is turned off, there is no EM field.

An EM field can ruin a video- or audiotape. The tape contains metal particles lined up in a pattern. This pattern is read when you play the tape. Because it is magnetic, an EM field can move the metal particles in the tape. When you play the tape, the picture or sound will be scrambled. Computer floppy disks and video games work in the same way as the tapes. They all should be kept away from EM fields. Compact discs do not have a magnetic pattern, so they are not damaged by EM fields.

The metal detector at an airport has an EM field. When you walk through the EM field, metal objects you are carrying affect it. If the field detects enough metal, an alarm sounds. After removing keys, coins, and jewelry, people can usually walk through the gate without affecting the EM field. The alarm does not ring.

Fill in the blank with the word or words that best complete the statement.

10 An EM field can affect metal because the field acts like a

_____.

Circle the number of the best answer.

11 Which of the following can be safely carried through an airport metal detector without damage?
 (1) an audiotape
 (2) a videotape
 (3) a computer floppy disk
 (4) a video game cartridge
 (5) a compact disc

Science Extension

Simple machines are all around us. Look in your home for examples of simple machines. (They may be part of a compound machine.) Make a table. In one column list these simple machines: inclined plane (ramp or wedge), lever, wheel and axle, gears. In the second column list all the examples you find. Here's one to get you started: Lever: bottle opener.

Science Connection: Physics and Whole Numbers

Lighter Than Air

For decades people have dreamed of flying around the world in a balloon. In 1999, Bertrand Piccard and Brian Jones were the first to realize this dream. Before them, however, the feat had been the goal of three dedicated balloon pilots—Richard Branson, Per Lindstrand, and Steve Fossett. Each had made several attempts to be first to fly around the globe in a balloon without landing.

In late 1998, Branson, Fossett, and Lindstrand made an unsuccessful attempt together. Their balloon, the *ICO Global,* carried them on a trip that could have lasted up to three weeks. In addition to using global jet streams, the men flew the craft by controlling the temperature of the balloon's gases. Adjustments to the temperature of the gases affected the density of the gases and their volume. This affected the altitude, or height, at which the balloon flew.

The pocket at the top of a balloon's envelope holds helium, a gas less dense than the air in the atmosphere. To keep the balloon high enough in the air, the helium has to fill the pocket. To fill the pocket, it has to be warm. This is no problem during the day when the sun is able to warm the balloon. As the sun warms the helium in the pocket and the air in the lower chamber, the balloon stays full and keeps the craft aloft. At night, when the sun no longer warms the balloon, burners must be used to keep the gases from cooling.

When a gas cools, its molecules move closer together. The gas is denser because the molecules take up less volume, or space. The more concentrated the gas, the heavier it is. When a gas is heated, its molecules move farther apart and the volume expands. As the gas in a balloon gets lighter than the air around it, the balloon will rise. As it cools and gets heavier, the balloon will fall.

Whole Numbers: How High Do They Fly?

Balloonists use an instrument called an altimeter to measure their altitude. Balloons designed to fly for long periods of time over great distances cruise in altitudes of 20,000 to 43,000 feet. One mile measures 5,280 feet. The peak of Mount Everest, the tallest mountain on Earth, is just over 29,000 feet.

ICO Global Balloon

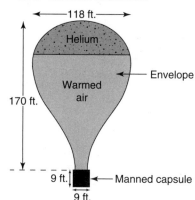

Use the material on the previous page and the table below to answer the questions that follow.

Big Balloons That Made History

Pilot or Balloon Name	Date	Description of Flight	Maximum Altitude
Montgolfier Brothers balloon	1783	A rooster, a duck, and a sheep fly in leashed basket of hot-air balloon for 2 miles.	1,700 feet
Steve Fossett in *Solo Spirit*	1997 1998	Fossett makes two unsuccessful solo attempts lasting 8 days and 10 days.	33,000 feet
Fossett, Branson, and Lindstrand in *ICO Global*	1998	Three-man crew, aloft for 8 days, travels over 6,000 miles.	43,000 feet
Piccard and Jones in *Breitling Orbiter 3*	1999	Two-man crew becomes first to circle the globe in a 29,000-mile, 19-day trip.	30,000+ feet

1 During the day, the helium in the pocket of a balloon's envelope
(1) is warmed by the sun and expands.
(2) is warmed by the sun and contracts.
(3) is cooled by the sun and expands.
(4) is cooled by the sun and contracts.
(5) is warmed by burners and contracts.

2 What was the approximate maximum altitude reached by the *ICO Global* balloon?
(1) 1 mile
(2) 8 miles
(3) 200 miles
(4) 5,280 miles
(5) 6,000 miles

3 If the gas in a balloon cools, the balloon will
(1) rise because the gas molecules move farther apart.
(2) fall because the gas molecules move farther apart.
(3) rise because the gas molecules move closer together.
(4) fall because the gas molecules move closer together.
(5) rise because the gas will be less dense than the air.

4 The average number of miles per day traveled by the *Orbiter 3* was
(1) 150
(2) 750
(3) 1,500
(4) 6,000
(5) 29,000

Posttest

Scientific Methods

Have you ever solved a problem by trial and error, by **observation,** or by making an informed choice? If so, you have used scientific methods. **Scientific methods** are organized, logical ways of setting up and solving problems. Suppose that you have an old table. Its wood finish is scratched and dull. You've also seen beautiful new shiny wood tables. As a result of these observations, you form the **hypothesis** that there is fine wood under the dull, scratched finish of your old table. How can you find out? You can remove the old finish.

What should you use to remove the old finish? You can ask people who have experience with refinishing wood. You can read about furniture refinishing. Or you can go to a hardware store and ask some questions. You can read the labels of several products.

By now, you should have narrowed down your choices to two or three products. One way to decide which one to use is to test them. This is an **experiment.** Try each product on a small area that doesn't show. Then compare the results. Which product does the best job of revealing the wood beneath the finish? Is the wood as fine as you hypothesized? After you look at your results, you should be able to draw a **conclusion** about the quality of the wood. You should be able to choose the best product to remove the old finish.

Fill in the blank with the word or words that best complete each statement.

1. Comparing your old, battered wood table to other new, shiny wood

   tables is a process called _____.

2. After making these comparisons, you formed a(n) _____:
   your old scratched table actually has beautiful wood underneath.

3. To find out whether this is so, you _____ with several
   products to see which one best removed the old finish.

4. As a result of these tests, you draw some _____ about
   the quality of the wood and the effectiveness of the products.

5. The approach you used to set up and solve this problem demonstrates

   the use of _____.

Go on to the next page.

How Viruses Replicate

A virus is a tiny particle made up of genetic material with a protein coating. Viruses are not cells, and they do not reproduce the way cells do. A virus does not contain the raw materials needed to make more viruses. Instead, it gets these materials from a host cell. Each kind of virus needs a particular host.

To replicate, or make more, viruses, a virus takes over its host cell. The virus attaches to its host and injects its genetic material into the cell. The genetic material from the virus takes control. Soon the cell becomes a virus factory. When the cell is full of viruses, it breaks open. The new viruses are released. Each one is able to take over another host cell.

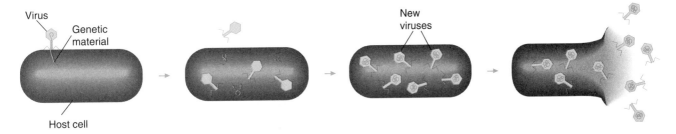

Circle the number of the best answer.

6. A virus needs a host cell to replicate because the
   (1) virus has the raw materials for making viruses.
   (2) host cell has the raw materials for making viruses.
   (3) virus has no genetic material.
   (4) host cell has the genetic material for making viruses.
   (5) genetic material of the virus and the host are the same.

7. After the new viruses are released, the host cell
   (1) becomes a virus.
   (2) makes several more generations of viruses.
   (3) returns to its original form.
   (4) dies.
   (5) reproduces to make more host cells.

Incomplete Metamorphosis

People love to see a butterfly visit a garden and drink nectar from the flowers. Everyone likes butterflies. They're pretty, and they don't chew up the leaves the way caterpillars do. Yet the caterpillar that you hate to see munching on leaves will become the pretty butterfly. This change is called complete metamorphosis because these two stages in the life cycle are so different.

Many insects do not go through such a dramatic change. The young insect, called a nymph, looks much like the adult. This slight change is called incomplete metamorphosis. The grasshopper goes through this kind of change. So does the praying mantis. There are two main differences between the nymph and the adult. Only the adult has wings. Only the adult is able to reproduce.

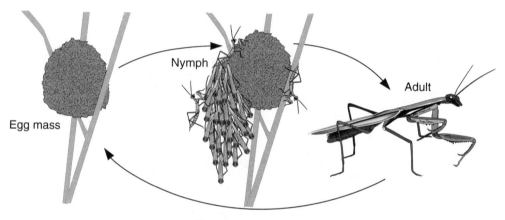

Egg mass   Nymph   Adult

Praying Mantis

Fill in the blank with the word or words that best complete the statement.

8. The change from a nymph to an adult grasshopper is called

    _____.

Circle the number of the best answer.

9. How does the appearance of a praying mantis nymph differ from that of an adult?
   (1) The adult is larger than the nymph.
   (2) The adult can eat, and the nymph cannot.
   (3) The nymph has wings, and the adult does not.
   (4) The adult is smaller than the nymph.
   (5) The adult has an egg mass, and the nymph does not.

Go on to the next page.

The Predator and the Prey

Snowshoe hares live in the forests of northern Canada. These animals get their name from their large feet. Like snowshoes, large feet spread out the animal's weight. As a result, the hare can walk on snow without sinking into it. Snowshoe hares are caught and eaten by lynxes. A lynx is a large cat. Like the hare, the lynx has large feet that help it walk on top of deep snow.

The lynx is a predator. It kills and eats its prey, the hare. The populations of these two animals are closely linked. The populations grow and shrink in a cycle.

In years when there are many hares, hunting is easy for the lynxes. There is plenty to eat. As a result, the lynx population increases.

In a year or two, there are many lynxes feeding on the hares. Many hares are caught and eaten, and the hare population goes down sharply. After the hare population goes down, there is less food for the lynxes. Hunting becomes harder, and fewer lynxes survive. The lynx population goes down.

When there are fewer lynxes, fewer hares are eaten. Over the next few years, the hare population grows. Soon there are so many hares that hunting becomes easy for the lynxes, and the cycle repeats.

Fill in the blank with the word or words that best complete each statement.

10. An animal that hunts and kills its food is a(n) ———————————.

11. An animal that is hunted by another animal is the ———————————.

Circle the number of the best answer.

12. The snowshoe hare is also eaten by wolves. If a disease suddenly killed off many wolves, the first change you would see is that
    (1) there would be more hares.
    (2) there would be fewer hares.
    (3) there would be fewer lynxes.
    (4) lynxes would catch the disease.
    (5) hares would catch the disease.

Respiration

Most living things need oxygen to survive. In the process of respiration, cells use oxygen to break down food to give the body energy. Carbon dioxide is given off as a waste product in this process. Respiration goes on in cells all the time. As a result, the body has a constant source of energy. Plants, animals, and some bacteria carry on respiration.

Plants also carry on photosynthesis. This process is the reverse of respiration. In photosynthesis, energy from sunlight is used to change carbon dioxide and water into sugar. The sugar is food for the plant. Oxygen is also produced. Photosynthesis goes on only when the plant receives light.

Plants produce more oxygen than they use. The extra oxygen is given off into the air. Photosynthesis is the source of all the oxygen used by living things.

Circle the number of the best answer.

13. How are photosynthesis and respiration related?
    (1) They are the same.
    (2) They both need oxygen.
    (3) They both need sunlight.
    (4) They both take place in animals.
    (5) Photosynthesis is the reverse of respiration.

14. Animals eat plants to get
    (1) carbon dioxide.
    (2) oxygen.
    (3) food.
    (4) sunlight.
    (5) air.

15. In the process of respiration, plants use
    (1) carbon dioxide.
    (2) water.
    (3) sunlight.
    (4) oxygen.
    (5) bacteria.

Go on to the next page.

Water Use

Between 1900 and 1980, water use in the United States grew faster than the population. Between 1980 and 1995, water use per person actually declined by 20 percent. The decline resulted from water-saving technology and practices such as improved irrigation machinery and toilets that use less water per flush. In addition, water in the United States has become cleaner in the last thirty years.

However, there are still threats to the future of the U.S. water supply. The best places for dams, which increase the amount of water available, have already been used. In addition, the water supply is threatened by increases in farm runoff water, which contains pollutants such as animal wastes.

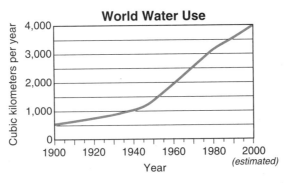

The growth of population, farms, factories, and cities in the last few hundred years has sharply increased the demand for fresh water. During the 20th century, water use grew almost eightfold. By 2025, some nations will not have enough water for both drinking and farming.

Source: "The World's Water 1998–1999" by P.H. Gleick, in William K. Stevens, "Water: Pushing the limits of an Irreplaceable Resource," *The New York Times*, Dec. 8, 1998, p. E7.

Fill in the blank with the word or words that best complete each statement.

16. In the future, some nations will have trouble supplying enough water for

    drinking and _____.

17. According to the graph, in 1900 the world used about

    _____ cubic kilometers of water per year, about one-eighth the present amount.

18. Between 1980 and 1985, water use per person in the United States has

    _____ by about 20 percent.

Circle the number of the best answer.

19. All of the following have contributed to improved water use in the United States in the last 20 years *except*
    (1) increased farm runoff.
    (2) improved irrigation machinery.
    (3) water-saving toilets.
    (4) water treatment plants.
    (5) cleaner rivers, lakes, and streams.

Pluto: Planet or Asteroid?

Recently, a disagreement among astronomers grew strong enough to make the news. It was started by Dr. Brian G. Marsden, director of the Minor Planet Center of the Harvard-Smithsonian Astrophysical Observatory in Cambridge, Massachusetts. Dr. Marsden, who is British, announced that he wanted to classify Pluto as a minor planet, or asteroid. His proposal caused an uproar, especially among American astronomers, perhaps because Pluto was discovered by an American in 1930.

Pluto has characteristics of both major planets and asteroids. Like the major planets, it is spherical, has an atmosphere, and has a moon. Unlike the major planets, its surface is icy and its orbit is very irregular. Pluto also has a lot in common with a group of icy asteroids beyond the orbit of Neptune. These asteroids, the first of which was discovered in 1992, are called the Trans-Neptunian Objects. Marsden predicts that eventually more Trans-Neptunian Objects as large as or larger than Pluto will be found in the far reaches of the solar system.

However, for the time being, astronomers have decided not to make a change: Pluto will remain classified as one of the major planets.

Fill in the blank with the word or words that best complete each statement.

20. The astronomers' argument over Pluto began when Dr. Brian Marsden

    proposed that Pluto should be classified as a(n) _____.

21. Since 1992, astronomers have found asteroids orbiting the sun in the

    area beyond the orbit of the planet _____.

Circle the number of the best answer.

22. Which of the following facts supports the argument that Pluto should *not* be classified as a major planet?
    (1) Pluto has a moon.
    (2) Pluto is shaped like a sphere.
    (3) Pluto's orbit is very irregular.
    (4) Pluto orbits the sun.
    (5) Pluto is much larger than the average asteroid.

Go on to the next page.

Oxidation

In the process of oxidation, a substance reacts with oxygen. The new compound that forms is called an oxide. Many metals oxidize when they are in contact with oxygen in the air.

You have probably seen some metal oxides. For example, iron combines with oxygen, forming iron oxide, or rust. Wrought-iron fences rust. So do the steel bodies of cars. Rust makes the metal look brown and scaly. Rust also weakens the metal. When flakes of rust fall off the metal, they leave more metal exposed to the air. This metal rusts and flakes off. Finally, the metal may rust through, leaving a hole.

Copper also oxidizes. As the red-brown copper oxidizes, it turns green. The green color is a layer of copper oxide. This layer does not flake off as rust does. Instead, the copper oxide stays on the metal and stops any further oxidation.

Aluminum is a metal that does not oxidize easily. That is one reason why aluminum is so useful for making garbage cans or other things that will stay outside in all weather.

Fill in the blank with the word or words that best complete the statement.

23. In the process of _____, a substance reacts with oxygen.

Circle the number of the best answer.

24. When silver is tarnished, it has oxidized. Why does covering silver objects in plastic wrap slow this process?
    (1) The plastic wrap keeps the metal warm.
    (2) The plastic wrap keeps the metal dry.
    (3) The plastic wrap keeps the metal away from oxygen.
    (4) The plastic wrap keeps the metal away from rust.
    (5) The plastic wrap keeps the metal away from copper.

25. Which of the following has not been oxidized?
    (1) iron oxide
    (2) copper oxide
    (3) silver oxide
    (4) aluminum oxide
    (5) silver chloride

Acids and Bases

Two large groups of compounds are acids and bases. These compounds can be identified with a substance called an indicator. Litmus paper is an indicator. An acid will turn litmus paper red. A base will turn litmus paper blue. A scale, called the **pH scale,** tells how strong an acid or a base is. The scale runs from 0 to 14. The strongest acid has a pH of 0. The strongest base has a pH of 14. A substance that is neither an acid nor a base is said to be neutral. Water is neutral. Its pH is 7.

Strong acids, such as sulfuric acid, can burn the skin. Weak acids have many uses. For example, vinegar is weak acetic acid. Vitamin C is ascorbic acid. Citric acid makes orange, grapefruit, and lemon juices sour.

Weak bases include soap and shampoo. Bases are able to dissolve fats, which is why soap removes grease from dishes. Ammonia, which is often used in cleaning solutions, is a base. Sodium hydroxide, or lye, is a strong base. This base is used in drain cleaners.

Match the pH range of the substance with its description. Write the letter of the pH range in the blanks at the left. Answers may be used more than once.

Description	pH range
_____ 26. turns litmus paper red	a. acid
_____ 27. turns litmus paper blue	b. base
_____ 28. water	c. neutral substance
_____ 29. ammonia	
_____ 30. vitamin C	
_____ 31. shampoo	

Circle the number of the best answer.

32. Which of the following lists of substances is in order from the lowest pH to the highest pH?
    (1) vinegar, water, soap, lye
    (2) water, vinegar, soap, lye
    (3) water, soap, vinegar, lye
    (4) soap, lye, vinegar, water
    (5) vinegar, soap, water, lye

Go on to the next page.

A New Type of Computer Chip

A typical personal computer has a silicon chip called a microprocessor, which processes data. It also has other chips that store software programs, data, and instructions. The fact that data processing and storage involve different chips slows a computer's functioning. Data must travel from chip to chip to be retrieved, processed, or stored. During this travel, data "traffic jams" often occur, affecting the computer's performance.

A new chip design solves this problem by combining processing and data storage on a single chip. In this design, the data storage parts of the chip are buried in tiny trenches. The surface of the chip is used for data processing. The chip, which is about the size of a thumbnail, has several times the processing power and memory capacity of the typical personal computer.

Because the new chip can do the work that used to be done by two or more chips, it is faster, requires less space, uses less electricity, and costs less. As a result, it can be used to make personal computers, cell phones, household appliances, and video games more compact and efficient.

Fill in the blank with the word or words that best complete each statement.

33. The data processing function of a personal computer is handled by its

_____ .

34. In a typical personal computer, data must travel from one

_____ to another _____ to be retrieved, processed, and stored.

Circle the number of the best answer.

35. All of the following are advantages of the new chip design *except*
    (1) greater processing power.
    (2) greater storage capacity.
    (3) greater efficiency.
    (4) less cost.
    (5) larger size.

Posttest Correlation Chart

The chart below will help you determine your strengths and weaknesses in the four content areas of science.

Directions

Circle the number of each item that you answered correctly on the Posttest. Count the number of items in each row that you answered correctly. Write the number in the Total Correct space in each row. (For example, in the Life Science row, write the number correct in the blank before *out of 15*). Complete this process for the remaining rows. Then add the four totals to get your total correct for the whole 35-item Posttest.

Content Areas	Items	Total Correct	Pages
Life Science (Pages 12–101)	1, 2, 3, 4, 5 6, 7 8, 9 10, 11, 12 13, 14, 15	_____ out of 15	Pages 14–19 Pages 50–55 Pages 68–73 Pages 80–85 Pages 80–85
Earth and Space Science (Pages 102–141)	16, 17, 18, 19 20, 21, 22	_____ out of 7	Pages 116–121 Pages 122–127
Chemistry (Pages 142–181)	23, 24, 25 26, 27, 28, 29, 30, 31, 32	_____ out of 10	Pages 144–149 Pages 150–155
Physics (Pages 182–215)	33, 34, 35	_____ out of 3	Pages 196–201

TOTAL CORRECT FOR POSTTEST _____ out of 35

If you answered fewer than 32 items correctly, determine which of the areas you need to study further. Go back and review the content in those areas. Page numbers for specific instruction in those areas of science are given in the right-hand column above.

Answers and Explanations

INVENTORY

PAGE 1

1. nucleus
2. cell wall
3. **(3) vacuole is empty** According to the diagram, the vacuole stores water and minerals, so the plant would need more water if the vacuole were empty. Options 1, 2, 4, and 5 are incorrect because these structures have functions other than storing water.

PAGE 2

4. contracts
5. relaxing
6. **(2) at the front of the thigh** According to the diagram, the paired muscles in the arm are on opposite sides of the arm. From this, you can infer that muscles that do opposite jobs are in opposite positions. If the muscles at the back of the thigh bend the knee, muscles at the front of the thigh would straighten the knee. Option 1 is incorrect because these muscles bend the knee. Options 3 and 4 are incorrect because these muscles move the ankle joint. Option 5 is incorrect because muscles around the hip bend the hip joint.

PAGE 3

7. Lactic acid
8. bacteria
9. **(1) Pasteurizing kills bacteria with high temperatures.** According to the article, pasteurizing involves heating and then quickly cooling the milk. The heat kills the bacteria. The rapid cooling is needed so that the milk does not cook. Option 2 does not kill the bacteria. Options 3 and 4 are incorrect because the bacteria are killed, not slowed. Option 5 is incorrect because no chemicals are involved in pasteurization.

PAGE 4

10. insects
11. insects
12. wind
13. insects
14. **(5) anthers and ovary** According to the article, these structures make the sperm and egg, which are needed for reproduction. Options 1 and 4 are incorrect because petals are not necessary for reproduction. The article states that some flowers have no petals. Options 2 and 3 are incorrect because both parts are necessary for reproduction.

PAGE 5

15. forest
16. grassland
17. cactus
18. **(2) drier** The article states that the grassland is drier than the forest, and the desert is drier than the grassland. Options 1, 3, and 4 are incorrect because the article does not indicate a pattern in these conditions. Option 5 is incorrect because the desert and grassland biomes are drier, not wetter, than the forest biome.

PAGE 6

19. c
20. e
21. b
22. a
23. d

PAGE 7

24. sedimentary rocks
25. metamorphic rocks

26. **(1) granite** According to the article, granite is an igneous rock. Options 2, 4, and 5 are incorrect because limestone, sandstone, and shale are sedimentary rocks. Option 3 is incorrect because marble is a metamorphic rock.

27. **(4) volcanoes** According to the article, volcanoes contain melted rock. When melted rock hardens, igneous rocks form. From this, you can infer that an area with many igneous rocks once had volcanoes. Options 1 and 2 are incorrect because rivers and sediment are associated with the formation of sedimentary rocks. Option 3 is incorrect because pressure is associated with the formation of metamorphic rocks. Option 5 is incorrect because earthquakes are not associated with the formation of rocks.

PAGE 8

28. b
29. c
30. a
31. c
32. a

PAGE 9

33. **(4) solid and liquid only** According to the table, these states of matter have a definite volume that does not change. Options 1 and 2 are incorrect because they list only one of the states with a definite volume. Options 3 and 5 are incorrect because the volume of a gas changes as the gas expands to fill its container.

34. **(1) Its shape changes from not definite to definite.** According to the table, a liquid does not have a definite shape, but a solid does. Option 2 is incorrect because it is the opposite of what happens. Option 3 is incorrect because both solid and liquid have definite volumes. Option 4 is incorrect because the change is to the lowest temperature range. Option 5 is incorrect because there is a change in a property.

PAGE 10

35. force
36. acceleration
37. **(1) acceleration** According to the article, when an unbalanced force acts on an object, the movement of the object changes. This is acceleration. All other options are examples of forces, not effects of forces.

UNIT 1: LIFE SCIENCE

SECTION 1

PAGE 14
Preview the Article
Answers will vary. Sample answer: How scientific methods were used on an experiment in space; the steps of the scientific methods; about observation, hypotheses, and conclusions
Relate to the Topic
Many answers are possible. Sample answer: Knowing about scientific methods can help me evaluate whether a science news story is supported by studies and experiments.

PAGE 16
a

PAGE 17
1. c
2. a
3. b

PAGES 18–19
1. scientific methods
2. observation
3. hypothesis
4. experiment
5. conclusion
6. a
7. b
8. b
9. a

10. **(5) a possible explanation for something observed** According to the glossary, a hypothesis is a guess about the answer to a question based on observations.

11. **(4) drawing a conclusion about the results of an experiment** This is a matter of evaluating data and thinking, not observation. All the other choices are examples of observation.

12. **(2) The eggs that were fertilized nine days before the launch would hatch.** This is the best prediction because it is the most similar to the results of the chicken embryo experiment.

13. Experimenting helps you gather evidence to support or disprove the hypothesis. Without experimenting, you cannot tell whether the hypothesis will be supported by facts.

14. Many answers are possible. Sample answer: No, because the risk to the unborn child is too great. We do not yet know enough about the effect of weightlessness on embryos to take chances with a human embryo.

SECTION 2

PAGE 20
Preview the Article
Answers will vary. Sample answer: how cancer affects cells; the parts of an animal cell
Relate to the Topic
Many answers are possible. Sample answer: I got a sunburn when I stayed at the beach too long. My skin burned and was painful. A few days later, the skin peeled off.

PAGE 22
a

PAGE 23
a

PAGES 24–25
1. a
2. d
3. c
4. b
5. f
6. e
7. Basal cell skin cancer looks like an open sore, mole, or shiny bump; this type of cancer rarely spreads to other parts of the body and usually can be cured. Squamous cell skin cancer looks like raised pink spots; it grows faster and can spread to other parts of the body. Melanomas are oddly shaped blotches that can grow and spread quickly.
8. b
9. a
10. Any three of the following: stay out of the sun from 10 A.M. to 3 P.M.; wear a hat and long sleeves; use sunscreen with an SPF of 15 or more; avoid tanning parlors; check your skin regularly
11. **(2) Skin color is closely related to the risk of developing skin cancer.** This sentence summarizes the main point of the paragraph. The other choices are all details.
12. **(3) Sunlight can cause skin cancer.** This sentence sums up the main point of the paragraph.
13. **(5) Preventing Skin Cancer** This section deals with ways to avoid getting skin cancer.
14. The doctor can check the moles for changes in size or color that might indicate skin cancer.
15. Many answers are possible. Sample answer: I will sit in the shade, wear sunscreen, and avoid the midday sun.

SECTION 3

PAGE 26

Preview the Article

Answers will vary. Sample answer: which foods have a lot of fat and cholesterol; how arteries become blocked; the different nutrients in low-fat and regular tortilla chips

Relate to the Topic

Many answers are possible. Sample answer: My uncle had a heart attack a few years ago. Afterward, he had to give up smoking and fatty foods and he began to exercise regularly.

PAGE 28

page 33

PAGE 29

1. a
2. three

PAGES 30–31

1. d
2. b
3. a
4. e
5. c
6. a
7. Extra cholesterol is deposited on the inside walls of arteries and clogs them.
8. a
9. b, c, d, e
10. **(2) 33** If you look up *heart* in the index, you will find an entry that says "heart, exercise and, 33."
11. **(2) saturated fat.** There is no wedge representing saturated fat in the circle graph for low-fat tortilla chips.
12. **(5) You cannot tell because the graphs do not show the salt content.** The graphs only show fat, carbohydrates, and protein, so you cannot tell how much salt is in either type of chip.

13. This is surprising because large amounts of saturated fat are usually found in animal products, not fruit.
14. Many answers are possible. Sample answer: It would be easiest to give up butter, cheese, and eggs. It would be hardest to give up ice cream and high-fat snacks like potato chips. I would eat more fruits, vegetables, and grains instead.

SECTION 4

PAGE 32

Preview the Article

Answers will vary. Sample answer: how walking helps bones and muscles; what the joints do

Relate to the Topic

Many answers are possible. Sample answer: I would recommend walking because it's safe, easy, and cheap. It's important to exercise regularly to keep your weight down and look good.

PAGE 34

b

PAGE 35

b

PAGES 36–37

1. joint
2. ligament
3. aerobic
4. osteoporosis
5. sprain
6. healthier lungs and heart, stronger muscles, stronger bones
7. When one muscle contracts, the bone moves one way. When the other muscle in the pair contracts, the bone moves the other way.
8. Your heart should be beating faster.
9. **(5) both can be aerobic exercises** According to the article, both walking and jogging can provide aerobic benefits.

10. **(2) it takes longer to walk a mile than to jog one** The other comparisons, while true, do not answer the question.

11. **(3) Walking does not put a lot of stress on joints.** According to the paragraph, joggers get stress injuries more than walkers do, and that implies that walking does not put a lot of stress on joints.

12. Many answers are possible. Sample answer: A hinge joint works like a door hinge.

13. Many answers are possible. Sample answer: I would choose walking because it would place less stress on my joints and ligaments.

SECTION 5

PAGE 38

Preview the Article
Answers will vary. Sample answer: how an unborn baby develops; the effects of drugs on the unborn; preventing birth defects
Relate to the Topic
Many answers are possible. Sample answer: I would tell her not to drink alcohol, because the development of her baby is too important to risk the damage that alcohol may cause.

PAGE 40

a

PAGE 41

a, c, d

PAGES 42–43

1. zygote, uterus
2. embryo
3. placenta
4. fetus
5. Thalidomide and DES
6. zygote, embryo, fetus
7. embryo
8. any three of the following: Thalidomide, DES, cocaine, nicotine (cigarettes), alcohol
9. a, b, d

10. **(3) the embryo is connected to the placenta, which is connected to the mother** The left side of the diagram gives you a view of the embryo, placenta, and mother's uterus and shows how they are connected to one another.

11. **(1) all of the body organs have formed** After the body organs have formed, any damage that occurs is more likely to be minor.

12. **(5) do all of the above** Diet, medical care, and no smoking or drinking will give a pregnant woman the best chance of having a healthy baby.

13. Many answers are possible. Sample answer: It is a good law because some women may not know that alcohol is dangerous and this would warn them.

14. Many answers are possible. Sample answer: I would tell her that she should not smoke because it is bad for her baby.

SECTION 6

PAGE 44

Preview the Article
Answers will vary. Sample answer: genetic screening; how traits are passed from parents to children; testing for inherited disorders; testing the unborn for genetic disorders
Relate to the Topic
Many answers are possible. Sample answer: I have my mother's nose and cheekbones and the same build as she does.

PAGE 46

1. no
2. yes

PAGE 47

1. fact
2. opinion; circle the word *feel*

1. dominant trait
2. traits
3. Genetics
4. heredity
5. recessive trait
6. a
7. dark hair, dark eyes
8. sickle cell anemia
9. Down syndrome
10. to help parents deal with possible inherited diseases and problems in their prospective children
11. **(2) amniocentesis** According to the article, this is a test performed during pregnancy.
12. **(3) two out of four** Two of the four boxes contain the dominant trait (H) for Huntington's. Therefore, the odds that a child will inherit the disorder are two out of four.
13. **(3) Some young people think it is better to be tested and know whether they will develop Huntington's in middle age.** The word *think* signals that this is an opinion.
14. three out of four, because three combinations include the dominant Huntington's trait, and one does not
15. Many answers are possible. Sample answer: Yes, because then we could prepare for any problems before the baby is born.

SECTION 7

PAGE 50

Preview the Article
Answers will vary. Sample answer: how people catch colds; parts of a virus and a bacterial cell
Relate to the Topic
Many answers are possible. Sample answer: I caught a bad cold from my son. My head was congested, my nose was running, and I had a headache. To feel better, I took decongestants and tried to rest.

PAGE 52

cell wall, cell membrane, genetic material, cytoplasm

PAGE 53

a

PAGES 54–55

1. e
2. c
3. b
4. a
5. d
6. b
7. a. virus
   b. virus
   c. virus, bacteria
8. b
9. a dose of a dead or weakened disease-causing agent that causes the body to form antibodies against the disease
10. a substance the body makes to fight disease
11. **(3) antibody** According to the diagram on page 53, the bacterial cell does not contain an antibody.
12. **(3) avoid people with colds** Since it's possible that colds are spread both by touch and by breathing air near people with colds, the best way to avoid colds is to avoid sick people.
13. **(1) they do not fight viruses** According to the article, antibiotics fight bacteria, not viruses, and colds and the flu are caused by viruses.
14. During the winter, people spend more time in small spaces indoors where it is easy to catch a cold or the flu from others nearby.
15. Many answers are possible. Sample answer: Try to stay away from people who are sick; wash hands frequently; avoid touching the face; eat well and exercise to improve fitness; get flu shots for older people in the family.

SECTION 8

PAGE 56

Preview the Article
Answers will vary. Sample answer: how plants are used to treat illness; parts of a plant, what plants certain medicines come from
Relate to the Topic
Many answers are possible. Sample answer: I eat plants—vegetables, fruits, and grains—every day. I use plants to make coffee and tea.

PAGE 58

a

PAGE 59

a

PAGES 60–61

1. f
2. a
3. d
4. b
5. e
6. c
7. by affecting the body's chemistry and by affecting disease-causing bacteria and viruses
8. a, c, d
9. to find out what they know about medicinal tropical plants
10. a, b
11. **(3) the chemical that works as a medicine** The paragraph contains the clue that the active chemical comes from the plant and that it has an effect on the cancer cells, bacteria, or viruses.
12. **(3) A typical seed plant has roots, stems, buds, leaves, flowers, and fruit.** The diagram illustrates a typical plant and shows its parts.
13. **(2) type of organism** Plant species are described as kinds of plants, so species must be kinds of organisms in general.
14. Many young people of the tropical rain forests are interested in modern culture, so they don't learn about rain forest plants. Also, the rain forest is being destroyed, which destroys plant species.
15. Many answers are possible. Sample answer: I used menthol in cough drops to relieve a cough.

SECTION 9

PAGE 62

Preview the Article
Answers will vary. Sample answer: how dolphins communicate by using whistles, echolocation, and language
Relate to the Topic
Many answers are possible. Sample answer: I saw dolphins perform at an aquarium show. They did tricks like jumping through hoops and balancing on their tails.

PAGE 64

clicks

PAGE 65

a

PAGES 66–67

1. mammals, language
2. sound waves
3. echolocation
4. density
5. Tyack invented the vocalight, a device that lights up when a dolphin makes a sound.
6. a unique sound that identifies that particular dolphin
7. a
8. a
9. **(3) mammals** Dolphins are not fish. According to the article, they are mammals.
10. **(4) a form of social communication.** Tyack inferred that Scotty had become quieter because Spray was no longer there.

11. **(1) have the ability to learn and think** Learning a simple language is evidence of the ability to learn and think, but it does not prove that dolphins use a language in the wild.

12. Many answers are possible. Sample answer: Yes, because they respond to humans the same way pets do.

13. Many answers are possible. Sample answer: I trained a dog to come, stay, and fetch a ball or stick by repeating the command and rewarding the dog when she obeyed it correctly. This shows that some animals can recognize words that refer to specific things.

SECTION 10

PAGE 68
Preview the Article
Answers will vary. Sample answer: the spread of the gypsy moth; the gypsy moth life cycle; and how to get rid of gypsy moths
Relate to the Topic
Many answers are possible. Sample answer: Baby: helpless, learned to walk and talk; child: learned a lot, played a lot; adolescent: grew up, understood more about the world; adult: became responsible for myself.

PAGE 70
1. pupa
2. egg, caterpillar, pupa

PAGE 71
1. about a month and a half
2. in July

PAGES 72–73
1. egg
2. pupa
3. caterpillar
4. adult
5. life cycle
6. A Frenchman brought gypsy moth eggs to the United States to use in the silk industry, and a few moths escaped.

7. It eats the leaves of certain trees, such as oak.
8. b
9. a
10. d
11. c
12. **(5) egg, caterpillar, pupa, adult** According to the life cycle diagram and the timeline, this is the order in which the stages of the life cycle take place.
13. **(1) egg** The longest segment on the timeline is that of the egg stage.
14. **(5) Soak the egg masses in kerosene, bleach, or ammonia.** According to the timeline, in March the gypsy moths are in the egg stage. Soaking them is one way to destroy them at that stage.
15. Many answers are possible. Some animals that look different at different stages of the life cycle include butterflies, mosquitoes, mayflies, frogs, and toads.
16. Many answers are possible. Sample answer: When we had ants in the house, we put an insecticide powder along doors and windows and in cupboards.

SECTION 11

PAGE 74
Preview the Article
Answers will vary. Sample answer: how much garbage we produce; what's in garbage; what happens to garbage in landfills and compost piles
Relate to the Topic
Many answers are possible. Sample answer: We have to separate out newspapers, bottles, and certain types of plastic and put these in a special recycling bin. Yard waste goes in special paper bags. Other garbage is put out in garbage pails. There are three separate collections for each of these types of garbage.

PAGE 76
1. 1970: about 45 million tons; 1995: about 80 million tons
2. none

PAGE 77

a

PAGES 78–79

1. degrades
2. inorganic
3. organic
4. decomposers
5. aerobic
6. a. organic
   b. inorganic
   c. organic
   d. inorganic
7. They all increased.
8. b
9. b
10. **(1) paper** The bar graph shows that in both 1970 and 1995, more paper was thrown out than any other type of garbage.
11. **(5) plastics** Plastics went from about 3 million tons to 19 million tons, about a sixfold increase.
12. **(1) vacuum-packing** Aerobic bacteria need oxygen to degrade organic material. In vacuum-packing, oxygen is removed to preserve the food.
13. Many answers are possible. Sample answer: paper: junk mail, catalogs, magazines, newspapers, business documents, tissues, paper towels, gift wrap. Possible ways to reduce paper in the waste stream are to use the backs of paper, recycle paper, get taken off the mailing lists of organizations that send out junk mail, etc.
14. Many answers are possible. Sample answer: I now recycle glass jars, newspapers, and some plastic containers.

SECTION 12

PAGE 80

Preview the Article
Answers will vary. Sample answer: what a tropical rain forest is; the carbon dioxide-oxygen cycle; where tropical rain forests are located
Relate to the Topic
Many answers are possible. Sample answer: I buy tropical fruits like bananas, pineapples, mangoes, and papayas.

PAGE 82

a

PAGE 83

a

PAGES 84–85

1. ecosystem
2. respiration
3. carbon dioxide–oxygen cycle
4. photosynthesis
5. tropical rain forests
6. Rice, bananas, coffee, and sugar first came from the rain forests.
7. a
8. farming, ranching, and logging
9. **(5) more photosynthesis** With fewer plants, there is less photosynthesis, not more.
10. **(1) increased** According to the article, burning fuel gives off carbon dioxide. So the increase in burning fuel has increased the amount of carbon dioxide in the air.
11. **(3) All tropical rain forests are located south of the equator.** According to the map, there are tropical rain forests both north and south of the equator.
12. Any three of the following reasons: Tropical rain forests have a wealth of plant and animal life. Tropical rain forests are the source of many medicines. Tropical rain forests are the source of many foods. Tropical rain forests help control the temperature of Earth. Tropical rain forests help add oxygen to the atmosphere.

13. Many answers are possible. Sample answer: I can buy rain forest products that are harvested without damaging the forest. I can refuse to buy furniture made from tropical woods.

SECTION 13

PAGE 86
Preview the Article
Answers will vary. Sample answer: the relationship of birds and dinosaurs; about feathers; about evolution
Relate to the Topic
Many answers are possible. Sample answer: Robins, crows, pigeons, geese, sparrows, blue jays

PAGE 88
b

PAGE 89
a

PAGES 90–91
1. mutation
2. adaptation
3. convergence
4. natural selection
5. evolution
6. The dinosaur fossils had feathers.
7. insulation; to attract females
8. a
9. **(2) are very different types of animals** Birds have feathers and lay eggs, bats are mammals and have fur, and butterflies are insects, so you can infer they are not closely related.
10. **(3) adaptation** According to the article, an adaptation is a change that permits an organism to better survive in its environment. Bacteria that are resistant to antibiotics have a better chance of surviving.
11. **(2) Human legs would gradually become weaker.** Through adaptation, as legs were used less, over generations of offspring they would become less important as a body part.

12. Many answers are possible. Sample answer: I think birds evolved from dinosaurs because there are so many structural similarities between them, including feathers, flexible wrists, wishbones, and air-filled skulls.
13. Many answers are possible. Sample answer: Yes. Before I read this article, I always thought of dinosaurs as slow, heavy creatures; now I realize that some were light (having hollow bones) and they may have been very fast, on their way to flight.

SCIENCE AT WORK

PAGE 93
1. **(4) hand weights**
2. **(2) He might get hurt from too much exercising.**
3. 1c, 2a, 3b

UNIT 1 REVIEW

PAGE 94
1. DNA
2. mitosis
3. **(3) the two new cells will have all the information they need** According to the article, DNA contains all the instructions the cell needs to live. This information is duplicated so that the cells produced by division will have all the instructions they need to live. Options 1 and 2 are incorrect because the parent cell has all its DNA and is finished growing by the time it divides. Option 4 is not true. Option 5 is incorrect because it doesn't matter to the cell if the chromosomes are easy to see.

PAGE 95
4. artery (The labels indicate that arteries carry blood to the lungs or the other parts of the body. Therefore, arteries are carrying blood away from the heart.)

5. left atrium

6. **(4) ventricle** The diagram shows that a ventricle has very thick walls when compared to an atrium, an artery, or a vein. Options 1–3 are incorrect because an artery, vein, or atrium has a thinner wall. Option 5 is incorrect because the walls are not all of the same thickness.

PAGE 96

7. antibodies

8. immune

9. **(3) identifying the virus that causes AIDS** Scientists have to identify the virus before they can do anything about it. Option 1 is incorrect because making the body attack the virus does not help in creating a vaccine. Options 2 and 5 are incorrect because you cannot weaken or kill something until you have identified it. Option 4 is incorrect because a vaccine does not contain antibodies.

PAGE 97

10. dominant

11. recessive

12. genetic material

13. **(3) both parents have the recessive genetic material for left-handedness** Traits are determined by pairs of genetic material, one type from each parent. From the parents' description, you can conclude that each parent has at least one type of dominant genetic material because each is right-handed. However, their left-handed child must have two types of recessive genetic material for left-handedness. Thus each parent must have passed on one of these types of recessive genetic material to the child.

PAGE 98

14. b

15. c

16. a

17. nitrogen-fixing bacteria

PAGE 99

18. food, shelter

19. protection

20. scavengers

21. **(1) A bird eats ticks that are on the back of an ox.** The bird gets food from this relationship, and the ox gets rid of parasites. Options 2 and 3 are incorrect because the only living species involved is the ant. Option 4 is incorrect because the lions don't get anything from the wild dog. Option 5 is incorrect because the two animals in the relationship are the same species, and mutualism is a relationship between two different species.

SCIENCE CONNECTION

PAGE 101

1. **(3) has a positive impact on an aging body**

2. **(4) Join the Newton Athletic Club now to improve your health.**

3. any three of these: Bone and muscle mass decreases. Heart pumping function decreases significantly. Breathing capacity decreases. Metabolism decreases.

4. improve body strength, slow down the loss of bone and muscle mass, keep the body flexible, heart and lungs work better, helps control weight

5. Many answers are possible. Sample answer: I'm a young person now. I'm only 27. I have two children, a job, and schoolwork. I'm afraid I don't get enough exercise. I think I should be getting more exercise so I won't have big physical problems when I'm older. I believe if I started a regular exercise program, my body would feel better and so would my mind. I would probably get some more energy, too. I think I could begin a regular walking exercise program. I could walk during my lunch hour or I could take my children on a half-hour walk after school.

UNIT 2: EARTH AND SPACE SCIENCE

SECTION 14

PAGE 104
Preview the Article
Answers will vary. Sample answer: how to read a weather map; what weather maps show
Relate to the Topic
Many answers are possible. Sample answer: An ice storm covered everything with a layer of ice. Although it looked beautiful, the weight of the ice broke tree branches and brought down power lines.

PAGE 106
1. a
2. a
3. b

PAGE 107
1. b
2. a

PAGES 108–109
1. air mass
2. front
3. forecast
4. meteorologists
5. weather map
6. stationary front
7. precipitation
8. a, c
9. b, c
10. a, d
11. b, d
12. from west to east
13. There are too many factors affecting the weather over a long period of time for accurate predictions to be possible.
14. **(3) stationary front** The map keys show that alternating triangles and half circles pointing in opposite directions are the symbols for a stationary front.

15. **(4) New York** Of all these cities, New York has the hottest weather with temperatures in the 100s—definitely a beach day.
16. **(1) occasional showers, high temperature in the 60s** Salt Lake City is in the middle of an air mass. In this air mass, temperatures are in the 60s and 70s and there are showers. Even if the cold front moves, the air mass is not likely to pass Salt Lake City by the next day.
17. The cold air mass in the west is probably a maritime polar air mass. It is cool, indicating polar. And it is moist (showers), indicating maritime origins.
18. Many answers are possible. Sample answer: The weather is cold and clear, so there is probably a continental polar air mass over the area.

SECTION 15

PAGE 110
Preview the Article
Answers will vary. Sample answer: how the atmosphere warms the Earth; whether the Earth is getting warmer; what can be done about global warming
Relate to the Topic
Many answers are possible. Sample answer: We use oil to heat the house; gas to cook; and gasoline in the car.

PAGE 112
1. a
2. a

PAGE 113
1. all over the world
2. a building (house) with plants (green)

PAGES 114–115
1. atmosphere
2. global warming
3. infrared radiation
4. greenhouse effect
5. fossil fuels

6. Radiant energy warms you when you sit out in the sun.

7. The greenhouse effect traps heat in the atmosphere the way a blanket traps heat.

8. carbon dioxide, ozone, chlorofluorocarbons (CFCs), methane, and nitrogen oxide

9. to reduce emissions of greenhouse gases

10. **(2) using light to combine substances into food** During photosynthesis, plants use light energy to combine carbon dioxide and water to produce food.

11. **(1) Trees take in carbon dioxide during the process of photosynthesis.** This statement explains how planting trees could reduce emissions of greenhouse gases. Options 2, 3, and 5 are true, but do not link statements (a) and (b); option 4 is not true.

12. **(3) The ice caps at the North and South poles would melt.** More water in the oceans would raise sea level.

13. Industrialized nations have more factories, trucks, cars, and power plants, all of which produce greenhouse gases.

14. Many answers are possible. Sample answer: Reduce energy consumption in the home and car. Recycle as much as possible. Plant some trees.

SECTION 16

PAGE 116

Preview the Article

Answers will vary. Sample answer: how water is transported; comparison of amounts of fresh water and salt water on Earth; where California's water comes from

Relate to the Topic

Many answers are possible. Sample answer: Our water comes from a reservoir in the next town. Our landlord pays for the building's water, and the amount is included in the rent.

PAGE 118

a

PAGE 119

1. opinion

2. fact

PAGES 120–121

1. renewable resource

2. groundwater

3. resource

4. glaciers

5. water cycle

6. from the mountains in the northern part of the state and from other states

7. rivers, lakes, and groundwater

8. Not enough precipitation falls on an area.

9. Any two of the following: take shorter showers; fix leaky faucets; install low-water-flow toilets; run the washing machine and dishwasher only with full loads; if doing dishes by hand, don't run the water continuously; turn off water when shaving or brushing teeth

10. **(1) there was not enough precipitation in the northern part of the state** Since California gets most of its water from the northern mountains, dry weather there will result in a statewide drought.

11. **(4) Some areas get too much precipitation, while others do not get enough.** According to the article, water shortages are caused by the uneven distribution of rainfall in the United States. Even though there may be plenty of water on average, there is not enough in specific areas, depending in part on their population and water use.

12. **(1) People should not live in areas that do not have an adequate supply of water.** This is an opinion that clearly many people do not share, since the population of many regions is far more than local water resources can supply.

13. Many answers are possible. Sample answer: Taking the salt out of seawater is one alternative.

14. Many answers are possible. Sample answer: I turn off the water when brushing my teeth and I water the grass only once a week.

SECTION 17

PAGE 122
Preview the Article
Answers will vary. Sample answer: about the outer planets: Jupiter, Saturn, Uranus, and Neptune
Relate to the Topic
Many answers are possible. Sample answer: No. The risks of a mission to an outer planet are too great and I would be away too long.

PAGE 124
1. 16
2. 84 years

PAGE 125
a

PAGES 126–127
1. outer planets
2. space probes
3. solar system
4. inner planets
5. c
6. b
7. e
8. a
9. d
10. Mercury, Venus, Earth, Mars, Jupiter, Saturn, Uranus, Neptune, and Pluto
11. The mission was to send photos and information about the outer planets.
12. its rings
13. **(3) Uranus** According to the table, Saturn is 892 million miles from the sun. Uranus is 1,790 million miles from the sun. This distance is about twice as far from the sun as Saturn.
14. **(3) Saturn** According to the table, Saturn has 18 known moons, which is more than the other planets listed in the table.

15. **(5) The cameras could be pointed at specific objects.** This is the only option that follows logically from the fact that the camera platforms were movable.
16. Many answers are possible. Sample answer: It is not practical because of the distances involved, the length of time required, and the hostile environments of the outer planets.
17. Many answers are possible. Sample answer: Yes, because eventually we may need to use resources found in other parts of the solar system.

SECTION 18

PAGE 128
Preview the Article
Answers will vary. Sample answer: what *Pathfinder* and *Sojourner* found on Mars; how Mars is similar to Earth; why Mars is likely to be the first planet visited by humans
Relate to the Topic
Many answers are possible. Sample answer: I have seen Mars in the night sky. It looks like a reddish star.

PAGE 130
b

PAGE 131
a

PAGES 132-133
1. c
2. e
3. a
4. d
5. b
6. to gather information by landing something safely—and cheaply—on Mars
7. Any two of the following: shaped by water, containing silicon, conglomerates
8. a
9. a, c, d, f
10. lack of oxygen to breathe and water to drink

11. **(5) rocky surface that would make getting around difficult** Of all the choices, this one is not as dangerous to humans as the others. The other choices are life-threatening, so people would have to be sheltered from the environment.

12. **(4) days about 24 hours long** Both planets have days that last about 24 hours.

13. **(3) has little surface water and Earth has a lot of surface water** This is one of the chief differences between Mars and Earth.

14. The air bags on *Pathfinder* and in a car are similar in that they inflate to protect against the force of impact. They are different in that the *Pathfinder* air bags inflated before impact and surrounded and protected the whole vehicle, but an automobile air bag inflates inside the car upon impact, protecting driver and passenger.

15. Many answers are possible. Sample answer: People have always been interested in Mars because of its distinctive red color and because so many legends and stories have been made up about it over the centuries. Also, *Sojourner* was an ingenious and attractive little robot, and people enjoyed the view from its cameras.

SCIENCE AT WORK

PAGE 135

1. **(4) sand and rock dust**
2. **(3) to make sure rain and splash water don't collect around the pool**
3. Many answers are possible. A sample answer is written below.
   We have a new apartment building going up in my neighborhood. There are construction workers there all the time. First I saw them level the ground and then I saw them dig the hole for the foundation. Now they are framing the building. They are nailing lumber to form the skeleton for the building. It is really neat to watch this part of the process.

There have been many safety issues for them to consider. At the beginning of the project they used huge, noisy machines to do most of the work. They had to be careful that nobody was in the way of the machines or what they were digging or carrying. Now, they must be careful when they're using hammers or nail guns. They must also be mindful of keeping their balance, as many workers are high up on the structure.

UNIT 2 REVIEW

PAGE 136

1. 90s
2. showers
3. **(2) hot, with showers** The map shows diagonal lines along the stationary front. According to the key, these lines indicate showers. The map also shows temperatures in the 80s, which is hot. Option 1 is incorrect because the map shows rain, not sunshine. Options 2 and 3 are incorrect because it is not cold along the front. Option 5 is incorrect because the map gives no indication of winds.

PAGE 137

4. oxygen
5. Ultraviolet
6. **(5) It is made up of CFCs.** According to the article, CFCs are damaging the ozone layer, but they do not form any part of it. Options 1–4 are incorrect because these are true statements that can be found in the article.
7. **(3) skin cancer** According to the article, more ultraviolet rays reach Earth as CFCs destroy the ozone layer. These rays cause skin cancer. Options 1 and 2 are incorrect because poisoning is not part of the problem caused by CFCs. Option 4 is incorrect because ultraviolet rays do cause sunburn, but people do not usually die of sunburn. Option 5 is incorrect because only Option 3 is correct.
8. 4

PAGE 138

9. continental shelf

10. **(4) waters of the continental-shelf region**
According to the article, these waters have the richest fishing. Options 1 and 2 are incorrect because nodules, which are found only on the ocean basin, are mineral resources. They are not food resources. Options 3 and 5 are incorrect because these waters are not as rich a food resource as the waters of the continental shelf.

11. **(5) coal** Options 1 and 4 are incorrect because these are resources from the continental shelf. Options 2 and 3 are incorrect because these minerals make up the nodules found on the ocean basin.

12. **(3) is shallow enough for sunlight to reach its bottom**

PAGE 139

13. sun

14. core

15. **(2) light** According to the article, most of the sun's energy is changed into light. A solar-powered calculator works only when placed in the light. Option 1 is incorrect because heat is not the form of energy that makes the calculator work. Option 3 is incorrect because nuclear reactions happen in the sun, but the sun does not cause them to happen on Earth. Options 4 and 5 are incorrect because they are not energy from the sun.

Science Extension Activity

Many answers are possible. Sample answer for a hurricane:

Bring outdoor furniture and objects indoors.

Tape up windows to prevent breakage.

Stock up on food and water for a few days.

Stock up on flashlights, batteries, and candles in case of power outage.

Follow instructions about evacuating, if this is recommended.

SCIENCE CONNECTION

PAGE 141

1. (3) 4 (Europe)
2. (2) 45
3. (2) gravity, temperature, and pressure are more difficult to control on Earth.
4. Belgium–4; Brazil–2; Canada–1; Denmark–4; France–4; Germany–4; Italy–4; Japan–5; Netherlands–4; Norway–4; Russia–5; Spain–4; Sweden–4; Switzerland–4; United Kingdom–4; United States–1

UNIT 3: CHEMISTRY

SECTION 19

PAGE 144

Preview the Article

Answers will vary. Sample answer: the chemistry of cleaning, what substances and mixtures are, chemical symbols and formulas, and chemical reactions

Relate to the Topic

Many answers are possible. Sample answer: bleach, ammonia, dishwashing liquid, detergent, soap

PAGE 146

1. nitrogen and hydrogen
2. one nitrogen atom and three hydrogen atoms

PAGE 147

1. a, c
2. b, c, d
3. four
4. c

PAGES 148–149

1. element
2. mixture
3. chemical reaction
4. substance
5. atom

6. compound
7. b
8. a
9. b
10. a
11. b
12. **(4) hydrogen and oxygen** According to the article, H is the chemical symbol for the element hydrogen and O is the chemical symbol for the element oxygen.
13. **(2) magnesium sulfide** According to the article, when a compound is made of just two elements, the suffix *-ide* is added to the root of the second element.
14. **(4) oxygen** According to the article, the suffix *-ate* means that the compound has oxygen.
15. Paint prevents the oxygen in the air from reacting with the iron in the steel.
16. Many answers are possible. Sample answer: chlorine bleach ($NaOCl$), to brighten white fabrics; ammonia (NH_3), to wash floors; baking soda ($NaHCO_3$), to clean porcelain surfaces (stovetop, sink)

SECTION 20

PAGE 150

Preview the Article
Answers will vary. Sample answer: changes from solid to liquid, like melting; and changes that take place when food is cooked

Relate to the Topic
Many answers are possible. Sample answer: My favorite cooked food is mashed potatoes. When the potatoes are raw, they are very firm solids. After you boil them, they soften and become hot. Mashing them breaks them down into smaller particles and so makes them even softer.

PAGE 152

a

PAGE 153

1. chemical change
2. physical change

PAGES 154–155

1. solid
2. liquid
3. gas
4. physical change
5. chemical change
6. solid—ice; liquid—water; gas—water vapor or steam
7. b
8. d
9. a
10. c
11. physical change
12. chemical change
13. **(4) Chemical and Physical Changes in Cooking** This title covers all the topics discussed in the article. Options 1–3 and 5 are too specific. They cover only parts of the article, so they are incorrect.
14. **(4) a physical change** The chocolate melted, a physical change from solid to liquid.
15. **(4) baking a cake** Baking a cake involves chemical changes in the liquid batter as it sets. Options 1–3 and 5 are all physical changes, so they are incorrect.
16. Many answers are possible. Sample answers: freezing leftovers, boiling water, melting chocolate, defrosting a turkey, melting snow, dew
17. Many answers are possible. Sample answer: I made pancake batter and cooked the pancakes on a griddle. A chemical change took place as the batter set into solid pancakes. I put butter on top and it melted, a physical change.

SECTION 21

PAGE 156

Preview the Article
Answers will vary. Sample answer: what a mixture is, what a solution is, what makes solutions form more quickly, the relationship of solubility and temperature
Relate to the Topic
Many answers are possible. Sample answer: orange juice

PAGE 158

1. b
2. b

PAGE 159

1. a
2. b

PAGES 160–161

1. solution
2. Distillation
3. solubility
4. solute
5. solvent
6. solution
7. mixture
8. solution
9. a
10. b
11. **(4) A solvent is present in a greater amount in a solution, and a solute in a lesser amount.** When two substances are mixed together in a solution, the solvent is the substance of which there is more.
12. **(3) They are all mixtures.** Even though these substances are in different states of matter, they all consist of mixtures of various substances.
13. **(4) 6 ounces** The answer to this question can be found by reading the solubility curve of sucrose (sugar) on the graph on page 159.

14. The water is the solvent, and the grape powder and sugar are the solutes. When I added water to the solutes, very little dissolved at first. Stirring for a few minutes made the grape powder and sugar mix evenly throughout the water.
15. Many answers are possible. Sample answer: I left a soft drink out on the counter and when I returned for it a few hours later, all the fizz was gone. The carbon dioxide gas that had been in solution had escaped.

SECTION 22

PAGE 162

Preview the Article
Answers will vary. Sample answer: what the by-products of combustion are, what a combustion reaction is, how a combustion heater works, indoor air pollution, and safety when using small heaters
Relate to the Topic
Many answers are possible. Sample answer: Once a potholder I was using caught fire on the stove. I put out the fire by dropping it in the sink and turning on the water.

PAGE 164

b

PAGE 165

a

PAGES 166–167

1. combustion
2. hydrocarbon
3. activation energy
4. kindling temperature
5. oxygen
6. a
7. b, c, e
8. a

9. **(4) More fires are caused by small heaters than by built-in heating systems.** Because small heaters are portable, they are more likely to be placed near flammable objects. Also, they are more likely to be knocked over. In both situations, a fire is possible. Built-in heating systems do not get as hot and are not subject to being knocked over.

10. **(2) The pollutants released by incomplete combustion would eventually overcome the people in the room.** According to the article, combustion uses oxygen. When the oxygen in the room gets low, people will have trouble breathing. In addition, combustion will be incomplete, producing deadly carbon monoxide and other pollutants.

11. **(2) Over time, people have burned fuels for many purposes.** The first paragraph gives an overview of people's use of combustion over the course of history. The other choices are too specific.

12. Many answers are possible. Sample answers: Heaters should be placed out of traffic and away from anything that might catch fire. Keep doors or a window open when using a combustion heater. Use high-quality kerosene in a portable heater.

13. Many answers are possible. Sample answer: Our car has a combustion engine that uses gasoline as fuel, and it produces pollutants.

SECTION 23

PAGE 168

Preview the Article
Answers will vary. Sample answer: what a nuclear power plant looks like, how it works, and what a fission chain reaction is
Relate to the Topic
Many answers are possible. Sample answer: Many people oppose having nuclear power plants in their areas because they fear accidents that might spread dangerous radioactive waste.

PAGE 170
b

PAGE 171

4. Heat from the coolant boils water, producing steam.
5. Steam turns a turbine, making electricity.
3. Coolant carries heat into a heat exchanger.

PAGES 172–173

1. Radioactive decay
2. fission
3. Nuclear energy
4. nuclear reaction
5. chain reaction
6. protons, neutrons
7. a
8. b
9. a
10. **(3) the splitting of an atom's nucleus** This is the definition given in the glossary. The other choices are incorrect.
11. **(4) boils water, producing steam** According to the diagram, the coolant transfers the heat produced by the fission chain reaction to the heat exchanger, where it is used to boil water, producing steam.
12. **(1) A neutron splits a target nucleus.** According to the diagram on page 170, the first step in a fission chain reaction is splitting the nucleus of an atom with a neutron.
13. Many answers are possible. Sample answers: The cooling system is designed to prevent the reactor core from overheating. The containment building has thick concrete walls designed to absorb radiation from the reactor core and prevent it from escaping into the environment.
14. Answers will vary depending on the region. Sample answer: Yes, some of our electricity is produced by nuclear power. People in the area take it for granted and do not worry about accidents.

SCIENCE AT WORK

PAGE 175

1. **(3) Body Plus**
2. **(4) Free and Clean**
3. **(5) Hair Today, Hair Dew, Wind Blown, Free and Clean, Body Plus**

UNIT 3 REVIEW

PAGE 176

1. mixture
2. graphite, clay
3. **(5) all of the above** According to the article, increasing the amount of clay makes the pencil harder. Harder pencils are given higher numbers. The lines made by harder pencils are finer and smudge less.

PAGE 177

4. exothermic reaction
5. endothermic reaction
6. chemical reaction
7. combustion
8. **(4) photosynthesis in a plant** According to the article, photosynthesis is an example of an endothermic reaction. All of the other options are incorrect because these reactions are exothermic and give off energy.

PAGE 178

9. **(5) oxygen, fuel, and heat.** According to the article, these are the three requirements for combustion. Options 1 and 2 are incorrect because carbon dioxide puts out fires instead of keeping them burning. Options 3 and 4 are incorrect because they are incomplete answers.

10. **(2) removing oxygen** According to the article, small fires can be smothered. Throwing a heavy blanket on a fire would smother it. Option 1 is incorrect because the blanket does not add carbon dioxide. Options 3 and 4 are incorrect because the fuel and heat will be under the blanket. Option 5 is incorrect because carbon dioxide is not needed by a fire.

PAGE 179

11. nuclear fusion
12. sun
13. helium

Science Extension

Many answers are possible. Sample answer: Mixtures: pudding, stew, chili, salsa, mustard, salad dressing; Solutions: milk, iced tea, soda, popsicles, kids' fruit drink

SCIENCE CONNECTION

PAGE 181

1. **(2) larger animals eating smaller animals and plants**
2. **(1) All toxins in the environment are man-made.**
3. **(3) India**
4. Toxin-Related Disasters: Love Canal, Union Carbide, *Exxon Valdez*, Salmon carry DDT and PCBs into the Arctic, DDT and PCBs found in glacial waters; Progress Against Toxins: European and North American nations agree to reduce emissions, European nations reduced acid rain problems, Norwegian scientists conduct polar bear studies

UNIT 4: PHYSICS

SECTION 24

PAGE 184
Preview the Article
Answers will vary. Sample answer: how a bicycle works, about force and work, about simple and compound machines
Relate to the Article
Many answers are possible. Sample answer: I used an old black bike with 3 gears.

PAGE 186
a

PAGE 187
a

PAGES 188–189
1. force
2. simple machine
3. compound machine
4. mechanical advantage
5. work
6. a
7. a
8. a
9. b
10. a
11. c
12. **(2) make work easier** According to the article, a machine is a device that helps you do work by multiplying your effort. The more the machine multiplies your effort (in other words, the greater the machine's mechanical advantage), the less effort you have to apply to get a certain amount of work done. Thus, work becomes easier for you.
13. **(1) friction** According to the article, friction is a force between surfaces that touch. In order to overcome friction, you must use extra effort.
14. **(5) no work will be done** If the resistance is larger than the effort, there will be no motion, and in physics, no motion means no work.
15. Standing on the pedals adds to your effort force because you can use your weight—the downward pull of gravity—to help move the pedal.
16. Many answers are possible. Sample answer: I went bike riding in the neighborhood and when I hit a bump in the street, the chain slipped off the gears. I had to stop and put it back on before I could go on.

SECTION 25

PAGE 190
Preview the Article
Answers will vary. Sample answer: what speed has to do with momentum, what energy is, how momentum is transferred, what corking bats means
Relate to the Article
Many answers are possible. Sample answer: I play golf, billiards, and table tennis. All three sports involve a transfer of momentum.

PAGE 192
a

PAGE 193
1. fact
2. opinion

PAGES 194–195
1. collision
2. momentum
3. elastic
4. Energy
5. a
6. a, b, c
7. a
8. b
9. a, b, c
10. **(5) a standing object will move if enough momentum is transferred** This is the only conclusion supported by the facts in the article.

11. **(3) A corked bat is lighter than a solid bat.**
This statement represents a measurement, which is a fact. The other options are statements of what people believe, think, or feel. These words indicate opinions.

12. **(4) are not very elastic** If cars were elastic, they would spring back into shape after a collision. Instead, they remain crumpled and dented.

13. The sport utility vehicle has more momentum because it is a much heavier car than the compact car.

14. Many answers are possible. Sample answer: I was in a car on a snowy day, going very slowly around a corner, when the car in front of me braked sharply. I too braked, but the snowplow behind me did not stop in time. The blade of the plow hit the trunk lid of my car, denting it. Luckily, we were all going so slowly that not much momentum was involved and no one was hurt.

SECTION 26

PAGE 196
Preview the Article
Answers will vary. Sample answer: how Deep Blue plays chess, what electronic components and microprocessors are, about the second match with Deep Blue
Relate to the Article
Many answers are possible. Sample answer: I sometimes play solitaire on the computer. The computer deals the cards, and I try to win the game. This involves stacking the cards in the proper order. If I get stuck, I can restart the same game and try again. The computer keeps track of my wins and losses.

PAGE 198
a

PAGE 199
a

PAGES 200–201
1. e
2. d
3. b
4. a
5. c
6. a
7. a device that controls the flow of electricity, for example, a transistor
8. a
9. b
10. b
11. **(4) Kasparov's human emotions interfered with his ability to play.** The author states that Kasparov was rattled by Deep Blue's change in strategy, so rattled that he even gave up during the last game. You can infer that his emotions were clouding his thinking.
12. **(5) became much smaller** The microprocessor was able to fit the complex circuits of a central processing unit on a single chip. This decreased the size of the computer dramatically.
13. **(3) It enabled Deep Blue's playing to be adjusted between games.** That was what the software was designed to do, and in fact the Deep Blue team changed its playing between games 1 and 2.
14. Many answers are possible. Sample answers: microwave oven, remote control, TV, CD player, computer, car, stereo system
15. Many answers are possible. Sample answer: No, because Deep Blue was basically an enormous calculator. The ability it had to evaluate chess moves was designed into its system by human beings.

SECTION 27

PAGE 202
Preview the Article

Answers will vary. Sample answer: how lasers are used in cosmetic surgery, the difference between ordinary light and laser light, how a laser works

Relate to the Article

Many answers are possible. Sample answer: I would have a surgical scar removed because it is unattractive.

PAGE 204
1. b
2. a

PAGE 205
a

PAGES 206–207
1. Light
2. frequency
3. wavelength
4. laser
5. b
6. They are all forms of energy that travel in waves.
7. a
8. a
9. a
10. **(4) distance between the top of one wave and the top of the next** The label "Wavelength" on the diagram points to the distance between the tops of two waves.
11. **(1) The atoms in the tube absorb the energy.** By looking at the diagram and reading the description of how a laser works, you can tell that the next step after the application of energy is its absorption by the atoms in the tube.
12. **(3) reflect the light back and forth** The arrows in the tube show the light reflecting back and forth and the label describes this as well.
13. Two treatments for the dyes in the tattoo, one for the blue and one for the red.
14. Many answers are possible. Sample answer: Yes, I would try the laser, because I don't like the idea of chemicals eating into my skin.

SCIENCE AT WORK

PAGE 209
1. **(3) spray foam**
2. **(5) foil insulation**
3. Sample answer: It would be a good idea to install insulation material under the floor between the room and the garage because garages are not usually heated. Therefore, when the outside temperature is cold and you want the room to stay warm, the insulation material would limit the amount of heated air escaping through the floor into the garage. If the room were being cooled by air conditioning, the insulation material would block the passage of warm air from the garage into the air-conditioned room.

UNIT 4 REVIEW

PAGE 210
1. inclined plane or ramp
2. Friction
3. **(4) pushing a wheeled 75-pound cart up a ramp three feet long** Options 1, 2, and 5 are incorrect because they involve lifting, which takes more effort force than using an inclined plane. Option 3 is incorrect because friction increases the resistance; thus you need more force to push a box than a wheeled cart.

4. **(3) weight and speed** According to the article, momentum depends on both weight and speed. Options 1 and 2 are incorrect because direction does not affect momentum. Options 4 and 5 are incorrect because how far the object has moved does not affect momentum.

5. **(1) Its momentum increases as the speed increases.** As the rock rolls down a hill, it moves faster. The faster it moves, the more momentum it has. Option 2 is incorrect because momentum does not decrease. Options 3 and 4 are incorrect because the rock does not get heavier. Option 5 is incorrect because the momentum does change.

PAGE 212

6. Sound

7. amplitude

8. **(2) high amplitude and short wavelength** The amplitude determines the loudness of the sound. The higher the amplitude, the louder the sound. The wavelength determines if the sound is high or low in pitch. The shorter the wavelength, the higher the pitch.

9. **(3) The wavelength will be longer and the amplitude lower.** The article says that lower pitches have longer wavelengths. Also, as sounds get softer, the amplitude of their waves gets lower.

PAGE 213

10. magnet

11. **(5) a compact disc** According to the article, a compact disc does not have a magnetic pattern, so it will not be damaged by the EM field of the metal detector. All other options have magnetic patterns and will be damaged.

Science Extension

Many answers are possible. Sample answers:
  Inclined plane: driveway, door stop, ax
  Lever: bottle opener, hammer, tweezers, nutcracker, crowbar, balance
  Wheel and axle: screwdriver, steering wheel, car wheel, wrench, faucet
  Gears: can opener, bicycle gears, salad spinner, car, mechanical clock, egg beater

SCIENCE CONNECTION

PAGE 215

1. **(1) is warmed by the sun and expands.**

2. **(2) 8 miles**

3. **(4) fall because the gas molecules move closer together**

4. **(3) 1,500**

POSTTEST

PAGE 216

1. observation

2. hypothesis

3. experiment

4. conclusions

5. scientific methods

PAGE 217

6. **(2) host cell has the raw materials for making viruses** According to the article, the virus does not have raw materials of its own, so it depends on the host cell for these things. Options 1 and 3 are incorrect because the virus has the genetic material but not any raw materials. Options 4 and 5 are incorrect. The genetic material of the host cell cannot make viruses because it is different from the genetic material of the virus.

7. **(4) dies.** The article states that the cell breaks open. The diagram shows that the cell is destroyed when this happens. Therefore, the cell dies. Option 1 is incorrect because cells do not turn into viruses. Options 2, 3, and 5 are incorrect because the cell is too badly damaged when it breaks open to return to its original form and produce anything more.

PAGE 218

8. incomplete metamorphosis

9. **(1) The adult is larger than the nymph.** The diagram clearly shows this. Option 2 is incorrect because it has nothing to do with the appearance of the praying mantis. The diagram shows that Options 3 and 4 are incorrect. Option 5 is incorrect because neither has an egg mass.

PAGE 219

10. predator

11. prey

12. **(1) there would be more hares** If many predators are removed, it becomes easier for the prey to survive, so there would be more hares. Option 2 is incorrect because it is the opposite of what would happen. Option 3 is incorrect because the loss of wolves would affect the hares first. If there were more hares, there would be more, not fewer, lynxes. Options 4 and 5 are incorrect because a disease that affects wolves might not affect the hares or the lynxes.

PAGE 220

13. **(5) Photosynthesis is the reverse of respiration.** According to the article, the substances produced by photosynthesis are used in respiration. The substances produced in respiration are used in photosynthesis. Option 1 is incorrect because these reactions are not the same. Option 2 is incorrect because only respiration needs oxygen. Option 3 is incorrect because only photosynthesis needs sunlight. Option 4 is incorrect because photosynthesis does not take place in animals.

14. **(3) food** Animals get both food and oxygen from plants, but only food is taken in through eating. Option 1 is incorrect because animals do not get carbon dioxide from plants. Plants get carbon dioxide from animals. Option 2 is incorrect because animals get oxygen by breathing, not by eating. Option 4 is incorrect because sunlight can come only from the sun. Option 5 is incorrect because animals do not get air from plants.

15. **(4) oxygen** According to the article, in respiration, plants use oxygen and sugar. Options 1–3 are incorrect because carbon dioxide, water, and sunlight are used in photosynthesis. Option 5 is incorrect because bacteria do not play a role in plant respiration.

PAGE 221

16. agriculture

17. 500

18. decreased

19. **(1) increased farm runoff** According to the article, one of the potential problems for water use in the United States is pollution from farm runoff, which contains animal wastes, chemical pesticides, and fertilizers.

PAGE 222

20. asteroid or minor planet
21. Neptune
22. **(3) Pluto's orbit is very irregular.**
    According to the article, Pluto's strange
    orbit sets it apart from the major planets.
    All the other choices are characteristics
    similar to those of the major planets.

PAGE 223

23. oxidation
24. **(3) The plastic wrap keeps the metal away
    from oxygen.** According to the article,
    oxidation takes place when a metal reacts
    with oxygen. Keeping these substances apart
    keeps the reaction from taking place.
    Options 1 and 2 are incorrect because
    keeping the metal warm or dry does not stop
    oxidation. Options 4 and 5 are incorrect
    because rust and copper do not have
    anything to do with the tarnishing of silver.
25. **(5) silver chloride** This is the only
    compound named that does not contain
    the word *oxide*. All other options are oxides,
    compounds formed by oxidation.

PAGE 224

26. a
27. b
28. c
29. b
30. a
31. b
32. **(1) vinegar, water, soap, lye** Vinegar is the
    only acid. So it has the lowest pH and must
    be listed first. Water is the only neutral
    substance, and has a pH of 7, so it must be
    listed second. The two remaining
    substances are bases. Soap, which is the
    weaker base, must be listed before lye, the
    stronger base, which has a higher pH. The
    other options are incorrect because they are
    not in the correct order.

PAGE 225

33. microprocessor
34. chip, chip
35. **(5) larger size** The new chip is smaller, not
    larger, than the chips it replaces, allowing
    for greater miniaturization and efficiency.

Glossary

activation energy the energy necessary to start a chemical reaction

adaptation a trait that makes a plant or an animal better able to live in its environment

adult the stage of an organism's life cycle in which it is fully grown and developed

aerobic needing oxygen to live

air mass a large body of air with similar temperature and moisture

amniocentesis a test performed on pregnant women that detects certain birth disorders

amplitude the height of a wave

antibiotic a drug that fights bacteria

antibody a protein made by white blood cells that attacks and kills invading germs

antigen a foreign protein

aqueduct a pipe that carries water from a reservoir

artery a large blood vessel that carries blood away from the heart to parts of the body

atmosphere the air around us

atom the smallest particle of an element

bacteria simple one-celled organisms

bar graph a type of illustration that is used to compare sets of information

bark the woody outer part of a plant stem

basal cell skin cancer a type of slow-growing cancer that often appears on the hands or face as an open sore, reddish patch, mole, or scar

biome a large region with a certain climate and certain living things

boiling the rapid change of matter from a liquid to a gas

bud on a plant, areas of growth that develop into leaves and flowers

carbon dioxide–oxygen cycle a process in which plants use carbon dioxide given off by other living things and make oxygen, which is in turn used by the other living things

caterpillar the wormlike stage in the life cycle of a butterfly or moth

cause something that makes another thing happen

cell the smallest unit of a living thing that can carry on life processes

cell membrane a layer around the cell that controls what can enter or leave the cell

chain reaction a reaction that keeps itself going

chemical change a change in the property of matter. A chemical change makes new substances.

chemical equation a statement that shows the reactants and products of a reaction

chemical formula a group of symbols used to describe a compound (example: H_2O is the chemical formula for water)

chemical reaction a process in which elements or compounds are changed into other substances

chemical symbol a kind of shorthand that chemists use in which one or two letters stand for an element

chemistry the study of matter and its changes

cholesterol a fatlike substance found in all animals

chromosome a strand of genetic material, or DNA

circle graph a graph used to show parts of a whole; also known as a pie chart

classifying grouping things that are similar to help understand how they work

collision the result of a moving object striking another object

combustion the chemical change also known as burning, in which oxygen reacts with fuel to create light and heat

compare to tell how things are alike

composting the breaking down of organic material in the soil by aerobic bacteria, fungi, insects, and worms

compound two or more elements combined chemically

compound machine a machine made up of two or more simple machines

conclusion a logical judgment based on facts

condensation the change from a gas to a liquid

conglomerate a type of sedimentary rock formed from large pebbles and stones

context surrounding material; you can often figure out the meaning of an unknown word by looking at its context—the rest of the words in the sentence

continental polar air mass a cold, dry air mass; for example, one that forms over Canada and the northern United States

continental shelf the nearly flat area of the ocean bottom where the ocean meets the continent

continental slope the sloping area that extends from the continental shelf to the ocean basin

continental tropical air mass a warm, dry air mass; for example, one that forms over the southwestern United States

contrast to tell how things are different

control group in an experiment, a group that is similar to the experimental group except for one feature

convergence the independent evolution of similar parts of unrelated organisms as adaptations to the environment (example: wings in bats, birds, and butterflies)

core the center of something such as the sun or Earth

crust top rocky layer of Earth

cytoplasm a jellylike material that makes up most of a cell

decomposer a living thing that breaks down organic material

degrade to break down

density the quantity of matter in a given unit of volume

details small pieces of information that explain or support the main idea

diagram a drawing that often shows steps in a process with arrows showing how one step leads to another

diode an electronic device that allows current to flow in one direction only

distillation the process for separating liquid mixtures

DNA the genetic material found in chromosomes

dominant trait a trait that can hide a recessive trait

Down syndrome a disorder caused by an extra chromosome. Children born with Down syndrome are mildly to severely mentally retarded and may also have other health problems.

Earth and space science the study of Earth and the universe

echolocation in certain animals, such as dolphins and bats, a system in which sound waves are sent out and their echoes interpreted to determine the direction and distance of objects

ecosystem an area in which living and nonliving things interact

effect something that happens as a result of a cause

effort the force that is being used to do work

egg in animals, the female reproductive cell

egg mass a clump of eggs

elastic able to be stretched or compressed and then returned to its original shape

electromagnetic field (EM field) the energy field around and caused by an electric current

electron a particle with a negative electrical charge that makes up atoms

electronics a branch of engineering concerned with devices that use electric current

element a substance that cannot be broken down into other substances by ordinary means, such as heating or crushing

embryo an organism in the early stages of development; a developing baby from the third to eighth week in the mother's womb

EM field *see* electromagnetic field

endothermic reaction a process in which heat is taken in (example: photosynthesis)

energy the ability of matter to do work

equator the imaginary circle drawn around the Earth halfway between the North and South Poles

erode to wear away

evaporation the slow change of a liquid to a gas

evolution the gradual change in a species over time

exothermic reaction a process in which heat is produced (example: combustion)

experiment a procedure used to test a hypothesis

experimental group in an experiment, the group being tested

fact a statement about something that actually happened or actually exists

fat a substance that provides energy and building material for the body

fetal alcohol syndrome (FAS) a group of birth defects that can occur when a pregnant woman drinks alcohol

fetus a developing baby from the third to ninth month

fission the splitting of an atom's nucleus

flower in a plant, the reproductive organ that produces seeds and pollen

flu *see* influenza

force a push or a pull

forecast a prediction, as of the weather

fossil the remains or imprint of a long-dead organism

fossil fuel a fuel, such as coal, oil, or natural gas, that is formed from the remains of plants or animals that lived hundreds of millions of years ago

freezing the change in matter from a liquid to a solid

frequency the number of waves that pass a point in a certain amount of time

friction a force between surfaces that touch

front the leading edge of a moving air mass

fuel a source of energy

fusion *see* nuclear fusion

gas a state of matter that does not have a definite size or shape and expands to fill its container

gear a wheel with teeth; each gear turns on its own center

genetic screening tests that can tell if certain disorders are likely to be inherited

genetics the study of how traits are inherited

glacier a mass of ice that forms when more snow falls than melts

global warming a worldwide increase in average temperature

glossary an alphabetical listing of important words and their definitions, located at the end of a text

gravity the natural force of attraction between two objects (example: the pull of Earth on humans)

greenhouse effect the warming of Earth caused by the absorption of infrared radiation into gases in the atmosphere

groundwater water that is found underground (examples: springs and wells)

hereditary capable of being passed from a parent to an offspring through a father's sperm or a mother's egg

heredity the passing of traits from parents to their young

hydrocarbon a compound made mostly of hydrogen and carbon

hypothesis an explanation of how something works, based on many observations

igneous rock rock formed when molten rock hardens

immune to be unaffected by a disease or illness because of a protective treatment or the body's natural resistance

implied not stated

incinerate to burn, as in burning garbage

inclined plane a simple machine with a long, sloping surface that helps move an object (example: ramp)

inference the use of information to figure out things that are not actually stated

influenza (flu) an illness caused by a virus

infrared radiation the energy Earth radiates back into the atmosphere

inherit to acquire a trait or disease that is passed on from one's parents (examples: hair color, Huntington's disease)

inner planets the four planets closest to the sun: Mercury, Venus, Earth, and Mars

inorganic substances that are made of things that were never alive

integrated circuit tiny electronic components linked together to form a circuit

ion an atom with a positive or negative electric charge

joint the place where two or more bones come together

kindling temperature the temperature at which a substance will burn

landfill an area of open land that is filled with layers of garbage

language a system of signs or sounds that refer to objects or ideas and that can be combined in different ways to produce different meanings

laser a tool that produces a narrow, strong beam of light in which all the waves have the same frequency and wavelength and are in phase

leaf the part of a plant that produces food from water, carbon dioxide, and sunlight

lever a bar that turns on a pivot

life cycle the series of changes an animal goes through in its life

life science the study of living things and how they affect one another

ligament a strong band that connects bones at joints

light a form of energy that travels in waves and makes vision possible

line graph a graph using lines to show how something increases or decreases over time

liquid a state of matter that takes up a definite amount of space but does not have a definite shape. A liquid flows and takes the shape of its container.

main idea the topic of a paragraph, passage, or diagram

mammal an animal with a backbone, hair or fur, and milk-producing glands to feed its young

maritime polar air mass a cold, moist air mass; for example, one that forms over the northern Atlantic Ocean and northern Pacific Ocean

maritime tropical air mass a warm, moist air mass; for example, one that forms over the Caribbean Sea, the middle of the Atlantic Ocean, or the middle of the Pacific Ocean

mechanical advantage the number of times a machine multiplies your effort to do work

melanoma a fast-growing skin cancer that may appear as oddly shaped blotches

melting the change in matter from a solid to a liquid

metamorphic rock rock formed in conditions of great heat and pressure

meteorologist a scientist who studies changes in Earth's atmosphere to forecast the weather

microprocessor an integrated circuit that functions as a computer's central processing unit

mitochondria the parts of a cell that give the cell the energy it needs to grow and reproduce

mitosis the process by which a cell's nucleus divides and therefore reproduces

mixture a combination of two or more kinds of matter that can be separated by physical means

molecule the smallest particle of a compound

momentum the property of a moving object that is a product of its mass and velocity

monounsaturated fat a type of fat found in some vegetable products

municipal solid waste organic and inorganic materials that are thrown away as garbage

mutation a change in a gene

mutualism a relationship in which two species help each other

natural selection the survival of organisms best suited to their environment

neutron a particle found in the nucleus of an atom that has no electrical charge

nitrate a substance made by soil-dwelling bacteria using nitrogen from the air

nuclear energy energy that comes from inside an atom

nuclear fusion the reaction caused by two nuclei combining to make the nucleus of a larger atom

nuclear reaction a change in the nucleus, or center, of an atom

nucleus in life science, a cell's control center, which contains genetic material. In chemistry and physics, the protons and neutrons forming the core of an atom (plural: nuclei)

observation the act of watching or using the other senses to gather information and learn about something

ocean basin the bottom of the sea

opinion a statement that expresses what a person or group of people think, feel, or believe about a fact

organic substances that come from things that were once alive

osteoporosis a condition of brittle bones common to older people, especially women

outer planets the five planets farthest from the sun: Jupiter, Saturn, Uranus, Neptune, and Pluto

oxidation the process in which a substance reacts with oxygen, causing the formation of a new compound called an oxide

ozone a form of oxygen

paleontologist a scientist who studies ancient forms of life

parasite an organism that lives on or in another organism and harms it

photosynthesis the process by which plants use carbon dioxide, water, and energy from sunlight to make food

pH scale a measurement from 0 to 14 of the strength of an acid or a base

physical change a change in the appearance of matter without a change in its properties (example: the dissolving of sugar in water)

physics the study of energy and forces and their effect on matter

pivot the point around which an object turns

placenta a structure that attaches the embryo to the uterus and allows substances to pass between the embryo and the mother

plaque deposits of cholesterol on the inside walls of arteries

pneumonia an infection of the lungs caused by viruses or bacteria

polyunsaturated fat a type of fat found in some vegetable foods and fish

precipitation water falling from the atmosphere in the form of rain, snow, or sleet

prediction a guess about what may happen

printed circuit board a board to which electronic components that form circuits are attached

product a substance that forms in a chemical reaction

proton a positively charged particle in the nucleus of an atom

Punnett square a diagram used to show all possible combinations of traits among offspring of two parents

pupa the nonfeeding stage in the life cycle of some insects when their adult tissues are formed

radiant energy energy that exists in the form of waves, such as light waves or radio waves

radioactive the state of atoms in the process of decay, in which the nuclei are giving off particles and energy in the form of radiation

radioactive decay particles given off by an unstable nucleus in an atom (an unstable nucleus has an unbalanced number of protons and neutrons)

reactant a substance that reacts in a chemical reaction

recessive trait a trait that will not appear if it is paired with a dominant trait

recycle to process materials to use again

renewable resource a resource that does not get used up (example: water)

reservoir a lake created by a dam

resistance a force that must be overcome to do work

resource a material that people need from Earth

respiration the process by which living things take in oxygen and release carbon dioxide to obtain energy

rhinovirus a virus that causes certain types of colds

ribosome a part of the cell that makes proteins that the cell needs in order to grow

root the part of a plant that holds it in the ground and absorbs water and nutrients from the soil

saturated fat a type of fat that is solid at room temperature

scientific methods organized ways of solving problems; the processes scientists use for getting information and testing ideas

sedimentary rock rock formed when particles are deposited and then harden over time

sequence the order in which things happen

silicon an element common in Earth's crust

simple machine a device to do work (example: lever)

software instructions that tell a computer how to perform a task

solar system the sun and the objects that revolve around it, such as the planets and their moons

solid a state of matter that has a definite shape and takes up a definite amount of space

solubility related to the amount of a solute that will dissolve in a given amount of solvent at a given temperature and pressure

solute the substance in a solution that is present in the smaller amount

solution a type of mixture in which the ingredients are distributed evenly throughout

solvent the substance in a solution that is present in the greater amount

sound a sensation caused by vibrations and perceived by hearing

sound waves vibrations transmitted through substances in waves with frequencies that can be heard

space probe unmanned spacecraft used for the exploration of space

spectrometer a device used to analyze what things are made of

species a group of organisms with similar characteristics that can interbreed to produce fertile offspring

sprain a joint injury in which the ligaments are stretched or torn

squamous cell skin cancer a type of cancer that looks like raised, pink spots or growths that may be open in the center

stationary front the zone between two air masses, caused when the masses stop moving

stem the part of a plant that provides support and transports substances

substance matter that is of one particular type

summarize to condense or shorten a larger amount of information into a few sentences

table a type of list that organizes information in rows and columns

timeline an illustration that shows when a series of events took place and the order in which they occurred

topic sentence the sentence that contains the main idea in a paragraph

trait an inherited characteristic such as hair color or blood type

transistor an electronic device used to amplify, detect, or switch electric current

tropical rain forest dense forest found near the equator where the climate is hot and wet

ultraviolet light a type of light with wavelengths too short to be visible to the human eye; also known as black light

ultraviolet rays a type of harmful energy in sunlight

uterus a woman's womb, in which her unborn baby develops

vaccination an injected dose of dead or weakened disease-causing agent. The body reacts to a vaccination by forming antibodies to fight the disease.

vaccine a substance containing weakened bacteria or viruses

virus a tiny particle of genetic material with a protein covering

water cycle the circulation of water on Earth through evaporation from the surface into the atmosphere and back to the surface as precipitation

wavelength the distance from the top of one wave to the top of the next wave

weather map a map showing where cold, warm, and stationary fronts are, as well as areas of high and low pressure

wheel and axle a simple machine composed of two objects that turn in a circular motion on the same center, multiplying both force and speed

work the process of using force to cause an object to move

zygote a fertilized egg resulting when the sperm from the father joins with the egg produced by the mother

Index

comparing, 35, 131, 158

composting, 77

compounds, 145–147

compound machines, 186

compound words,
        understanding, 113

computer chips, 225

computers, 196–199, 225

conclusion, in scientific
        methods, 15, 17, 216

conclusions
    drawing, 65, 118, 125, 192
    evaluating support for, 130

condensation, 151

conservation
    of energy, 113
    of water, 119

construction workers, 134–135

context, getting meaning from,
        58

contexts, applying knowledge
        to other, 77, 89, 153

continental polar air mass, 105

continental shelf, 138

continental slope, 138

continental tropical air mass,
        105

contrasting, 35, 131, 158

control group, 16–17

cooking, chemistry of,
        150–153

copper, 157, 223

cosmetic surgery, and lasers,
        203–205

crust (of Earth), 130

cytoplasm, 23

Darwin, Charles, 88

data storage, in computers,
        225

DDT, 180

decomposers, 76, 77

Deep Blue, 196, 197, 199

DES, 39

deserts, 5, 117

details, finding, 41, 46
    in a diagram, 52

diagram
    finding details in, 52
    finding main idea of, 40

Dick, Elliot, 51

dictionary, using, 17, 170

diet, and health, 26–29
    pregnancy and, 41

dinosaurs, 86–69

diodes, 198

Discovery, 16, 17

disease
    bacterial, 50, 53, 96
    genetic, 44–47
    and immunity, 96
    viruses, 50–53, 96

distillation, 157

DNA, 94

dolphins, 62–65

dominant trait, 45, 46, 97

Down syndrome, 47

drought, 119

drugs
    antibiotics, 53
    cancer treatments, 59
    from plants, 56–59
    and pregnancy, 39, 41

Earth
    gravity of, 15
    as planet, 123, 124, 131
    temperature of, 80, 82,
        111–113

Earth and space science, 102

eating habits, 26–29
    pregnancy and, 41

echolocation, of dolphins, 64

ecosystems, 80, 81

effort, 185–187

egg cell, 39

egg, of insect, 70–71

elasticity, 192

electricity, 113, 169, 171,
        196–199, 213

electromagnetic field, 213

electronics, 196–199

electrons, 8, 197, 198

elements, 145–147
    chemical symbols for, 146

embryos
    chicken, 16, 17
    human, 39, 40

endothermic reaction, 177

energy, 182, 191
    activation, 163
    and cellular respiration, 220
    and changes of state, 151
    and chemical reactions, 142,
        163, 177
    electrical, 205
    heat, 111, 139, 151, 158,
        162–164, 171, 177
    human, 28
    laser, 203
    light, 139, 177, 182,
        202–205
    nuclear, 169–171, 179
    saving, 113
    sound, 182
    from the sun, 111, 179

energy conservation, 113

engines, 155

environment, 12
    pollution of, 74–77, 118,
        119, 180

erosion, 130

evaporation, 151

evolution, 86–89

exercise, 29, 32–35, 92, 100

exothermic reaction, 177

experiment, in scientific
        methods, 15–17, 216

experimental group, 16, 17

FAS (fetal alcohol syndrome),
        41

fact, distinguishing from
        opinion, 47, 119, 193

fat, 26–29
    and exercise, 33

feathers, 87–89

fetal alcohol syndrome (FAS),
        41

fetus, 39, 40, 47

fire, 142, 163, 164, 178

fission, 170, 171

fitness instructor, 92

tables, reading, 124
taxol, 59
temperature
   and bacteria, 3
     of Earth, 80, 82, 111–113
     kindling temperature, 163,
       178
     and solubility, 159
     of sun, 139
Thalidomide, 39
Three Mile Island, 168, 171
timelines, reading, 71
toxins, 180
traits, and heredity, 45, 46, 97
   and evolution, 88, 89
transistors, 198
Trans-Neptunian objects, 222
trees, and insect pests, 68–71
   destruction of rain forest, 82
   and global warming, 113
triceps muscle, 2
tropical rain forests, 56, 57,
   80–83
Tyack, Peter, 63, 64

ultraviolet light, 21, 23, 137
universe, 102
uranium, 170
Uranus, 122–125
uterus, 39, 40

vaccination, 53, 96
Valium, 59
Velociraptors, 86, 87
Vellinger, John, 15–17
Venus, 123
Viking space probes, 129
viruses, 50–53, 57, 96, 217
Voyager space probes, 123–125

walking, 32–35
warm fronts, 105, 106, 136
water
   changes of state, 151
   chemical formula for, 146
   on Mars, 131
   in photosynthesis, 82, 177,
     220
   pollution, 221
   as precipitation, 6
   as resource, 116–119, 221
   as solvent, 158, 159
   use, 221
water cycle, 6, 118
weather, 102, 104–107, 136
weightlessness, 14–17
wheel and axle, 186
white blood cells, 96
womb, 39, 40
work, 185, 186, 210

yard waste, 77

zygote, 39